Cruise of the Heart

Memoir of a Transatlantic Voyage

Robert D. Ferré

©

ISBN (print version)
978-0-9779612-5-2

Published by Labyrinth Enterprises, LLC

www.labyrinth-enterprises.com

Accompanying website for this book with color photos:
www.cruiseoftheheart.com

Descriptions of other cruises by Robert D. Ferré:
www.retiredgonecruising.com

Personal website and blog:
www.robertferre.com

Dedication

to my
sweetie
Linda
for finding me
loving me
restoring me
inviting me on
that first cruise
for that first kiss
for marrying me
being in my life
whether on
land or sea
next to you
is the only
place I want
to be

Contents

Introduction

It seemed like a simple idea. Write a detailed account of a transatlantic cruise. There are very few accounts in print about the actual experience of cruising. Sure, there are many books and articles filled with information on how to find a good bargain, but little is available about the nature of the cruise itself. This book fills that need.

During our cruise I took copious notes, planning on knocking off a quick travelogue. But something unexpected happened on the high seas. The enormity and mystery of the ever-passing ocean empowered and inspired me to make relevant observations of myself and my life as well as the cruise. Hence, elements of a memoir.

Travel, labyrinths, prison, cancer, spirituality, Gothic cathedrals, gambling, happiness, new love, renewal—it all came tumbling out, as if it had long been waiting to find expression. Yet even that wasn't enough for my curious mind. I delved into the fascinating history of ocean liners, famous disasters, health and safety issues, and more. The book grew in depth and width—and thickness.

The original manuscript came out to 125,000 words—far too long. It was enough words to fill two books. "Oh," I thought one day, "two books. Great idea." Thus was born *Cruise of the Heart Volume Two: The Rest of the Stuff*. That may not be the final title, so I will simply refer to it as *Volume Two*.

Like so many others, I found the search for agents and editors and publishers to be discouraging. Discovering the growing field of digital self-publishing, I dove in. The result is in your hands. The many books inside of me waiting for expression are joyful and excited. Perhaps one day they, too, will find a place in the world.

First Cruise, First Kiss

My friend Rosette spoke demurely, tilting her head and raising her eyebrows, as if uncovering a great secret.

"You've found someone new in your life."

"No, no, no," I replied too quickly, speaking through a mouth full of pasta. The restaurant was noisy, crowded for a Wednesday night. "It's way too soon. Ruthie's barely gone a year." I swallowed my food to speak more clearly. "We're just friends. Linda's nice enough."

"I don't think so-o-o-o-o," Rosette persisted, dragging out the last vowel. "When you talk about her, you light all up and your energy level really takes off." She waited for details.

"Do you think so?" I asked as a delaying tactic.

"I know so. It's quite obvious. It's all over your face."

"That's tomato sauce," I jested, dabbing my mouth with the white linen napkin. "Hm-m-m-m-m. Very interesting. I hadn't noticed."

I tried to act nonchalant, but inside, something stirred—a recognition simultaneously wonderful and terrifying. Disparate unattended bits coalesced. The veil thinned. Surely Rosette was wrong. Or was she astute? I told her our story.

Linda and I met in San Antonio at the reception following a lecture I gave on labyrinths. True, I now realize with greater clarity, she stood out as the person who most caught my attention. Thin, attractive, she actually laughed at my puns. She actually *got* my puns, which I took as a sign of high intelligence. Atypically, Linda gave me her business card and said, "Let's stay in touch."

I remember thinking, "Under different circumstances, I would really like to get to know this woman." However, after what I had just been through, the thought of a new relationship was the furthest thing from my mind. I wasn't looking. No, sir. Too soon. Way too soon.

My Ruthie had died only seven months earlier. For the first five years of her cancer journey, by employing a variety of alternative treatments (including going to a clinic in Germany), we succeeded in maintaining a decent quality of life. But the breast cancer persisted, spread to the bone, and threatened the brain. Her oncologist, who had been heroically patient with us, convinced us that we needed to get more aggressive. And so, we made a horrible decision (relief from which comes only from the knowledge that it was mutual), followed by a year of chemotherapy and radiation hell. Those treatments killed my Ruthie, slowly, agonizingly, as certainly as the cancer it presumed to treat. It was aggressive, all right.

I served as caregiver, helped by her amazing circle of faithful friends. Hospice attended her at home that last week, her bed occupying the living room. Incoherent, pacified with morphine, her sensitivities and dignity gone, her bodily systems failing, she died resembling a skeletal, eighty-five–pound old woman, rather than her youthful, vigorous, beautiful sixty-three years, her long golden hair and distinctive front braids but a faint memory. I had never seen death before, especially so close up, so personal. It was ugly and unrelenting.

By the end, my own health was in shambles. Nowhere within me was there an inkling of interest in starting all over again. To me, a relationship is a spiritual path, requiring diligent attention, communication, and release from the ego. I had no energy for that. I couldn't imagine myself in a relationship with anyone other than

Ruth. Totally exhausted, I went into social hibernation and attended to myself.

However, the universe had other plans. Linda and I stayed in touch by email. We shared poetry. My labyrinth business took me back to San Antonio again. I stayed in her guest room. We talked and listened to music late into the night. On one occasion, we drove to south Texas for a three-day silent retreat at Lebh Shomea.

Two years passed. One day, Linda invited me to accompany her and a group of friends on a cruise—a fourteen-day voyage from Barcelona to Galveston. The cruise would be the following November, 2009. I had never cruised before. I learned that cabins are priced per-person, double occupancy. A single traveler pays double the amount. If we had separate staterooms, it would cost four times the standard fare. Wouldn't it be more economical to share a stateroom? As roommates only, of course. Traveling companions. When asked about the configuration of the room, we discretely ordered two single beds.

I have a long history of traveling in France, but Linda had never been there. We decided to fly over a week early and work our way down to Barcelona. I showed Linda some of my favorite places, including Paris, Chartres Cathedral, and Taizé. She cried, so wonderful did she find these places. I noticed. I feel the same way. We shared hotel rooms. Even if our beds were only inches apart, we maintained our distance, dressed and undressed separately, often in the cramped bathrooms.

Linda, it turns out, is a great traveler—energetic, inquisitive, and fun to be with. Slowly, I began to come out of my shell. Had we flown directly to Barcelona and jumped immediately aboard the ship, we would have missed that important week of relaxing and establishing rapport.

The morning we boarded *Voyager of the Seas*, I was on tenterhooks, having no idea what to expect. Arriving at the dock, I was totally agog. What a huge and beautiful ship! Never had I seen anything like it. The boarding procedure was well-organized and quick. We soon arrived at our stateroom on Deck 8, opened the door, and walked in. Behold, it was a tidy little room, but the beds were not arranged singly, as requested. Rather, they were pushed together and made up in a queen-size unit. We looked sheepishly at each other and shrugged our shoulders, unconcerned, and maybe a little grateful. "Oh, well."

The outside wall was all glass. We opened the sliding door and ventured out onto the balcony. The view faced away from the city, toward the brilliantly blue Mediterranean, the fall air crisp and refreshing. Puffy clouds dotted the deep blue sky. I knew I had to kiss Linda, but still I paused, terrified, frozen in place. I stood behind her, my arms around her waist, looking over her shoulder at the restless sea. I released my grip and she turned toward me. I looked into her eyes, then at her lips for a moment, and then ... we kissed.

Wow, what a shock! I expected a little introductory peck—puckered lips lightly touching puckered lips—like you get from your grandmother, like French people greeting or departing. Not Linda! Her lips were parted, ready for full involvement. Quickly, clumsily, I adjusted my lips to hers. Thankfully, we kept our tongues in check, or I might have jumped overboard. Oh, my! Our first kiss. Not romantic, exactly, as it was too self-conscious. No violins or choirs. More monumental than that, I had overcome my doubt and hesitancy. Rosette had correctly predicted my future.

Our friendship and mutual exploration had already deepened into something we both knew would last. When we saw Linda's friends around the ship, they observed, "You two really glow." We smiled. It was true.

Our new intimacy continued cautiously. Linda herself had been divorced for more than twenty years. As an Episcopal priest, she had found relationships difficult to begin and maintain. When men she met through dating websites discovered she was a priest, they usually ran the other way. When she told me her experience, I responded, "Why would they run? I think it's a big plus." I love Linda's spirituality and sensitivity.

Married the following May, we took our honeymoon to England and back to New York on Cunard's *Queen Mary 2*. More cruises followed. And the kissing? Well, just use your imagination.

Embarkation and Departure

Day 1, October 26, 2011

Linda thinks we shouldn't keep telling our friends about all of our cruises because they will think we are rich or putting on airs. *Au contraire ma cherie,* it's just the opposite. We should tell *everyone* about how wonderful cruises are, including what a good *bargain* they are, perfect for people just like us who *aren't* rich. So, that's what I plan to do: tell everyone. The cruise in this book took place in the fall of 2011 on *Mariner of the Seas*, departing from Civitavecchia (the port for Rome) to Galveston, Texas—a voyage of seventeen days.

Our big adventure begins with breakfast at nine, at our hotel. The rain has lessened, although the fog remains. After consuming coffee, pound cake, yogurt, and dry cereal, we pack our bags. Linda's weighs in at about forty-three pounds, mine forty-eight. Plus we have a third, smaller one with our formal cruise clothes and several carry-on bags. At the reception desk, we check out and wait for the 11:00 a.m. shuttle to return from its first run to the port. Our comfortable stay at Tenuta dell'Argento, an active cattle ranch up on the hill overlooking the city and port, has proven to be surprisingly affordable, especially considering we had the best room with the best view. Below, the foggy outline of seven cruise ships—lined bow to stern along two piers—pulls us like a magnet. We're coming, we're coming! Wait for us!

The shuttle arrives late, its cargo space filled with boxes of vegetables, bottles of olive oil, cases of wine, and other provisions for the hotel kitchen. We wait for them to be unloaded and then pile in to take our seats. At dinner last night, we met eight people going on *Norwegian Jade* today, part of a group of twenty-nine people celebrating someone's sixtieth birthday. Several of them join us now, taking seats in the back of the van. From the driveway, we can still see the harbor. Royal Caribbean ships have a distinct outline, due to the futuristic disk-like Viking Crown Lounge perched on the afterdeck, wrapped around the single funnel as if a spaceship from *Star Trek* had just landed there. Hello, Jean-Luc Picard? Of the seven cruise ships in port, it appears that three are Royal Caribbean. Can that be true? Which one is *Mariner*?

The light rain can't dull our excitement during the bumpy ride down to the port in Civitavecchia. As the old but solid shuttle bus bounces through the potholes, it clatters and rattles. We loved being perched up on the hill. Now we are steeply descending. We didn't take any chances, leaving the hotel with plenty of time before the departure deadline. The sooner we get there the better. The moderate traffic poses no problem. Stores and buildings catch our attention, along with cars and people on the street.

"Look, a gelato stand!" we cry.

Just another working town, neither pretty nor ugly, Civitavecchia pays little attention to us. Most of the people we see are concentrating on going to their jobs, as they do every morning. Been there, done that. Now retired, our lives have changed. We have removed our noses from the grindstone, straightened our spines, and are headed, hand-in-hand, into our sunset years. As we all know, sunsets are beautiful. So are sunset years, affording time to catch up on all we've missed in the first part of our lives.

Untypically, we never explored Civitavecchia during our two days here. Whether there are parks with wooden benches, or bars in which to sip cold coffee shakeratos, or other lovely Italian attractions, we can't tell you. I know a fort here was designed by Michelangelo and a church dedicated to San Francesco d'Assisi. Founded by Emperor Trajan in the second century, Civitavecchia (pronounced *chee-vee-ta-VEK-ya*), like any important port, was a prize captured periodically by various parties in various wars for various purposes. Heavily damaged during World War II by American bombing, the town was rebuilt in an unremarkable way. Its main claims to fame stem from being the port of Rome (eighty kilometers distant) and serving as a major link to Sicily and other Mediterranean ports.

Never before have I seen a harbor that can simultaneously accommodate seven major cruise ships plus many ferries, freighters, and tankers. The best cruise ports allow passengers to disembark and walk easily right into the heart of town. That's not the case here, however. The commercial working port sprawls northward, creating an impassible barrier to reaching town on foot.

Our shuttle winds its way around warehouses and storage lots to Pier 28. We catch tantalizing glimpses of other ships, most of which are docked along Pier 12, on the other side of a narrow channel. Even though from a distance the cruise ships dwarf their surroundings, being visible from miles away, we can't see *Mariner* as our view is blocked by low buildings. At last we arrive. I tip the driver 5 euros. Exiting from the shuttle van, everyone cranes their neck to look up at the massive vessel towering over the terminal building, rather like looking up at the Eiffel Tower or an Egyptian pyramid or perhaps a grand Gothic Cathedral, boggled by the scope of the artifact. Rising more than twenty stories (207 feet to the top of the funnel) and longer than three football fields end-to-end, *Mariner of the Seas* will be our home for the next seventeen days.

Our suitcases display tags indicating 8598, our stateroom number. They will be delivered there in a matter of hours. How much easier could it be? Ditto for taking a cruise. The hardest part? Showing up, passport, paperwork, and credit card in hand. Pretty straight forward.

Granted, we were overly cautious in arriving in Civitavecchia two days early, just to make sure there were no complications in reaching our destination. On our train from Rome, we encountered several couples arriving one day before departure. Pretty safe. But an older couple, struggling with their red suitcases, had just arrived by air that morning and needed to be at their ship by 4:00 p.m. Getting off the train around 1:00 p.m., we saw them hail a taxi for the port, so they made it. But what if their plane had been delayed? Or their luggage misdirected? Such a tight schedule is too rich for our blood. Instead, here we are, calm and well-rested with four or five hours to spare.

The taxi drivers at the train station have a unique system. Virtually all the vehicles are nine-passenger vans, which go only to the cruise port. At 10 euros per passenger for a short distance, it must be quite profitable. Getting a taxi to go elsewhere seems nigh impossible. It's a good thing our hotel had a free shuttle. An alternative is to arrive on departure day, walk from the train station for ten minutes, downhill, to the port entrance, where you can utilize a free shuttle to the cruise terminal and your ship.

Our terminal bustles with activity. Five large busses disgorge their passengers and mountains of luggage. Porters load suitcases onto wire-cage pallets that will be forklifted into the ship.

I remember a passage in a book about an around-the-world-cruise in 1913, describing the lines of "half-naked natives" streaming up the gangways with luggage and supplies on their shoulders. And then there was the bunkering (refueling) of the great steamships, with men precariously balanced on small ledges along the hull, dumping 250-pound bags of coal into the hold.

Historically, loading a ship was a sweaty, noisy activity, with lots of shouting and confusion, sometimes taking several days. Embarking was further encumbered by hundreds of well-wishers, gathered to see off their friends and loved ones on their dangerous voyage. Nowadays, loading a cruise ship involves the whine of electric tailgates and propane-powered forklifts, swiftly moving tons of materials with the push of a button, finishing the task in a matter of hours.

One aspect of loading has changed little—registering the passengers as they board. We could just as easily be second-class passengers in the 1920s, standing on the great hinged wharf in Liverpool, but instead, here we are in Italy in 2011. I dawdle a little, taking photos. More buses arrive, so we go into the terminal building to beat the crowd. I look at my watch: 11:30 a.m. We wonder how long this will take.

The high, arching roof of the terminal creates a spacious interior. The line of passengers snakes around the perimeter of the room. Immediately upon entering, we are handed a health form to fill out, verifying that we don't have several listed contagious conditions and symptoms. How effective can this be as a screening device, I wonder. Won't sick people just lie? Still, that would place the blame on them and not the cruise line. I notice that the rows of chairs in the waiting room are largely empty. Can that mean people are already boarding the ship? I'm getting excited.

A friendly, uniformed employee divides the wheat from the chaff—I mean, the suite and diamond passengers from us commoners—assigning each to their respective lines. Repeat customers rightly receive an ever-increasing array of perks and special privileges.

Our check-in queue extends forty yards or so, meandering back and forth, like an airport security line. We move forward at a steady pace. Around us we see our fellow passengers-in-waiting. White hair clearly predominates. Our destination is a long counter staffed by forty-five (!) check-in agents.

When ready for another passenger, the agents raise a wooden paddle, about the size of a badminton racket, which displays the number of their station. The next person in line goes there. We go to agent number 37. While many of the agents are fluent in several languages, English predominates, as two-thirds of all cruise passengers are Americans. Since we're heading for Galveston, an inordinate number of Texas drawls can be heard. The agent takes our paperwork and passports.

"For security reasons," she informs us, "all non-European passports will be held and returned later in the voyage." She puts a sticker on each of our passports with 8598 on it. I submit my American Express card for paying our extraneous charges, such as purchases in the shops, liquor, specialty restaurants, and the like.

A few vestigial euros remain in our pockets, but on the ship we all spend U.S. dollars. That's not true of all ships, as P & O uses the pound and Europe-based lines, such as Aida and Costa, use the euro. We are given magnetic cards the size of a credit card, which will serve as our ID cards, charge cards, and room keys. The agent points us toward the hallway that leads to the ship.

First, we encounter the ubiquitous cruise-photo opportunity. We put down our carry-ons and stand against the backdrop. The photographer works fast, about fifteen to twenty seconds per photo. One shot. Click. Next passenger. Click. Next passenger. Click. After days of sleepless travel, some people don't look their best at boarding time. One travel writer suggests taking another photo upon debarking, thereby allowing a before-and-after comparison. One needn't purchase any of the photos, which are displayed in vast arrays in the gallery area. An air-headed passenger once reportedly asked, "How will we know which ones are ours?"

Leaving the terminal, the great shining white hull of the ship fills our vision, a Taj Mahal of a wall. I take photos of everything in sight. The readout on my camera indicates 1,647 photos remaining. I snap a photo of the photographer taking photos and one of the backdrop, which has an aerial photo of our ship.

We cross the gangway, which has nonskid ridges on the walking surface and railings on both side. The land-end of the gangway has wheels plus a steel plate that hinges down to the ground. When the ship rocks slightly, the wheels on the gangway allow it to move in concert. When this happens, the end plate scrapes audibly on the ground. I suspect that gangway design hasn't changed for a very long time.

Finally, our feet are on the deck! Whew. Once aboard, our pass cards are scanned and identity photos taken. From now on, any time we leave or reenter the ship, our cards will be scanned, which will bring up our pictures on the monitor, thereby thwarting the use of someone else's card. Our carry-ons pass through the scanner and, *voila*, we are embarked. We made it.

People crowd the hallway, waiting for the elevators, so we head up the stairs. We plan to use stairs rather than elevators whenever possible, for the exercise. I glance at my watch: 11:50 a.m.. The entire boarding process took only twenty minutes. Our friends Jim and Fran told us they have avoided cruise ships because they don't like waiting in long lines, which they assume must be common with so many passengers aboard one ship. Not so. In fact, the largest ships process passengers the quickest.

Lunch beckons us to the Windjammer Cafe on Deck 11. En route, we stop at Deck 5 to verify our preferred dining time of 6:00 p.m. for the entire cruise, which the maître d' confirms. Then we go up for lunch. On embarkation day, everyone eats lunch at the buffet.

The spread in the Windjammer is famously extensive. The buffet line closest to the entry door has a queue, but we go further along and find duplicate buffets with no waiting. Some of the hatted and booted Texans were happily loading their plates with burnt animal flesh in the form of charred hamburgers—a bit repulsive for a long-time vegetarian such as myself (more than thirty years). Around two hundred feet of buffet counters overflow with all kinds of temptations.

At one of my favorite buffet tables, I gather up a variety of salads: fresh lettuce, Waldorf, Greek chopped, and chick pea. For good measure I add chopped beets, mozzarella cheese, and hummus. I don't even look at the two different hot bars. At the soup counter, I get a bowl of potato and leek soup. Lemonade to drink. A crowd presses in around the dessert buffet, where I abscond with key lime mousse and chopped fresh fruit. I spend a few minutes taking photos of the food. (At www.cruiseoftheheart.com I have posted my photos of our voyage.) Linda likewise fills her plate with delicacies.

We sit wearily, not really tired, just relieved. Eight months of anticipation was followed by six weeks of land travel in France and Italy, two nights in Civitavecchia, and twenty minutes of registration. Back during the sixteen years that I guided people on pilgrimage trips to France, my groups never had an emergency greater than a bit of flu, a chipped tooth, or a stolen passport. As director of One Heart Tours, I attended to myriad details. The organization and direction of a well-executed tour should go unnoticed. Only when things go wrong do group members see the machinations of management. Even with my excellent record, when the last day arrived and the final participant got on the train for Paris, departing from my responsibility, I would let out a sigh of relief that nothing had gone wrong and head to my favorite cafe for a *pastis*.

I feel that same sense of relief now. So many things could have gone wrong, but didn't. Our itinerary unfolded flawlessly. Our luggage was not stolen or lost. Our persons were never in danger. In fact, people were universally friendly and helpful, the weather cooperated, and our plans went smoothly. Not a bad record. We look at each other, repeat our gratitude for enjoying such a great life together, and take turns going back to the buffet.

After lunch, we stay on Deck 11, going outside to stand along the rail, surveying the dock area, town, and hills beyond. We try to pick out our hotel, Tenuta dell'Argento up on the hill, reversing our first view from there down to the harbor. We can't find it. The rain stops and blue sky appears. Below, on the dock, we see acres of containers the size of eighteen-wheeler trailers, stacked in long rows four or five high, waiting for their respective cargo ships to take them to their final destinations. How do they keep track of them all? What do they hold?

To the right, huge cranes jut into the sky. No lighthearted cruise port, this. No marketplace filled with welcoming vendors, no costumed dancing natives on the quay, no palm-lined walkways. Just concrete and fences, warehouses and equipment, parking lots, trucks, buses. The immaculate white ships seem like interlopers, fantasies imposed upon a grimy reality of black, rusty freighters and long, low tankers. We passengers anticipate parties and dances and gourmet dinners, whereas the low-paid commercial crews know only hard, dangerous work, unpleasant conditions, and 340 days a year at sea. Quite a contrast.

Two p.m.—all staterooms can now be occupied. We go down to deposit our carry-ons. Our new abode holds no surprises, other than feeling noticeably smaller than some staterooms we have had. Scandinavian-like decor, blonde wood, king-size bed, window wall with a sliding glass door, small balcony—everything in proper order. In the middle area, a couch hugs one side, paired with a glass coffee table. Opposite is a make-up table with a large mirror, drawers below, and to the right, a flatscreen TV and more cupboards. Next to the hallway, acting as a sound buffer, we find a closet and the tiny bathroom.

I would guess this cabin encompasses around 184 square feet (with forty-six more for the balcony). Room size remains one area in which land-based resorts claim superiority. Yet there is a mystique about this efficient little stateroom that is an integral part of shipboard life. More than adequate, scrupulously cleaned and maintained, it becomes our unique refuge.

A knock at the door. Our steward Michael introduces himself. He has one of our suitcases. Among the great wonders of cruising are the constant efforts and personal service provided by the steward. The long hours and hard work require diligence and dedication. After Michael closes the door behind himself, we go out onto the balcony and embrace, repeating our legendary first kiss of two years earlier.

Well, that's not quite accurate. That's the way I had envisioned it—a romantic replay of our memorable first cruise aboard *Voyager of the Seas*. Here's what really happens: We go out on the balcony and look briefly at the scene before us. As I move into position to plant a big one, Linda puts her finger on my lips. "Let's not kiss," she says gently, "I don't want your cold." Right. Well, I don't want to give her my cold, either. So I settle for a big hug. That's it.

Not otherwise distracted, our attention soon turns to the impressive row of cruise ships along the narrow channel. Directly across from us sits *Liberty of the Seas*. Also part of the Royal Caribbean fleet, it is a bit newer and larger than *Mariner*, accommodating 4,375 passengers, compared to *Mariner's* 3,114. Behind it, the next ship causes us to look at each other in surprise and wonder. *Voyager of the Seas*, our first ship! The past two years have made full circle.

Seeing *Voyager* reminds me how Linda saved my life, not just from loneliness and overwork, but literally. During that first cruise, I caught some kind of respiratory infection, sending me to the infirmary to see the doctor. My blood pressure proved to be 180 over 105, high and dangerous numbers, which, left untreated, could cause major problems. When I returned home, my doctor prescribed a gentle drug that now keeps my blood pressure within acceptable limits. Had Linda not invited me on that cruise, which led to my seeing the doctor, who knows what my current state of health might be.

After the delivery of our other two suitcases, we hang our clothes in the closet and place items in drawers. We have room left over. The suitcases fit under the bed. As one becomes accustomed to the dimensions of the stateroom, it seems to expand a bit. This level of comfort easily surpasses first class in the heyday of ocean liners, a century ago.

Perhaps my current cold resulted from my concern about getting to the ship and ending our land travels successfully. I had planned the itinerary, made the reservations, drove the car, lugged the luggage (that must be how it got its name), shepherded us onto the trains, and more. Now all of those responsibilities are finished. As the more experienced cruiser, Linda is now the leader. Whew! We lie down on the bed and take a relaxing nap. Soon comes the announcement we expect to hear.

"All passengers report to your muster stations. This is a mandatory drill. The number of your station is on your room card." By international maritime law, all passengers must attend muster, no matter how many times they have cruised before. The procedure varies slightly from ship to ship. Every passenger reports to his or her particular muster station, a deck below the lifeboats designated as the gathering place in the event one must evacuate the ship. Here, the lifeboats hang above Deck 4, the promenade deck. The lifeboats are large, dual-engined, covered boats that can hold eighty-five people.

Ever since *Titanic* sank in 1912, with enough lifeboats for only the first-class passengers, ships have been required to have an adequate number for everyone. A recorded message comes over the loudspeakers:

"In case of emergency, put on the life vests found in the closet of your stateroom, dress warmly, and bring along any necessary medication. The signal to commence this emergency procedure comprises seven short blasts on the ship's horn, followed by one long blast. Please note, this is *not* the signal to abandon ship, only to report to your muster stations." So, don't jump overboard!

The warning comes at 4:15, as scheduled. We haven't yet left port. Hoping to beat the rush, we get to muster station 08 at about 4:10, only to discover a substantial group already in place. After the sirens, another ten minutes transpire while bewildered passengers look for their muster stations. Even numbers are on port side, odd numbers starboard, arranged in ascending order. How hard can it be? It takes another ten minutes or more before the drill finally begins.

Already we've been standing in the hot sun for half an hour. It took less time than that to go through the entire boarding process. Two different older couples in our group had to be excused because they weren't strong enough to stand for so long in the heat. They go to a designated place inside where they and others unable to participate outside receive the same instructions that we are given. Special preparations are also made for those in wheelchairs or who otherwise have limited mobility, to make sure they are properly assisted in the case of an evacuation. Crew members wearing matching T-shirts give instructions on how to put on our life vests.

"The two sections of floatation material Velcro together. You just put the vest around your neck and press the two sections together in front of your chest. Tighten the belt around the whole thing to keep it from falling off."

Royal Caribbean claims to hold guest health and safety as their first concern. In this instance, however, the muster drill was very poorly organized, leaving us tired and sweaty. Surprisingly, it takes only five minutes for the crowded deck to clear.

We go directly to the drawing for prizes at the spa. We have attended similar drawings on several cruises. A clever ploy—the contest mostly advertises spa products and services. Even if you win something, the value may be elusive. Once, a couple gave us their prize: a coupon offering 33 percent off, which reduced the cost of a fifty-minute massage from $180 to $120, still more than either of us wanted to pay. Located right above the fitness area, the spa sets prices that reflect the value of its significant square footage, not to mention its captive audience.

We decide to skip the spa and go to the stern of Deck 4 to take photos of the other cruise ships all lined up in port. Below, we watch a small drama that delays *Mariner's* departure. It appears that the thick lines (ropes) that moored the rear of the ship to a huge bollard on the pier have tangled with similar lines stretching from *Ivory Girl*, a freighter docked directly behind us. Rarely do cruise ships and freighters moor in such proximity.

Meanwhile, Norwegian's *Jade* pulls out first. Norwegian ships have colorful graphics splashed across the bow and sides. While that makes them distinctive, I find them gaudy and ugly. After a tug pulls it into the channel, *Jade* slips away from the lineup that includes the other two Royal Caribbean ships, *Costa Concordia*, and two I can't identify: one has a single blue funnel and one a whale tale, *a la* Carnival, but all blue.

Built five years ago at a cost of nearly $600 million, *Concordia* is about 25 percent smaller than *Mariner.* Nevertheless, she carries 3,780 passengers and 1,068 crew. Who would predict that in just a few months, only three hours after leaving this port, *Concordia* hit rocks off the Island of Giglio, foundered, and rolled onto its side.

We figure that only *Concordia, Mariner of the Seas,* and *Jade* took on new passengers here. The other ships have stopped en route as a port of call, with tours into Rome. They will likely leave much later. We had noticed while we were in Civitavecchia that, by late at night, all the ships docked during the day had left.

Up on Deck 11, also called the Lido deck, a sail-away party gains momentum. Virtually all cruise ships designate the upper, open pool deck the Lido deck. What does that mean you might wonder? Wikipedia says this:

> *The term* lido *is an Italian word for beach and forms part of the place name of several Italian seaside towns known for their beach, e.g. Lido di Venezia, the barrier beach enclosing the Lagoon of Venice. Possibly the term found its way into English from returning English visitors to Lido di Venezia, where sea-bathing took place from the late nineteenth century.*

Although some cruise ships have had real sand by the pool, these days most have indoor-outdoor carpeting, wood, or tile. Not exactly beaches. Still, the association remains.

An archetypal experience embraces all who pull away from the safety of dry land to embark on a sea voyage. Such departures have inspired many poets. In his book, *Super Ships,* Noel Mostert describes the moment as "shaking off the shore." Despite the differences in time, place, culture, purpose, and type of ship, we're repeating what millions have done before us—boarding a ship and excitedly watching it drop its moorings and head for open water. There, free from its burden of anchors and ropes, the ship takes on its true nature and rightful function, exercising its *raison d'être* like a sea creature. It expresses its delight in its newly gained freedom with three loud blasts from its fog horns.

Far more than just offering transportation to Texas, *Mariner* will embrace, nourish, and protect us feeble land creatures as we venture out of our element and onto the notoriously perilous sea. On the shore, as we pull away from the dock, no crowds wave *bon voyage*, no white handkerchiefs, no bands playing. We don't throw confetti. Whereas departures once represented a joyful (and tearful) spectacle and important event, ours draws little attention being just one of fifty taking place this week. No big deal. Along the dock, a few forklifts move the last pallets of recycled materials, tidying up for the next cruise ship, which will arrive in a matter of hours. Though not necessarily a life-changing or life-threatening event, setting sail still delivers an emotional impact to those of us onboard.

The horizon once hid unknown worlds. Unlike the immigrants of a century ago, who knew not what lay ahead, Linda and I have crossed the Atlantic before, so we have a good idea of what to expect—a comfortable stateroom with a balcony, entertainment every evening, scrumptious food, and plenty of romance—all of which we anticipate with great relish. No longer does leaving land lead to fear and trepidation.

This port offers no visible security, in contrast to our departure from New York City on *Queen Mary 2*. We were accompanied by a Coast Guard boat with a sailor standing behind a machine gun on the bow. Here we simply clear the channel and turn directly toward the open sea. When a boat labeled *Piloti* pulls up next to the hull, a local pilot climbs down a rope ladder from our ship and jumps onto the deck of his small boat, which immediately heads for shore. This procedure plays out at every port—entering and departing—during which a local pilot informs the captain of relevant conditions with which he may not be familiar. Some ports, such as Nawiliwili on the island of Kauai, Hawaii, are extremely difficult to enter. For others, the pilot seems a bit extraneous.

Shirking the Lido departure party, we head for Top Hat and Tails dining room on Deck 4, where dining follows three distinct schedules. The early and late sittings take place at 6:00 p.m. and 8:30 p.m., usually at fixed tables with the same people. Families and older passengers typically favor the early seating, whereas the later time tends to draw the sophisticated, Continental, younger group.

Historically, the great ocean liners seated all first-class passengers in a single sitting. It would have been indiscrete to rush their dinner to vacate in time for a second group. As ships became larger and larger, a single seating became unwieldy. Two seatings are now the norm.

Mariner's impressive main dining room features three decks with an open atrium in the center. Each level has a different name. For Deck 5, "The Sound of Music," for Deck 4, "Top Hat and Tails," and for Deck 3, "Rhapsody in Blue." Who thinks up these names, anyway? Capacity totals 1,862 diners.

A number of years ago, Norwegian Cruise Lines introduced Anytime Dining, which led to their motto, "Freestyle Cruising." It proved to be popular, so most cruise lines now follow suit, giving the third possible schedule for dining. One can go to any venue at any time and sit either alone or with others. Some people like such flexibility and the opportunity to meet many new friends. For the freestyle folks, dining at an assigned time and table is just too regimented.

We have Anytime Dining mainly to avoid getting stuck permanently with people we don't like. We are still able to reserve a specific time, in our case 6:00 p.m., although we generally arrive at 5:30.

Hand cleaner dispensers grace the entrances to all dining venues. Use is mandatory. Many people probably wouldn't bother, considering themselves to be an exception to the rule, so a crew member (disguised as a greeter) stands at the entrance and makes sure that everyone partakes. We sit at table 708, a table for two, smack up against the floor-to-ceiling windows with a sweeping view of the passing sea. Our waiter, Subash, introduces himself and his assistant Michelle. The whole six weeks on land we were frugal and avoided paying for fancy meals, saying that we would have plenty onboard the ship. Well, that time has come.

What a wonderful task, selecting from the many delicious choices on the menu—recommendations from the chef, healthy suggestions from the spa, plus an array of vegetarian and ethnic dishes. Since we eat fish, we're in good stead. But we don't want to overdo it on the first day. Linda orders a spinach salad for her first course, and I have a tasty Vidalia onion tart. For the main course, we each have the sea bass, served on a bed of lentils, green beans, and snap peas—a rather odd combination, but somehow, it works.

This easily ranks as the best meal of our trip to date. (Well, a couple of meals in Cortona came close.)

We're both a bit disappointed with the dessert. That's OK, because we don't want to eat too many sweets. We also try to avoid eating too much bread, but the choices are so tempting, proffered in a wide wicker basket—especially those little round rolls with sesame seeds on them. M-m-m-m. As we eat, the sun sets languidly into the sea. Linda watches for the rare green flash that comes the instant the sun disappears. Not tonight.

We know that cruise ships must take on provisions for the entire cruise, much of it frozen. However, for this first meal, I think they tried to get our attention, perhaps having acquired fresh sea bass in port. It worked. We're duly impressed. Moments like this entice us to go on cruises. That and the inescapable expanse of water that speaks directly to my soul. Since our first port of call, Majorca, lies only four hundred miles away, the ship pokes along at a conservative 12 knots. At full speed, we would arrive tomorrow evening, which wouldn't give people time to see anything. Instead, by going slowly, we have a sea day tomorrow and will arrive in Majorca the following morning. The casual pace suits our sensitivities.

Mimicking the two dinner seatings, the evening entertainment presents an early show (seen before dinner by the late diners) and a late show (seen after dinner by the early diners). Got that? Not being night people, we prefer both to eat early and see the first show. Tonight, however, they have scheduled only a single show at 7:30, due to reduced demand (frequent cruisers often skip this introduction).

Typically, we get to the theater half an hour ahead of time to claim our favorite seats. We prefer the front row on the upper balcony, to the left of the stage. With a little time to kill, we break out the Phase 10 deck and play cards. Around for decades, Phase 10 is a rummy-like game in which ten combinations must be achieved (the ten phases), such as two sets of four or a consecutive run of eight. The first player to complete all ten phases wins. Not a very demanding game with respect to concentration or strategy, it can be played in the background, as we keep an eye on our surroundings.

To occupy those who are waiting, the screen on either side of the stage displays trivia questions.

"Shrimp have no heart—true or false?"

"False. They do have a heart, which is located in their head."

"Little known fact: Armadillo meat has 740 calories per pound."

The quizzes and factoids cover a wide range of subjects. After the second or third time around, we know all the answers and go back to our card game.

The Savoy Theater soars three decks high, with a steeply banked main floor and sweeping balconies, back, and side. It seats almost 1,400 people, which, while spacious, still cannot accommodate all the passengers, even in two shows. Although we rarely miss a night, some folks never attend at all.

The first night's program consists of comments from the cruise director, Paul, and brief numbers by *Mariner's* resident singers and dancers. The entertainers work hard and present enjoyable shows, often with elaborate costumes and cleverly designed sets. They're not the best we've ever seen, but they are enjoyable. Paul makes the usual jokes and introduces his staff. He polls the audience.

"How many newlyweds are there?"

No response.

"Yeah, well, we know where they are ... There are five newly wed couples aboard."

"How many first-time cruisers?"

No response.

"Well, this isn't the typical cruise for first timers."

He's right. The longer the cruise, the older and more experienced are the passengers. I was an exception to that rule, as my very first cruise, aboard *Voyager of the Seas,* took fourteen days.

Looking around, the median age clearly exceeds sixty. Paul says we have more than three thousand passengers from thirty countries and 1,200 crew from fifty countries. I can't even name fifty countries. Talk about cultural diversity! Some two thousand of the passengers have cruised with Royal Caribbean before. The captain hails from Denmark. That's typical, as most cruise captains are Italian, British, or Scandinavian, with only a smattering coming from the United States or Canada.

Paul announces that the schedule includes more than one thousand activities over the next sixteen days, from karaoke to wine tasting, from origami lessons to bridge, from rock climbing and roller-blading to ballroom dancing. Most of what he mentions we plan to avoid. Not being very demanding, we just want a good dance band, a dexterous piano player, a quiet library, and the occasional interesting lecture.

If everyone were as dull as Linda and me, the cruise lines could save big bucks in their activities budget. In turn, the cruises could cost even less. Hey, maybe I've come up with a great niche market—those who don't need to be distracted every minute of the day. Who should I tell? Skip the ports, while you're at it, and cut the ticket price even more. Certainly there must be other "pure" cruisers out there, like us.

A couple from Russia follows the cruise director. They once worked at the famous Moscow Circus. I saw the Moscow Circus once, and I particularly enjoyed a sequence of balancing acts using a ladder. Tonight's performer does something similar. The man climbs a straight ladder, perhaps ten feet tall, which he stands upright without resting it on anything. He ascends in small spurts, constantly fine-tuning his balance. While high on the ladder, he leans side to side, walking the ladder in tiny steps, as if he were on stilts. He then climbs over the top and down the other side.

Some performers make the difficult look easy. Not here. His hesitancy and concentration make it look hard. Perhaps that's deliberate. Meanwhile, his wife (I suppose) strikes stately poses. If you research "free standing ladder" on the Internet, you will find numerous videos of this stunt. Next, they do some very good juggling routines, which must take a lot of practice. As a finale, the man climbs the ladder again and does nearly impossible juggling routines while balancing at the top.

The program finished, the theater empties quickly. We go up to Deck 5 to stroll the length of the atrium, called the Royal Promenade, a spectacular feature of Royal Caribbean ships. Four decks high and almost four hundred feet long, this enormous public space serves as a hub for popular activities. At each end, an open circular area called the centrum houses stairs and elevators that extend up to Deck 12. *Voyager*, built in 1999, was the first to introduce this feature, which must be technically very difficult to achieve. Some 138 interior staterooms on Decks 6, 7, and 8 have bow windows facing into the atrium. Looking up at their shutters, I am reminded of a small square in Céret, France, where we enjoyed a three-course lunch.

Earlier, walking down the stairs, I noticed extra space between Deck 8 and Deck 9. This must be to accommodate the large girders needed to stabilize such a huge open span. Designed to resemble a London Victorian street, the Royal Promenade was reportedly inspired by Burlington Arcade. The latter is an enclosed indoor shopping arcade extending from Piccadilly to Burlington Gardens in London, near Bond Street. This precursor to the shopping mall first opened in 1819 "for the sale of jewellery and fancy articles of fashionable demand, for the gratification of the public." On rainy days in Paris, I sometimes seek out similar nineteenth century arcades, which often house tea rooms with tiny, round tables along the perimeter of the passageway. Other famous arcades include the *Saint-Hubert Gallery* in Brussels, the *Galleria Vittorio Emanuele II* in Milan, and the *Passage* in St. Petersburg.

We walk past the Cafe Promenade, which is open for coffee, desserts, and light fare twenty-four hours a day, seven days a week. Across the atrium, the fashion and cosmetics shop awaits. Next to the wine bar, a side stairway winds down to the casino on Deck 4. We stroll past an English pub, a jewelry store, and a souvenir shop. Reaching the other end, we pass the Champagne Bar. At Boleros Bar, the trio doesn't start playing until 10:00 p.m. That's a perfectly reasonable time for dancing, but we want to be in bed early, so we head back to the stateroom.

Once in bed, we both read for a while. Linda turns out her light and appears to go to sleep. We have left the balcony door open, filling the room with fresh air and ocean sounds. Well, most of the sound proves to be the ship plowing through the water, which, at only 12 knots, doesn't kick up much wake. I peruse the various flyers and newsletters, eventually turning off my light as well. Usually we read out loud to each other for a while (currently being midway through our third Linda Greenlaw book), talk about our day, and express at least three things for which we are grateful (first on the list: each other!). Quiet ensues.

We hug. Civitavecchia lies seventy miles behind us.

A Note about Civitavecchia

Being a memoir, this book travels through time, both backward and forward. So here I can disclose that a year after this cruise, we returned to Civitavecchia on another cruise. We took the shuttle from our ship to the port entrance gate. From there, we walked easily into town, visited a large Saturday market, found a great Internet coffeehouse, and discovered an extensive park bordering the sea (the perfect place for a new, convenient cruise port). In the park we encountered an unusual statue called *Il Bacio Della Mare* (The Kiss of the Sea). This huge, three-story statue reproduces the famous V-J Day photo taken by Alfred Eisenstaedt of a sailor kissing a nurse.

Copies of this work by sculptor J. Seward Johnson have appeared in temporary or permanent form in the United States and around the world (Paris, Japan, Germany, Switzerland, Sydney, Hong Kong). A permanent bronze version, entitled Unconditional Surrender, stands in Tuna Harbor Park in San Diego. Now, here's a copy in Italy, with a name that makes no sense. The work is not without controversy. As the story goes, the drunken sailor grabbed a woman he didn't know and subjected her to his intentions. Many feel that this nonconsensual act is not proper material for acclaim. Others feel the computer generated statue is too derivative and not very interesting, artistically. It's like a big, three-dimensional cartoon. Of course, like a good tourist, I took the obligatory photo of Linda standing at the base. We emailed it to her son, Mike, a Navy pilot, and his wife, Audrey.

Interest in the Eisenstaedt photo has grown over the decades; currently a dozen men claim to be the sailor and three women to be the nurse (the most likely one was a dental hygienist, not a nurse, who had left her office to celebrate). Several of the claimants have been honored in parades and other events. The photo (and statue) certainly capture the exuberance of the moment that peace was declared. The U.S. Navy had seen action in Civitavecchia, but it still seems to me a strange subject matter for a huge statue in an obscure city.

Our First Sea Day

Day 2, October 27, 2011

I awake before dawn. In my sleepiness, I see some lights flashing against the wall. How can that be? There's nothing out there but water. I rise up on my shoulder and look out into the night. On *Voyager of the Seas*, the railing had been steel, and opaque. We had to sit up straight and look over the rail to view the sea. *Mariner*, being a second-generation voyager-class ship, has a glass railing, allowing us to see through it. Something must be wrong. I see a long thin line of lights along the horizon. Linda is awake, too.

"Africa?" she offers.

"Too far. We wouldn't go that far south. It must be France."

"We're on the port side," she reminds me (that's the left side). As we're going west, our balcony faces south. It can't be France.

"Maybe Sicily," I guess.

"Can't be." Clearly we are both geographically challenged.

"We can look it up in the morning."

"Maybe we can find a map on the TV, like the progress map they have on airplanes."

"I want to go back to sleep."

"Me, too."

And so we do. But with dawn, the mystery deepens. Bright orange clouds fill the sky. Land remains quite close to the starboard side. In fact, we clearly see a conical-shaped island or peninsula with a lighthouse on it. Every five seconds, the light blinks. We can't stand it anymore. We turn on the TV and find a map. Although not to scale, it does show the islands of the Mediterranean. It seems that we are sailing between Corsica (to our right, which we can't see) and Sardinia, on the port side. On the Internet I try to find a photo of the lighthouse that we saw but don't succeed. So—it remains a mystery of sorts.

Breakfast arrives at our door at 8:00 a.m. They call just before delivery, so there are no surprises. Before going to bed, we filled out a breakfast order and hung it on the doorknob. We checked items on the list, including eggs and hash browns, tomatoes and granola, tea, decaf coffee, pastries, and fresh fruit. Yum!

We are obliged to leave the room at least for a short while each morning so the steward can do his work. He cleans the room, makes the bed, replaces towels, and resupplies the necessary tissues, toilet paper, shampoos, and other items *twice* a day. Since we take afternoon naps, we mess up the bed twice, as well. And so, he makes it during the morning cleaning and again while we're at dinner, at which time he turns down the covers. What a luxury!

Before we leave our stateroom, we each visit the tiny bathroom—surprisingly and adequately efficient and compact. The triple mirror, counter top, and medicine cabinet allow plenty of room for our toiletries, to wash and to brush our teeth. The toilet functions on a vacuum system that has great power. You always put down the toilet lid first, and then flush, which makes a startlingly loud whooshing sound. Even experienced travelers can be taken aback at this toilet—I once read of a travel writer who admitted to being *afraid* of the toilet, so powerful did it seem.

During our previous cruises, we have heard the following joke several times, by different comedians, including twice on the same cruise. It seems that there once was a rather large lady who inadvertently pushed the flush button while still sitting on the toilet. The resulting vacuum action pulled her so tightly against the toilet seat that she was unable to free herself. She called her husband, who called for the engineer. To cover his wife's exposure, the husband took a straw hat that he had acquired in Mexico and put it on his wife's lap. In due time, the engineer showed up and examined the situation. "Well, we won't have any trouble extricating your wife," he assured the husband, "but I'm afraid it's too late to save the Mexican."

Next to the toilet stands a circular shower, about three feet in diameter, with Plexiglas doors that separate in opposite directions for you to enter, and then pull together again. The doors allow in light from the fixture above the mirror. The shower head is attached to the end of a flexible hose that rests in a saddle adjustable in height by sliding it up or down a chrome rod. I like to have the shower above my head and let the water cover me completely. Linda, on the other hand, likes to direct it from the neck down, to keep water out of her face and off her shower cap. Although less than gushing, the water pressure suffices. The more expensive staterooms and suites feature marble tubs, Jacuzzis, and other comforts not applicable in our price category.

Like the bathroom, our stateroom also benefits from efficient design. To walk around the end of the bed to reach the balcony would be near impossible if the bed were rectangular, as the cabinet (which holds the TV, refrigerator, cupboards, counter, and desk) and the corner of the bed would touch. To create more space, the designer could have made the counter shorter, but that would reduce the size of the amenity. The solution? The end of the bed curves—being full length in the middle but rounded where the corners usually are, thereby opening up plenty of room to walk past the bed.

The sliding glass door to our balcony adjusts to whatever degree we wish it open during the night, for fresh air and to hear sea sounds. In one stateroom we occupied (*Queen Mary 2*), the door hinged outward—a very clumsy arrangement. Sliding is sterling.

On our first cruise, on *Voyager*, we had great weather—80 degrees every day and calm seas the whole way. Today will be 76 degrees, with brilliant sunshine. Perhaps we will have a repeat performance of favorable weather. I can get my daily dose of vitamin D out on our balcony while typing these notes. Such was my purpose for choosing the port (sunny) side.

Traditionally, passengers wanted to avoid the hot sun. Traveling from England to India, they wanted to be on the port side going east and the starboard on return. On their forms and luggage was written the acronym "POSH" (Port Out Starboard Home), a word we now associate with luxury and opulence.

We consult our "Cruise Compass." The newsletter placed on our bed every evening outlines the next day's activities. Slowly, leisurely, we get into the rhythm of life at sea. One maritime writer said that on a cruise, there's nothing that you need to do, and never enough time to do it. On *Voyager*, I tried to do so much that my schedule was stressful. Not this cruise. I spend much of the morning writing, using the Pages app on my iPad. No longer do I drag my clumsy laptop around with me traveling. Reading about the future of Apple and Mac computers, I find that virtually all research and development now concentrates on mobile computing. Laptops will be like trucks—useful for heavy-duty work, but not the choice for an everyday vehicle by most people.

I told you about Ruth back in the first chapter. Our two decades together were formative for me and they continue contributing in many positive ways to my deepening relationship with Linda. In 2007 Ruth lost her six-year battle with breast cancer. As the primary caregiver, I was left in very poor health. My teeth were brittle and troublesome (I lost seven of them), my adrenal system barely functioned, foot problems kept me on crutches or canes. I walked slowly, bowed and wobbling like an old man. My wellness doctor put me on a four-year program of recovery. I liked that. Four years seemed reasonable. If he had just given me a bottle of pills to relieve the symptoms, I would have been skeptical.

After Ruth's memorial service that February, I went to Budapest and soaked in their healing spas every day for two weeks. Back home, I joined a gym and centered my recovery on working out daily. In the spring of this year, I passed the four-year mark in excellent health.

Changes will come quickly. In a few months indications of coronary artery disease will lead me to a strict low-fat, vegan diet. Meals such as I describe throughout this book will become a thing of the past. Psoriatic arthritis will reintroduce pain into my walking and exercising routines. Yet, even as I negotiate these limitations, I look forward to more cruises in my future. Indeed, what better place to heal than on a cruise? I see people who are barely mobile, pushing their walkers ahead of them or rolling in their wheelchairs with oxygen bottles on the back. Good for them.

Upon learning that cruises are one of our favorite pastimes, a friend immediately asked: "All I hear from people who take cruises is how much food they ate and how much weight they gained. Is cruising only about eating?" We assured her that while eating represents one of the great attractions of cruises, it's not the only one. In these pages, you will see for yourself the nature and composition of our meals. While we like to take advantage of the great quality and wide-ranging options, I don't consider undisciplined pigging out as eating well. It is, in fact, eating poorly.

But we might well be in the minority—cruisers consume an astounding quantity of food. We always check out the cruise information sheet, as it presents some mind-boggling numbers. The following list is supposedly week's consumption:

Beef—20,000 lbs.
Chicken—12,000 lbs.
Potatoes—18,000 lbs.
Eggs—28,000
Lobster—1,400 lbs.
Seafood—6,500 lbs.
Fruit—35,000 lbs.
Ice Cream—8,000 gal.
Vegetables—65,000 lbs.
Flour—15,000 lbs.
Pizza slices—18,000
Beer—8,500 cans

I have a sense for numbers, and these seem a bit skewed. Let's say we have four thousand passengers and crew onboard. That means the per capita beef consumption equals five pounds a week. Considering some people don't eat beef, per capita consumption would reach one pound per day. Really? The same for fruit—more than a pound per day. Plus two gallons per person of ice cream in a week, and daily consumption of two pounds of vegetables, two cans of beer, and a slice of pizza. Surely the ship's kitchens make more food than is necessary; even the largest person onboard would have trouble consuming all of that in a week. The rest of us wouldn't even come close.

Consider this statistic: the galley prepares 105,000 meals a week. That's twenty-six per person, or three-and-a-half per day. Furthermore, in the same period, they prepare 234,000 appetizers and 300,680 desserts. Some of the desserts and appetizers get consumed in the cafes during the day, as snacks. Still, twice the appetizers and thrice the desserts as the number of meals—I find that hard to believe.

The morning behind me, I head to the fitness center for the first time in a while. I intend to work out every day on this cruise. At the same time, I have a single goal: don't hurt myself. I remind myself to be patient and not do too much too soon. I walk up the stairs to get to the fitness center. From Deck 1 to Deck 8 are 170 steps, with fifty-six more from Deck 8 to Deck 11, and sixteen to Deck 12. A grand total of 242! On previous cruises, I have done several laps up and down the staircases from the bottom deck to the top. A sweaty proposition.

I'm impressed with the facility. Some twenty treadmills line up along the windows, behind which lies a row of elliptical machines and bicycles. To the right is an open room for classes, such as spinning (stationary bike exercises). To the left are three rows of strength-training machines, and beyond that, a small free-weight area.

I limber up with ten-pound dumbbells. Once on the machines, I do fifteen reps rather than my customary ten, at lower weights. This reminds my body what it's like to work out. I feel pathetically wimpy. Even ridiculously low weights seem a challenge. My left bicep is sore before I even get started, perhaps from dragging luggage through Italian trains. On the upside, my usually sore right shoulder doesn't bother me today. Perhaps during my period of inactivity while traveling it had a chance to heal.

The fitness area features a hot tub the size of a small swimming pool. Back on the *Voyager*, Linda would come and do her stretches about the time I finished working out, after which we would both go into the hot tub for a while. Today, she isn't here, so I don't go in. The thought of germs notwithstanding, I really appreciate the benefits of saunas and hot tubs.

I walk down the steps back to Deck 8 and return to our stateroom, where I shower and get dressed for formal night. Wow, where did the day go? Morning in the stateroom, lunch in the dining room, a nap, fitness center, and now time to get cleaned up for formal night. I open that extra suitcase we dragged all the way through Europe.

For formal dress, some men go so far as to wear tuxedos and women may bring fancy ballroom attire. Often these are the more experienced cruisers—couples who have accumulated the relevant wardrobe. Such extremes may be apropos on *Queen Mary 2*, but on Royal Caribbean it seems a bit much. Still, I enjoy dressing up, as it makes the evening seem special. Linda has a knack for wearing the same long, slinky black dress and accessorizing it with beautiful scarves and shawls for a different look each time.

For this cruise, I brought only my Travel Smith blue blazer. I don't know what material it is made from, but I can cram it into my suitcase and when I take it out, there isn't a wrinkle. On some trips, I wear it as a jacket or take it on the airplane. It has many handy pockets, including an inside zippered pocket the size of a passport and another inside pocket, with a button, that is the depth of a plane ticket. Add gray slacks, white shirt, patterned tie, and I can get by. Feeling pretty snazzy, we have the ship's photographer take our picture.

They hold many events in the Royal Promenade. We could tell by the quantity of free champagne that tonight's after-dinner event involves the captain. Waiters arrange hundreds of glasses on a long table and then fill them in one continuous pour until each bottle is empty. They deliver them on small round trays to eagerly awaiting hands.

We've seen this party before. At the appointed time, the captain will address the assemblage from a bridge-like platform that stretches across the promenade. Not fond of crowds, we decide to forgo the captain's welcome. Instead, we head down to Deck 4 to the Schooner Bar. Having stopped in before dinner to check out the piano player, we wanted to catch a little more music before heading over to the theater.

Sergio is at the piano tonight. Older, with short gray hair, one would assume he's been doing this for a long time, and thus should be excellent. He starts out playing standard piano hits. The melodies are fine but the accompanying chords seem clunky, routine, and even inaccurate. No arpeggios or whimsical riffs, just melody in right hand and bouncing chords in the left. When Sergio plays, he doesn't talk to the audience, or sing, or relate. I guess he sees himself as background music. Unfortunately, he's at a great disadvantage: Linda and I keep comparing him to Ian West, the piano player on-board our *Voyager* trip whom we greatly adored.

When the seats start to fill up, some people sit at a bar built around the curve of the piano, placing them almost in Sergio's face. Even then, he hardly acknowledges them. He adds prerecorded music and rhythm tracks, some with vocals, and then mostly plays the melody line, almost like piano karaoke. He produces a full sound, which is entertaining. Some people sing along. It's danceable. However, we won't be here every night as we were with Ian.

Once, on a Holland American cruise, a young woman played piano and sang so poorly that no one even sat in the bar. Linda and I went in out of pity, seeing her playing to empty chairs, but we couldn't stand it. We left, too.

Last night, we heard Darren, the other piano player in the Schooner Bar. He's quite young. His playing is basic, and his voice rather artificial. It's as though he's trying to have a big voice, or imitate someone, or perhaps meet some kind of standard beyond his ability. His singing doesn't sound natural or authentic. Darren tells us his parents were both cruise-ship entertainers, and his mother is now a cruise director. I suspect he some inside help getting this gig. He has a good personality, driven by plenty of ego. I suspect he will grow into the job.

As usual, we get to the evening entertainment in the Savoy Theater thirty minutes early. Typical of older passengers, many had already claimed their favorite seats, including the front two rows, middle seats in middle rows, and the front rows of the balconies. We choose the front row of the second section of the right-side balcony, looking down at the stage at about a forty-five degree angle. Under the railing, a small ledge gives us a surface on which to play cards.

The theater encompasses three deck levels: the floor in front of the stage at Deck 2, the lower entrance at Deck 3, and the main entrance at Deck 4. The ceiling soars high above our heads, with banks of stage lights pointing in all directions. The front curtain sparkles with a glittery design of dancers all in a row.

Tonight's entertainment features the Beatles, a group that you may know from Liverpool, England: Not *the* Beatles, of course, but this group does a credible imitation. In their late twenties or early thirties and sporting the iconic mop-like hairstyles, the boys call themselves John, Paul, George, and Ringo. The instrumentals closely resemble the original songs, and their British accents are spot-on. Only "Yesterday" falls short of believability, being weak and too fast. "George" and "John" do some individual numbers, during which, from our side-balcony seats, we can see a front section of the stage descend. A mechanical arm stretches a net across the opening to catch anyone who accidentally falls into the hole.

Given this little preview, we wonder what will happen on that part of the stage. The next piece starts in darkness, with a piano solo leading into "Let It Be." Then, as the lights come on, "Paul" rises slowly from the depths, playing a white grand piano. Very dramatic and showy. "Hey, Jude" follows, which appears to be the last song. The group says its goodbyes and the cruise director comes out. Many people get up and leave, attempting to be the first out.

Instead of ending the show, however, the cruise director asks, "Do you want some more?" The audience roars in the affirmative. So the Beatles return and do three more songs, all of them heavy rock songs, the last one being "The Twist." Old hippie girl, down on the left side of the stage, easily dating back to the first Woodstock, has been up and dancing in the aisle the whole program, lost in her own little world (still on drugs?). Now, most of the audience rises to its collective feet and dances, including Linda and me. Down below, we see a woman dancing along in her seat. In the adjacent seat, her husband sleeps peacefully, head back, mouth open, unperturbed by the decibels.

The performance lasts from 9:00 to 10:10 p.m. The group will repeat the entire program for the second show at 10:45. I give some thought to attending a second time, but decide in favor of nursing my cold by going to bed early.

Returning to our stateroom, we find the bed turned down, adorned with tomorrow's newsletter and an animal (opossum?)

made of towels, wearing my sunglasses. Towel art seems to be a big deal among stewards. Seems to me that it would take a lot of time.

Conspicuously missing from our pillows are two chocolates. Yes, a small touch, but one that connects the present to an age-old tradition. Many of the cruise lines have discontinued the practice. How much of a savings can be gained? What was their chocolate bill? The drapes are closed, which we open, along with the sliding door to the balcony. Refreshing 60-degree sea air wafts into the room. Since cruise ship staterooms are similar in design, everything already seems very familiar to us. I find the bed a bit hard, but comfortable. We do our readings and review our day, expressing three things for which we are each grateful. Then, off goes the light. Good night to day two.

Sardinia

I have heard of Sardinia in my work as a labyrinth builder because one of the oldest datable labyrinths decorates a cave-like tomb there, entered through an obscure hole in a farmer's field. The tomb dates to around 2,500 BCE. If the labyrinth scratched onto the wall is original, then it must be 4,500 years old. In fact, the oldest known labyrinths seem to be associated with tombs, perhaps as a symbol of the challenging passage through the underworld.

Before passing it on *Mariner,* I never really knew where Sardinia is located, much less its size. To my surprise, it's the second largest island in the Mediterranean Sea, smaller only than Sicily, but bigger than Cyprus, bigger than any of the Greek isles, bigger even than Corsica and Majorca. It was named after Sardus (a.k.a. Sardus Pater), the son of Makeris, a Libyan mythological figure. He led a large group from Libya to inhabit the island, the name of which was subsequently changed from Ichnusa to Sardinia in his honor. Linda and I have come to really appreciate how traveling offers opportunities to learn about the world around us. Discovering the facts about this island is just one example.

Bathrooms

The functionality of the shower on *Mariner* contrasts well with one we had at our hotel in Menton, France, which was similar in size, but worked very poorly. Instead of being circular (a circle encloses more area than any other geometrical shape), the French shower was built into the corner of the room, forming a quarter-circle, producing much less interior room. The shower curtain would stick to my body, requiring me to continually pull it away. Ugh. Worse, the curtain hung two inches short of the floor, guaranteeing that water would escape and form a lake in the middle of the room.

I should say that having a shower curtain at all puts Menton ahead of many other bathrooms we experienced in France, which had none. Commonly, the tub has a shower head attached to a flexible hose. Apparently you are meant to sit in the tub and spray yourself. That means you must take your shower one-handed, which is made even more challenging by the lack of ledges or shelves to put down the soap or shampoo. Nor does there seem to be any way to avoid spraying water all over the bathroom. I've heard that the French save water by spraying themselves, then turning off the water to soap up (two-handed), then tuning it on again to rinse off. That would at least explain the minimalist design.

Stereotypes poke fun at the French for taking few showers or baths. In past epochs, bathing was thought to be unhealthy. After sex, one would sit astride a basin of water to clean one's private parts. Like the chamber pot, a basin was typical bedroom furniture in the seventeenth and eighteenth centuries. With the advent of plumbing and running water, both pieces moved into the new separate bathroom.

Americans traveling to Europe for the first time are sometimes surprised to see an extra porcelain fixture in the bathroom, a bidet, with two small faucet handles on the top and a third to control the stopper. In many French homes and hotels, the facilities are divided between two rooms, with an actual bathing room (bathroom) and a second room which houses only a toilet (water closet, or WC). Many are the stories of travelers unfamiliar with this two-room system who have mistaken the bidet in the bathroom for the absent toilet. Only when they go to flush do they discover the absence of such a mechanism and a drain inadequate to handle what they have just deposited therein. Their ignorance must be quite tedious for the housekeeper.

Back in the days when I led groups on tours to pilgrimage sites in France, I would explain (short of an actual demonstration) how the bidet works. You straddle it, facing the wall, and sit in such a way that your private parts are nicely presented for washing. From this "riding" position the bidet gets its name, coming from an old French word meaning pony. A porcelain pony. Rather poetic, no?

Our bathroom at Tenuta dell'Argento in Civitavecchia had a rather modern-style design with more than just a faucet for the water. It had a small adjustable nozzle that sprayed upward. I was very curious about the ergonomics of that design, but I did not take it upon myself to personally investigate. A quick visit to the Internet reveals a bidet industry alive and well. One company at www.biobidet.com uses the word "impressive" to describe its personal ponies. I can't remember the last time a bidet impressed me. A second company offers a toilet seat with a spray attachment allowing any toilet to double as a bidet. Be still my heart.

During my first visit to France forty-six years ago, I rather urgently rushed to the men's room, only to discover that someone had taken the toilet, leaving only a hole in the floor. I left, still in my urgent condition, only to find similar thefts elsewhere. I had just been introduced to Turkish toilets, also known as footprint toilets. While primitive, they are quite sanitary, as you don't touch any part of the fixture with any part of your body other than your feet, which are placed on slightly raised, foot-shaped plateaus.

The key lies in squatting fully. Don't try to stand up or lean against the wall and aim at that distant little hole in the floor. If you are in a full squat, feet properly aligned, your excrement will land quite efficiently in the designated place. Now *that's* impressive. By fighting the system and assuming other positions, you are likely to miss the target hole, leaving an unsightly pile on the porcelain where it oughtn't be.

This can create a problem when you pull the flush knob, as the powerful surge of water meant to wash the porcelain clean projects your mis-located refuse through the air and against unintended objects, including the wall and/or your legs or shoes. In defense against high water pressure, I have learned to open the door, make my exit from that small room, then reach back, pull the flush knob, and run, remaining ignorant of any further developments.

So, in contrast to my European experiences, ship's toilets are quite acceptable. Further, the vacuum system requires little water—a valuable commodity onboard. All black water (from toilets) is treated before being released into the ocean. I'm sure the fish must love it.

What We Eat

We can get a broader view of cruise dining by comparing ships or cruise lines. The *Queen Mary 2* carries 1,433 items in its food inventory on an average sailing—roughly three times as much as full-service hotels. A Carnival ship's provision list contains 950 to 980 food items. I imagine *Mariner* finds itself somewhere in the middle. Estimated annual purchases of food and beverages by all cruise lines top more than $1.3 billion!

Cruises provide better food than most resorts or restaurants, offering more food items, yet at a lower per capita cost. The luxury cruise lines (six stars) may spend $25 to $30 a day per person on food, not counting labor and overhead. Upscale cruise lines typically spend $10 to $16 per capita per day. For mass-market ships, such as *Mariner*, food costs run $9 to $13 a day for each passenger. That computes to under one hundred dollars a week. Rather a low cost for the pleasure and abundance it represents.

In the 1970s, I managed an all-you-can-eat buffet restaurant (King's Table) in Irving, Texas. Our goal for food cost was to stay under 30 percent of revenue. Using that ratio, a daily expense of $13 extrapolates to a value of $43 for our daily meal cost on *Mariner*. Since that calculation refers to cost, the retail value exceeds even that. Comparing the quality of what we receive here to what we would have paid for similar meals in France or Italy, I think the tab on land would be in the $85 to $90 range. Ironically, that price represents close to what we paid per day for the whole cruise, not just for food.

I can't deny that cruising equals eating. Everyone makes that inescapable association, with food venues everywhere, specialty restaurants, dining rooms, buffets, cafes, special events, and more. Eating's not the only draw, but food definitely tempts many people to cruise, including us. We marvel at the convenience of it all—we need only to show up.

Traveling on land in Europe, our rental car cost us $50 a day, plus gas at the equivalent of $9 a gallon. This ship burns fifty gallons of fuel *per minute*. What does that cost us? Nothing. We've already received the value of our ticket in the food. Entertainment? Costs nothing. Fitness center? Nothing. Lido Deck, dancing, bridge lessons, lectures? Nothing, nothing, nothing. What frugal person wouldn't love cruising? Our friends think we must be rich to cruise so often. Ha! Little do they know.

Cruise ships realize a greater economy in numbers than land-based operations, using bulk contracts and companywide purchasing power. Another advantage lies in consumption predictability. Hotels or restaurants may be full one night and empty the next. If they buy too much food, and no one shows up at the restaurant that night (or fails to order that item), much goes to waste. Buying too little risks running out.

Cruise ships use the same menus company wide, on all the ships, which they repeat cruise after cruise. Not only do they know exactly how many people will show up for dinner, they have accumulated statistical data that allows them to predict very accurately how many will choose the prime rib and how many the salmon, how many the Indian pakoras and how many the chicken. This allows them to be extremely efficient in planning, thus offering a greater selection than could a resort or land-based restaurant.

As if all of this weren't enough advantage for the cruise lines, consider also the human element. Each table has a waiter, an assistant waiter, a supervisor for that part of the dining room, and an overall maître d'. Their procedures for ordering and serving food have been whittled down and choreographed to eliminate superfluous effort. Rarely on land would you have so much attention and such good service at an equivalent cost. Cruise lines further economize by hiring crew members from Third World countries and paying them far less than their land-based equivalents. We all appreciate how hard our servers work. Yet, I have heard of tightwads who fail to tip anyone, thinking they will save a few hundred dollars. Let them walk the plank. The crew deserves (and depends upon) our generosity.

Our Favorite Pianist

Ian West has been playing piano in bars and other venues for more than thirty years. At thirteen, he was the organist for his church. Typically, Ian places an electronic keyboard on top of the baby grand piano, while down by his feet he has organ-like bass foot pedals. He also uses an electronic rhythm machine. His playing is extremely dexterous, occasionally throwing in a classical piece or two.

Ian lives in Andorra and works aboard ships about eight months of the year. A true showman, he has played all over Europe. Thus, he often speaks to guests in their own language and plays some of their national favorites. He maintains constant contact with the audience, including his trademark move, standing up on the piano bench and throwing out his arms wide, as if to exclaim, "Da da-a-a-a, here I am." On *Voyager* we became Ian groupies, going to the Schooner Bar every night from 9:30 to 12:30. That seems shocking to us now—especially the late hours.

To pass our time while listening, we played cards. Some evenings, friends joined us, as they knew where we would be. The two hat ladies, who wore different outrageous hats every day, were also Ian groupies. We invited them and Ian to lunch one day, and they all came. Of course it was only to the dining room, so the invitation was more of a gesture than a gift.

Ian's technical ability produces very interesting and complex versions of songs. He also sings along with many of them. His voice is mellow and natural in a pleasing way, which also keeps him from straining his voice during the nightly (and sometimes daytime) performances.

He filled the bar to overflowing every night, with people standing along the rails that divided the bar from the passageway. The Schooner Bar was on Deck 4, Outside the bar were stairs leading up to the Royal Promenade, one deck higher. In front of the stairs we used a wooden section of floor for dancing from time to time, when there wasn't a lot of foot traffic.

One thing that horrified us was Ian's collection of loose leaf pages, comprising his repertoire of songs. He didn't have a binder or an iPad, just an unruly stack of dog-eared pages of many different sizes. He would pass them out into the audience to let people look through them to pick a favorite. The pages seemed so fragile and easy to lose or damage.

We have stayed in touch with Ian by email. He switched to Norwegian Cruise Line for an increase in pay. The last we heard, he was putting together his own headline show to be one of the evening events in the main theater. He would be perfect for that. We would consider booking a cruise just to be on the same ship with him again sometime.

Majorca

Day 3, October 28, 2011

I usually start writing just after 6:00 a.m. to work in three or four hours per day. Even at that rate, the iPad slows me down and I'm falling behind. I have auto-completion turned on, as I am a very sloppy typer. Half the time that serves me well, and the word I have started to write gets magically corrected and/or completed for me. A little box pops up to tell me the word it thinks I want and is about to give me. If I don't want that word, I must hit the little X in the box to stop it and revert to my spelling. When starting long words, such as Mediterranean, after three or four letters, Pages (my word processing app) begins guessing what the word will be. If it's right, there's no need to type the rest of the word. I just hit the space bar and the whole word appears. The trouble comes when I am typing fast and not watching that little dialogue box. I frequently fail to cancel a wrong guess by the computer, thereby getting an unintended word. Typically, it gives me a possessive when I don't want it, such as *ship's* when I want *ships* or *it's* when I want *its*.

Under such circumstances, typing requires vigilance. When I accidentally run two words together or put in an extra space or make a typo, Pages takes a wild stab at a whole phrase rather than a single word. It changes what I have written to odd, often comical, things that make no sense. If I don't catch it while I'm typing, then later when I reread the sentence, I sometimes can't remember or reconstruct my intended words. Here are some examples:

"Just the opposite" became "musty el posits"

"And you can use" became "Andy UVA use only"

"Probably reading" became "Pro an greasing"

"Down to one part per" became "downtown online partner"

"Many teeth being changed" became "MA utter being hanged"

Of course, the original phrase is totally obliterated, usually to my amusement, sometimes to my absolute consternation.

Typing, typing, typing this morning, our second one (third day) on *Mariner of the Seas,* I pay little attention to the view outside our windows until a casual glance reveals a dim row of buildings. Unnoticed by me, we have arrived in Palma de Majorca. The ship pulls parallel to the pier, then slowly slides sideways to achieve docking position. Besides one fixed propeller, *Mariner* has two azipods, which are propellors mounted on columns that extend down from the hull. The column can turn 360 degrees, thereby propelling the ship in any direction. Side thrusters in the front of the ship also move it sideways. Wouldn't parallel parking be easy if cars had wheels that could turn sideways?

Like most ports, authorities here require a local pilot to guide ships into the harbor. The usual process goes something like this: Arriving in a motorboat, the pilot grabs onto a rope ladder and climbs a few feet up to a doorway, through which he enters the ship. Once on the bridge, he doesn't handle the controls himself. Instead, he advises the captain of local conditions and circumstances, pointing out where to go and at what speed. All of this has happened already, as the ship is only twenty feet from the pier.

As dawn lightens the sky, the outlines of the whole city start to appear. We can also see the name of another cruise ship coming into port behind us—*Bella,* from the Aida line. Cleverly, they have painted their website, www.aida.de, on the side of the ship in large letters. In case you are curious, the "de" stands for Germany, which is *Deutschland* in their native tongue.

Yesterday's prediction for rain seems accurate—the sky hangs low, gray, and threatening. The gangway to disembark from *Mariner* extends out to the shore with a bang, almost directly below our balcony.

To go into town, even for just a few hours, Royal Caribbean requires passengers to buy a shuttle ticket, which costs $12. We pass up the official tours, most of which would cost the two of us a hundred dollars or more just to see the three main sites: the cathedral, the castle on the hill, and the bull ring—two of which we don't really care to visit. Taxi tours cost less, albeit with a bit more risk. If you're on an official tour and there are delays, Royal Caribbean will hold the ship for you. If you're on your own, they won't. According to our information sheet, Michael Douglas, the actor, has lived in Majorca for more than twenty years.

The largest island in an archipelago belonging to Spain, Majorca (also spelled Mallorca) joins adjacent islands Menorca to the northeast and Cabrera, Formentera, and Ibiza to the southwest. Because of their location and sunny climate, these islands have become popular holiday destinations.

Prehistoric findings indicate that these islands have been occupied for a very long time. Everyone seems to have gotten into the act, including the Phoenicians, Greeks, Romans, Carthaginians, Byzantines, Moors, and, to everyone's dismay, pirates. The entire population of Formentera once fled en masse in the face of pirate invasion. By the mid-thirteenth century, the islands were part of the Kingdom of Aragon. During much of the eighteenth century, Menorca was part of the British empire, which left behind many traces of its culture.

Not being in a hurry to go to town, we mosey up to the Windjammer Cafe for some breakfast. I take full advantage of the buffet and have a good sample, including fresh watermelon, stewed prunes (maybe too many, I could get myself into trouble), spicy potato frittata, smoked salmon with cream cheese and capers, scrambled eggs with salmon, two small pastries, decaf coffee, and orange juice. Whew! That's much more than I would consume at home.

When finished, we return to the room and pack our things for the day's excursion: jackets, umbrella, euros, notebook, our room/ ID cards. No passport. They're still holding them. Because cruise-ship passengers are well documented, few countries check passports, and so they are safer left onboard with the staff.

From our balcony, we can see the sweep of the wide, store-lined boulevard that borders the bay, Old Town, and the Gothic Cathedral of Santa Maria of Palma. The buttresses of the cathedral are so close together that the space between them looks narrower than the width of the buttresses themselves. From a distance they look almost like a windowless wall. Yet, behind them, the windows still get plenty of light.

As we exit the ship, they scan our cards. After a short bus ride, we find ourselves looking up at the cathedral. An interesting series of events brought about this particular building. For a while, starting in the tenth century, the island was inhabited by Arabs, who built a mosque on the most propitious spot. In 1229, King James I defeated the Arabs and took control of the island. En route to Majorca from Barcelona, the seas had been very rough, causing him to fear for his life. He prayed for deliverance, promising that in return for his survival, he would build a church on the island. He kept his promise, razed the mosque, and began building the cathedral. Ironically, kneeling Christian worshipers still face the direction of Mecca.

Although started in 1229, work on the cathedral didn't begin in earnest until 1300, with the main facade not completed until 1601. From 1904 to 1914, work was undertaken to open the space, add windows and light, and relocate the altar. That work was led by the renowned Catalan architect, Antonio Gaudi, identified for his work on *La Sagrada Família* in Barcelona. (His work on this cathedral is described in the book, *Gaudi at the Cathedral of Mallorca* by Pere-Joan Llabres.) As recently as 2007, the Chapel of the Holy Sacrament was renovated, with new stained-glass windows by Majorcan artist Miquel Barceló. In buildings of this size and age, renovation, maintenance, and restoration are ongoing necessities.

We walk past a large pond and fountain, across a broad plaza, and up a long, wide staircase to reach the hilltop level of the cathedral. Entry is not through the main doors but from a side plaza. First, however, we are distracted by a souvenir shop, which we enter. Several small items catch our eye. As usual, Linda examines the scarves—always a favorite. In the back of the store, in a small alcove, we find a wallet lying on a shelf. It becomes immediately apparent that it had been stolen, the money removed, and the rest ditched here. The ID is still there, revealing a Spanish name and local address. It appears that the victim was not a tourist. We turn it in to the cashier at the front of the store, where we pay for the necklace Linda picked out.

The line to enter the cathedral reflects considerable diversity. In front of us is a Japanese couple, while the folks behind us are speaking German. Our tickets cost 4 euros each, which includes entrance to the museum. The latter is located in the former chapter room (where the priests, called canons, would meet) and vestry (where the clergy don their robes). Not surprisingly, the museum holds paintings of a religious theme, but the ornate silver work especially catches the eye. Among the reliquaries and chalices, two gigantic and very intricate silver candelabra stand five feet tall and must weigh sixty pounds each.

We enter through a side door into the nave of the cathedral. The vaulted ceiling towers above us. The dimensions of the space are remarkable. If for no other reason, the restored cathedral would be interesting for its sheer size alone. Most of the visitors have no appreciation of the technology that made such size possible. (I have a lot more to say about Gothic construction, having visited Chartres Cathedral in France fifty-three times over a period of forty-eight years. I elaborate more at the end of this chapter.)

The cathedral here in Majorca has almost delicately thin pillars, the proportions of which are emphasized by the extreme height of the bays. We know the original builder wanted the pillars to be as thin as possible, because his experiments caused the building to fall down several times. A few centuries later, in 1698, part of the church crashed in again and had to be rebuilt.

The open interior expanse and accentuated height reminds me of the cathedral in Bourges, France, built by masons not from the Paris Basin, as with Chartres, but from Burgundy, further south. Again, Gothic principles pertained, but the expression differed. The cathedral in Bourges remains today an astounding building, truly one of a kind, with an enormously open interior. It was built without transepts (the arms that give cruciform shape to most cathedrals), as are most examples of Catalan Gothic, including this cathedral.

The dimensions of this place are quite extraordinary, surpassing even Amiens Cathedral, the largest Gothic church in France. The ceiling is forty-four meters (144 feet—around fourteen stories) tall. Looking at this height, it's hard to conceive that *Mariner,* at 207 feet, is half again as tall. Wow!

The ornate decoration is very Spanish. We can see a beautiful pipe organ, but don't know the maker. I speculate that it might be Jordi Bosch, the eighteenth-century Majorcan pipe organ builder who influenced the young Aristide Cavaillé-Coll (whose organs are found all over France), but none of the literature I find makes that connection. Probably replacing an older organ, this one dates to 1795, restored in 1993. (Before my twenty-year marriage to Ruth, I was married for a decade to Susan Ferre, world-class concert organist. I've turned pages and pulled stops in some spectacular settings. Don't even get me started describing these magnificent instruments.)

The modern stained-glass windows flood the interior in a vivid rainbow of colors. The huge rose above the altar (a unique location) casts brilliant yellows and oranges onto the pillars and floor inside, to dazzling effect—hence often referred to as the Cathedral of Light. My main goal for visiting Majorca is to see this cathedral for the first time. Mission accomplished. One final tidbit. For some reason, both the cathedral in Barcelona (1289–1460) and in La Palma de Majorca (1229–1601) are called *La Seu.* I can find no relevant translation for this word. I would love to know what it means.

Finding ourselves in the midst of Old Town, we walk down the narrow streets, passing many interesting buildings. Signs point toward the Arab baths. One of the attractions of Islamic architecture is often the intricate decoration. My work as a labyrinth maker led me to delve into this subject in some depth. Since Islam prohibits art portraying living creatures or people, its architecture developed extremely beautiful and ornate patterns. (Think of the Alhambra in Granada, Spain.) Any serious student of geometry soon discovers the rich treasures of the Moslem world.

Everything in the physical world has dimensions, which can be expressed in numbers, ratios, and proportions. The patterns found in nature reflect the underlying blueprint of creation. Pumpkins and squashes always have ten divisions, for example. The eyes of potatoes line up in three parallel spirals. Always.

Where did these laws, these design principles, this specific blueprint come from? The Creator! Their geometry represents the direct expression of the Divine Mind. Hence, due to their origin, these principles have come to be called sacred geometry—used widely in art and the construction of temples and cathedrals. The highest development of geometric intricacy took place in the Arab world. I have spent many fascinating hours examining books about Islamic geometry and design.

The Arab Baths on Majorca are the ruins of Medina Mayurqa, a former Arab city. Photos I have seen of the baths show a far more rustic structure which holds little interest for me. My mind is still filled with impressions of the cathedral, which I don't want to dilute. And my foot is sore.

So, we don't turn in that direction. Instead, we follow a narrow street that meanders past an English bookstore. The owner invites us in for a look, but we shake our heads and keep walking. After sharing a quick coffee in one of the cafes, we head back toward the shuttle bus. En route we pass the Palau de l'Almudaina, which was once an Islamic fort, but now is one of the residences of the King of Spain, as well as a venue for special events.

We contemplate walking back, but decide against it. Our entire excursion takes only a couple of hours, so we arrive back to the ship in time to have lunch. They check our IDs twice and scan our bags. That's reasonable. I have nothing against good security. We ditch our things in the stateroom and head up to Windjammer, where I choose butterfish with coconut curry sauce, vegetable moussaka, cauliflower Mornay, and French fries.

Passing the library after lunch, I pick up the day's sudoku. Something is amiss here. Whoever handles these puzzles doesn't know or understand sudoku. For the third day in a row, the puzzle is impossible. I don't mean that figuratively, to express difficulty. I mean it literally. The puzzles are poorly designed. I have books of the hardest sudokus, such as the Mensa fourth-level book and the Friday *New York Times* puzzles. I have a book called *Sudoku Hell*. Difficulty levels in the books are called extreme, fiendish, cranium crushing, and the like. I can do even the hardest puzzles, using a variety of techniques. But the onboard puzzles from the last three days can't be solved using any method I know of.

Besides being a waste of time, puzzles this hard aren't any fun for the beginner or intermediate player. Or the advanced player, for that matter. The grid is printed needlessly huge, so that one puzzle fills the whole page. Why? Why not offer several—a variety of easy, intermediate, and hard—four or six on a page? Why not try Hyper-sudoku or KenKen or some other version? Sudoku should exercise the brain, not engender frustration.

That brings us to nap time. Then we sit on our balcony. On the hill above the city we see Bellver Castle, a circular construction of rather unusual design that took ten years to build. There must be a commanding view of the whole area from its battlements. This was one of the stops on the organized tour. Another tour featured the Dragon Caves, near the village of Porto Cristo, which included such touristic pleasures as commentary about the strange stalactites, a violin concert on Lake Martel, and a boat ride with a gondolier. Us? We're enjoying our balcony.

Soon the clock shows 4:00 p.m. We can see the arrival of tour and shuttle buses below, as the deadline for returning to the ship approaches. As always, a sail away party takes place up on the Lido deck. We can watch just as easily from our balcony, without the noise. *Aida Bella* has not yet left. We notice that she carries bicycles onboard, so passengers can explore the area. Good idea. There are also hammocks, a well-established sea-going tradition, since sailors once slept in them.

Although formal dress is not required every night, we still choose to get spiffed up for dinner. I wear dress pants and a collared shirt. Tonight, we are again seated at table 730 with its vast pano-rama of the sea. We are getting to know Valentin and Jude, our waiters.

At dinner last evening, we had a conversation with a couple from Austin, Texas, who were seated nearby. The husband, perhaps in his late thirties, a bit rumpled and pudgy, with curly hair and a goatee, revealed that he is a writer of pseudo-historic horror fiction, especially vampires and werewolves. Like me, he finds ships a mar-velous place to write, although the research is difficult considering the cost and slow speed of internet access. He chose Royal Caribbean specifically because of its older clientele, assuring a more genteel voyage. He and his red-haired archeologist wife find it more relaxing among us older folks. I don't remember his name, so Linda and I refer to him as Mr. Horror.

We speak with them again and learn that today Mr. and Mrs. Horror discovered the same English bookstore in Majorca that Linda and I had passed by. Similarly, the proprietor invited them in, promising it costs nothing to take a look. So the Horrors went in. They told us that they experienced a marvelous step into the past, with three floors of books comprising not just an English language bookstore, but a very British one, including a whole section of rare books and first editions. Mr. Horror asked about a first edition Tolkien, but the owner said he wouldn't even give the price, it was so high. He dropped the fact that he and Tolkien had been acquaintances. So Mr. horror ended up buying, instead, a first edition of a Charles Dickens work. Quite the find on a narrow back street of Old Town Majorca.

Tonight I order the vegetarian option, an Indian dish accompanied by naan, raita, and papadums. So tasty is the cold fruit soup appetizer, that I have it again for dessert.

The evening program in the Savoy Theater features *Mariner's* resident troupe singing and dancing. The professional effort put into the sets, costumes, and choreography shows. The performers are all young and mostly from Florida or Canada. Since Royal Caribbean offices are in Miami, they probably recruit locally. I like to pick one performer and watch him or her throughout the number. The movements seem automatic, repeating the same show every cruise, dozens of times. Still, everyone on stage smiles and looks like they're having fun. As one would expect, most are lithe and in good physical condition.

The music is a bit young for my taste, and I have to admit we were spoiled by the quality of the performers on *Queen Mary 2*. Most of the dancers in its productions were from former Soviet states, which made a difference. Physically they looked lean and wanton. They performed numerous shows of vastly different styles, which was very impressive. *Mariner's* performers don't reach to the level of *QM2*, but, as with everything else on this cruise, tonight's show proves perfectly fine, plenty good enough for the cost of our ticket. We enjoy it.

After the show, we again choose not to stay up late dancing or partying. It wouldn't matter, as we can sleep as late as we wish, but we keep to our accustomed schedule, old fogies that we are.

Gothic Construction

In France, the Age of Faith was a time of architectural experimentation and innovation. Most of it took place in dozens of small churches in the Paris Basin during the eleventh and twelfth centuries. In one place, someone invented the flying buttress, in another the ogival arch, in a third, the triforium, and so on.

In Chartres, France, between 1194 and 1224, some great mason, anonymous to us but likely famous in his own era, put the pieces together. If the small discoveries can be seen as individual instruments, at Chartres, for the first time, the full orchestra played. That's a good analogy, because its visual harmony is to the eyes what musical harmony is to the ears. During the past forty-seven years, I have visited Chartres Cathedral fifty-three times. If you find my commentary sounds like that of a tour guide, you would be right. During many of those years, as director of One Heart Tours, I served as the tour guide.

The story is all about stone. For all of history, builders had to deal with the limitations of stone. If they piled stones too high, the structure tended to tumble down. To make a tall building, they obligingly made the walls enormously thick to assure adequate stability. They dared not pierce the walls lest they become too weak. Hence, windows were few, leading to small, dark churches.

During the Middle Ages, a number of factors in France led to a huge building boom and a desire for the churches to be taller and more light-filled. The ultimate solution was unity. Rather than each stone being a separate, discrete unit, groups of stone were put in tension against each other.

For example, the weight of the roof used to be borne equally along the entire length of the wall. But when the roof rested on ogival arches, the thrust of the weight followed the diagonals of the vaults to the four corners, which rested on columns, thereby removing the weight from most of the wall. As a result, the wall could be opened for windows, eventually becoming completely glass (as in Sainte Chapelle, in Paris).

Bearing so much weight, the column tended to fall outwards. So they were connected to horizontal braces called flyers, which in turn connected to massive buttresses, located away from the building. These flying buttresses directed the forces outward, allowing the columns to be relatively small and decorative. To conceive these relationships, medieval masons envisioned gravitational forces as if they were liquid, noting carefully how and where they flowed. This unified system eventually came to be known as Gothic. Every component has its own job, each working in concert with the others. As a result, stones no longer represented units of dead weight. They became part of a dynamic whole, which led to cathedrals of soaring height with several levels of windows. For the first time in all of history, human ingenuity overcame the limitation of stone, with audacious results.

Churches already existing before Chartres, such as Notre Dame in Paris, re-constructed their buildings to adopt the Chartrain formula. Not only was the problem of weight overcome, soon stone would be carved as intricately as a wedding cake, as if they were just playing with it. These principles, brought to Majorca in 1300, were utilized according to the same physics, but in a different style. There are still ogival arches and quadripartite bays, still flyers and massive outer buttresses, but, whereas in France the roof was very tall and steep, an impressive part of the building's visual appearance, here the roof was made so low it is not even visible from the ground, as if no roof exists at all. That certainly solved any wind shear problems, but at a cost of looking much less impressive. To me, it looks like something is missing.

Stained-glass is another feature for which the cathedral in Chartres is rightly famous. Its windows were made using jewelry techniques normally applied to make glass look like precious gems, especially sapphires (blue) and rubies (red). The windows consist of layers of glass, some scored with parallel lines, which trap the sunlight, causing the windows to glow. People write poetically of the floor of

Chartres cathedral, bathed in color. Wrong. Oh, there are little bits of color scattered here and there, but they represent the repairs made in modern times, as we don't know the techniques used 800 years ago. In fact, the light stops at the windows and just glows—like the gems they are imitating. The cathedral itself remains so dark that it requires lighting even during the day.

In Majorca, the light does indeed pass through the contemporary brilliantly colored windows and bathes the floor, walls, and pillars.

A Bit of History

I love research! And my interest in cruises made me want to know more about the whole history of getting around on ships. It took me back in time, to the era of ocean liners, and I have to say there's a considerable difference between "lining" and cruising. Don't worry, we won't go into a full history lesson here, but the highlights really are fascinating. If you want more, look to the second volume companion to this book, in which I write about the nuts and bolts of the ships, history, and technicalities of ocean cruising.

In past centuries, passengers found space on cargo ships, whose itineraries were unpredictable. They would wander from port to port as opportunities presented themselves. Such ships, called tramp steamers, proved to be an unreliable way to get to one's destination in a timely manner.

The development of the steam engine allowed ships to follow a schedule from one specific port to another in a reasonably straight line. Hence, they were called ocean liners. Such ships moved millions of immigrants who were crammed into the cargo holds with unbelievable density. Travel was long, arduous, and dangerous.

Eventually, limits were placed on the number of passengers allowed within a certain space. Shipping companies began reinventing their ships to become more passenger-friendly. In their heyday, ocean liners became purveyors of status and luxury. Maritime newspapers reflected the social register, naming the famous people who would be crossing the Atlantic on a particular voyage. Ships became status symbols, famous for their glamorous appointments or their speed.

During the world wars, ocean liners served heroically, at a great cost. After World War II, the industry reached its most vibrant point. The United States entered the fray of competition, building the *SS United States*, the fastest and most innovative ocean liner ever built. Yet, all of that progress came crashing to an end when air travel arrived, offering a speedy alternative to many who would have once, through necessity and lack of other choice, traveled by ship. Only a few of the liners made the transition into a new industry: pleasure cruises. The Caribbean was one of the first pleasure destinations, drawing middle-class vacationers from middle America. Speed lost its importance. The voyage and the ship itself became parts of the entertaining diversion.

Just as the ocean liners grew in size and capacity because of the demand fueled by immigration, now vacationers became impetus for cruise ships to be designed and built ever larger and taller, with more and more balconies and amenities. If ocean liners can be seen as floating palaces, cruise ships become floating resorts, with casinos, floorshows, sports facilities, spas, fitness centers, childcare facilities, and much more.

If there was a Golden Age of ocean liners, we now have the Platinum Age of cruising. Never before have ships been more magnificent, safer, or more affordable. Now astoundingly complex entities, mechanical failure can be devastating. If the generators go out, for example, a ship can lose air conditioning and become uninhabitable. A small fire in the wrong place can cripple the whole ship. The demands of a modern cruise ship have completely changed the nature of maritime travel, for both crew and passenger.

In the second volume companion to this book, I will go into greater depth on these subjects. The old ocean liners still engender a palpable mystique. Just looking at their long, low profile, with several funnels slanted at rakish angles, brings to mind images of romance and risk. Some liners had lengthy and glorious careers, while others lasted only a few years before meeting ignominious ends. *Ti-*

tanic is a household word, synonymous with foolish pride and trag-edy. We should be equally familiar with *Mauritania, Leviathan, Normandie, Queen Mary,* and *United States.* They deserved to be remembered.

Cartagena

Day 4, October 29, 2011

Linda and I anticipate a long and wonderful future together. We set our goal at thirty years, which would fit into my previous patterns. My first marriage (Merle) lasted one year, my second (Susan) ten years, and my third (Ruth) twenty years—all multiples of ten. So, this marriage should last thirty years. I'm starting to get the hang of it.

Because our history together is rather limited, many of the things Linda and I do together are for the first time. In the area of cruising, however, we have a growing body of mutual experience. On *Voyager*, which left from Barcelona, Cartagena was the first port of call, on Day 2. In this city, we have a shared history of romance. We were less than twenty-four hours beyond "the kiss," experiencing our first morning waking up as a couple rather than as travel buddies.

I remember that giddy morning. Our love, newly liberated, filled everything we did. Here in Cartagena, on our first port of call together, we listened to a musician playing the accordion along the waterfront and walked the Calle Mayor, the pedestrian shopping street. Arms around each other's waist, everything seemed alive and fascinating. We looked and acted no different from any two lovers you might see on any street and then say, "Aren't they cute, so enamored with each other."

Not puppy love. Nor frivolous. For Linda, having lived alone for more than twenty years, a partnership now loomed. For me, devastated by Ruth's horrific death and my own physical issues, I was astounded at my good health, and that I could love again so easily. It was like shedding a huge burden of doubt and uncertainty, releasing my gloomy prospects for the future. Without the emotional lead weights, I soared like a bird set free from a cage. "Wow, look at this. Oh, look at that." Although we hadn't yet verbalized our lifetime commitment to each other, it was clear to me that I had an option other than holing up in my house in St. Louis for the rest of my life, writing boring books.

We don't hesitate to express these feelings of togetherness. At night I'll say, "Hey, there's a man in your bed," with an excited grin. We embrace often and laugh at the wonder of it all. We stay in physical contact all night, if only holding feet. It's unbelievable that we found each other, and fit together so harmoniously. Ours is no marriage of convenience to assuage our loneliness, nor to enjoy certain economies. We stumbled upon the real deal. Love! Deep, pervasive, unconditional.

I have firmly set my intention: to love *everything* about Linda, no matter how quirky or dissimilar to my way of doing things. When Linda does something that makes no sense to me, I don't dismay or try to change her or even try to understand. I embrace our differences and declare her ways endearing. She has complete freedom to be exactly who she is (not that she would accept any other possibility). I love the person, the ego, the spirit, soul, and body. M-m-m-m-m-m, that petite frame. I love *Linda*, not some hokey manufactured Hollywood fantasy. Her job description does not involve complementing my deficiencies or keeping me amused or satisfied, even though that happens pretty darn often. Rather, we are obligated to be fully Linda, and fully Robert, together, freed and enabled by our love and support for each other.

So here we are, back in Cartagena, where an isthmus of land protects the deep harbor. Its advantageous location has been appreciated in peace and in war for thousands of years. There remains a

Roman theater, with parts of castles and fortresses perched on a dozen of the surrounding hills. Here, ships dock right in the heart of the city—no long walks or shuttle buses. Again we reject organized tours. We sleep late, having stayed up to watch the seventh game of the World Series in the middle of the night. Hurray for the Saint Louis Cardinals! Linda showers and washes her hair before breakfast. She looks fresh and put together, but we are both tired and grouchy, impatient with the details of things. Quite a different mood than our first visit.

At breakfast, three days into our voyage, we finally discover the location of the oatmeal pot, our preferred morning meal. Conversation is minimal. Linda says her throat is still sore and she's conserving it. So far, this doesn't appear to be the auspicious return to Cartagena I was expecting.

A photo of Linda standing in front of *Voyager* in this port remains one of my favorite keepsakes of that first cruise. Although *Mariner* has docked at a different pier, I take a matching photo of Linda in front of this ship. Behind us, the pier extends a hundred yards to shore, past a marina filled with bobbing boats on one side, and low port buildings on the other.

Once we begin walking, our tiredness dissipates as the flood of pleasant memories overcomes sleeplessness. Strolling hand in hand through the park along the water's edge, we hear a familiar sound— the same accordion player as two years ago, with the same toothless smile. We don't sit and listen this time, as the benches are wet from a morning shower. Instead, we put a euro in the tip basket, pause for a minute or two, and walk on. He doesn't remember us, of course— probably half a million cruisers have walked past since we last did.

The town exalts in large open spaces that easily accommodate thousands of cruisers. Calle Major climbs a hill, rife with restaurants and cafes and stores of all kinds. Soon they will be filled with Americans. Signs advertise the fare, such as half a liter of sangria for 2.25 euros (a little over $3). Location is vital. Just half a block down the side streets, stores languish, completely ignored.

We window shop. Statistics rate how much money cruisers spend per day in various ports. Usually it runs from $75 to $125. Sometimes more. We clearly drag the average down. At our stage in life, we are divesting ourselves of possessions, not accumulating them.

At the tourist office, we ask for a post office, to get stamps for the postcards we bought in Majorca. As in France and Italy, tobacconists sell them in tiny, crowded shops. We buy the appropriate denominations. The mail boxes, large yellow cylindrical affairs, display CORREOS in towering letters. We release the cards, destined for our four-year-old granddaughter Anna, down the chute.

Another great joy in my life has been meeting Linda's friends and family. Thanks to Linda, I now have grandchildren. Being "Grampy Robber" is certainly a new role for me. I've also been especially impressed by her connection with her parishioners. When we go to Greenfield and Andover, Massachusetts, where Linda served as parish priest, hundreds of people remember her fondly and welcome her visits. Her churches have been small and intimate, perfect for her sensitivities and compassion, allowing close connection with her parishioners.

How proud I am when I see her celebrate her priestly duties, dressed in her long white robe and colorful stole. I'm especially touched during communion, when she holds up the round host toward heaven and then breaks it in two. It gives me shivers. Her sincerity is palpable.

Linda holds very specific and progressive ideas about liturgy. When we attend St. Mark's in San Antonio, or other Episcopal churches, she adjusts the readings to change all the male pronouns for God from "His" to "God's." I've taken up the banner, perhaps a bit too enthusiastically, reading loudly, "and blessed be GOD'S kingdom."

Women priests have had to work for their rightful place in the Episcopal church hierarchy and leadership. At this writing, for the first time, the top position, Presiding Bishop, is occupied by a woman, The Rt. Rev. Katharine Jefferts Schori.

In the fall, from late October to early December, cruise ships head west from the Mediterranean to their winter locations for cruising in the Caribbean. These, and their springtime eastward counterparts, are called repositioning cruises. Particularly affordable, they are our favorites. We have crossed the Atlantic five times and the Pacific once and look forward to many more.

Our last visit to Cartagena was at the end of November. Now, in late October, the city seems more active, with most cafes still open. I'm not sure how many ships stop here. I suspect some businesses will close down for the winter and then open back up when the tourist-bearing ships return in the spring.

Even though the weather looks threatening, the streets are full. Especially crowded is the small store in which everything costs 2 euros. Some of the jewelry and scarves look like good bargains. Linda asks the availability of a scarf on display, but they are sold out and the clerk won't take down the one on the wall. With no purchase in mind, all we want to do is escape. We slowly make our way through the masses toward the exit. Yes, we were intrigued by the shop, too, but pushing and clamoring for bargains does not present Americans at their best. I feel embarrassed by the whole scene.

After a little more than an hour, we make our way back to the ship. We pass the waterfront restaurant where during the last visit we ordered paella and met a couple who invited us to visit them in France. Before we reboard, I take several photos of the harbor, with traditional sailing vessels in the foreground and the humongous cruise ship in the background.

No paella his time. We opt instead for a leisurely lunch at a window table on Deck 11, looking out at the beautiful view over the harbor. I choose small portions of coconut rice, fish masala, papadums, raita, stir-fried vegetables, green bean salad, and pumpkin custard.

What is the value of our lunch? If there had been a high-rise building in the port, with a restaurant on the twentieth floor that offered this kind of view, what would they charge for a meal such as this? A considerable amount, I'm sure. It would be a special event. Yet, we lunch as casually as if it were an everyday thing. Oh, that's right, on *Mariner* it *is* an everyday thing. Adventurers have gone to sea for millennia, but never has anyone enjoyed the style, safety, convenience, and comfort that is now possible with modern cruise ships. I will make this point repeatedly. Ancient mariners would be wowed. On some of their unexpectedly long voyages, some crew members starved to death.

As the ship pulls out of Cartagena, thirty or so people gather on the dock to watch us leave, waving to those of us standing on our balconies or at the deck rail. Somehow, their gesture pleases me, as if we represent more to them than just dollar signs. I learn that a small ceremony was held aboard the ship for local dignitaries celebrating this first visit by *Mariner of the Seas* to this port (even though *Voyager* has been here frequently).

As we ease into the afternoon, the sudoku puzzles from the library remain problematic. Sometimes they don't show up on the table until evening, rather than at 9:00 a.m., as scheduled. The typical grid for a sudoku puzzle has nine large squares, delineated by heavy lines, inside which are nine smaller squares delineated by thinner lines. Today's puzzle has no heavy lines, just one big grid of eighty-one squares. Who created these? Does someone onboard make them on a computer, using some kind of strange software? Whoever it is doesn't get the gist of the game. I'm contemplating writing another book called *Cruise Ship Sudoku*, that will present sudoku as a way for us retired folks to stay mentally sharp. Perhaps one day I can teach sudoku on cruise ships, much as bridge is taught today.

The day passes—gym, showering together, donning our clothes, dinner. Wait, let's go back to the part about showering together. I find it one of our most pleasurable and erotic activities. It symbolizes, for me, a kind of tantric interaction not associated with horizontal sexual activity.

First, we shower while standing upright (I almost said standing erect, the implications of which wouldn't be completely unwarranted). The geometry and gravity of our bodies are different from when we are in bed.

Second, we share this event only with each other, making it immensely personal.

Third, how often can we wash our own backs? Certainly showering together represents improved hygiene.

Fourth, there are no intentions or expectations, other than enjoying each other and, I suppose, as a side benefit, getting clean.

Linda usually is under the water first, as her hair is thick and plentiful, while mine is short and sparse. When we are all soaped up, our bodies slip and slide nicely against each other. Shower arousal leaves me tingling and excited. The details are even better than I can describe here but I must exercise a certain amount of discretion. Some things we like to keep to ourselves.

At dinner, we are again placed at table 730. We banter with our servers. Valentin is from Romania and Jude is from India. The ship sails directly toward the setting sun, then turns south, heading for Madeira. My dinner: shrimp ceviche, filet of Atlantic salmon with assorted vegetables, and the appetizer, cold blueberry and yogurt soup, for dessert. I have been listing my food choices to give you some idea of the typical cuisine. The following account of an entire evening's menu offers a broader picture.

Appetizers: shaved cantaloupe and honeydew melon; shrimp cocktail; escargot Bourguignonne (I think this should be called escargot a la Bourguignonne); lobster bisque; oxtail broth; papaya and pineapple soup; Caesar salad; blueberry and yogurt soup

Main courses: filet of beef; shrimp ravioli; grilled seafood brochette, roasted duck; sautéed seasonal mushrooms; potato curry

Every-night staples: linguini with marinara sauce; filet of Atlantic salmon; chicken breast with seasonal herbs; Black Angus top sirloin

Desserts: bittersweet chocolate soufflé with espresso custard; low-fat berry mousse; double strawberry cheesecake; marinated cherry cake; sugar-free coconut vanilla layer cake; ice cream

Specialty Beverages (extra cost): espresso; cappuccino; latte; cafe mocha; wine; and cocktails

Eating is one of the great pleasures of cruising. No shopping, cooking, preparing, or cleaning up required. Just show up and order. For me, food has always been an integral part of my health regime. My diet has changed frequently, depending on the situation. Here, on *Mariner,* other than eating no meat, I have few restrictions

Soon that will change. Six months after this cruise, tests will suggest I have advanced coronary disease. So on my next cruise (*Rhapsody of the Seas*), from Sydney to Honolulu, I strictly followed a vegan, low-fat, low-sugar diet. Very restrictive. Although feeling a bit deprived, I succeeded in reducing my cholesterol level to an acceptable range (187). Further tests have shown that my heart is doing quite well.

Then psoriatic arthritis showed up, introducing me to chronic pain (wrists, elbows, shoulders, feet) and restricting some of my more energetic activities. Again, I experimented with different dietary regimes and discovered that eliminating wheat from my diet curtailed virtually all of my arthritis pain. So, during our next transatlantic crossing (on *Crown Princess*), I followed a gluten-free diet. While I passed on the lovely looking dinner rolls, to my delight, they offered one or two gluten-free desserts daily, plus special off-menu dishes that fit my requirements. In the pay-extra gourmet restaurant, they dusted my calamari rings with rice flower rather than wheat. They were delicious. The best I have ever had. Tender. Tasty.

A few months later, in Mexico for three weeks, I took a different approach. Recovering from a life-threatening bout of double pneumonia, I decided that I should have more calories and protein, including dairy, some fats, and even a smattering of meat to build up my strength. I ate corn chips and avocado and steak fajitas (my first meat in almost thirty years). I had gelato almost every day. (Yes, I know gelato is Italian, but along the *malecon* in Puerto Vallarta is this great little gelato stand ...)

Upon returning home, I felt younger, more rested, and more energetic than I had in years. Then a blood test showed my cholesterol had soared one hundred points (288) and my triglyceride level was totally unacceptable. Sheesh. As I do the final editing on this chapter, I am back to a more modest and responsible diet, mostly vegetarian and fish, similar to the Mediterranean Diet, still gluten free. Now, after all of that, I am almost without pain, and I feel stronger and younger than my chronological age (I turn 70 in 2014).

Meanwhile, back on *Mariner,* we head to the theater. The evening entertainment features a well-known Israeli "mind reader." (My notes have failed me—I forgot to write down his name. Googling "Israeli mind reader" gave me too many choices to be helpful.) He does a number of things that astound the audience, such as having people pick words randomly from pages in books and then divining what they are. I have seen this trick before, at a booth at World of Concrete in Las Vegas. Tonight's performer explains that many of the clues come from minute body language observation. Whatever the explanation, he guesses the word every time.

He stages an elaborate grand finale. I'm able to figure out how he does part of it, but some elements seem impossible to control.

Watching him, I again get a glimpse of what it means to be an entertainer. Imagine being out on the stage all by yourself in front of a thousand people with the assignment to keep them engaged and mystified and amused (or fascinated or titillated or even horrified, depending on the act).

I became aware of that essential quality for entertainers during our honeymoon on *Queen Mary 2*. A performer needs much more than just talent. He or she needs pizazz, a catchy style, showmanship. In many cases, style can trump talent. Sometimes, I thought comedians were being downright corny, even condescending, but the audience just lapped it up. The sound system contributes another aspect. I remember one musician who played about ten musical instruments, each so highly amplified that it filled the huge theater with vibrant sound, making a relatively ordinary number seem impressive. Of course, amplification also reveals any mistakes, so precision, pitch and dexterity become important.

This evening's mind reader invites people up on the stage and involves them, which pleases the crowd. To counter any suspicion that the people he picks are secretly part of his act, he asks someone in the audience to help make the choice. He extends his arm and points his finger. Closing his eyes, he swings his arm from far left in a semicircle to far right. Somewhere during that arc, the audience member says, "Stop." He opens his eyes, looks down his arm, and chooses whomever he is pointing at.

Later, I talk to someone so fascinated by this act that he watched both shows. The people were different and the answers were different, but the style and methods were the same. The evening held our attention and spurred reflection and speculation. Well done.

Leaving the theater, many head for the coffee cafe (that's redundant, isn't it) or to their favorite bar or lounge. The disco doesn't open until 10:00 p.m., swinging until the wee hours of the morning. The casino fills with smoke and a cacophony of mechanical sounds, ringing and spinning, with the occasional chink chink chink of quarters or nickels being dropped into the winner's tray. Some passengers go to the Lido Deck to smoke or play cards, while others walk the track on Deck 12.

We wander into the Wig and Gavel Pub, where we find that the guitar player spends more time talking between songs than singing. The pub is full; apparently people find his chatter engaging. Hoping for more music, even though he sings quite well, we leave disappointed.

Mounted on the ceiling of the Royal Promenade are different types and colors of lights that can make the area as bright as day, or, as now, subdued in a bluish color that gives the feeling of evening. We stroll a bit and then head back to our stateroom. Tonight's towel animal dangles from a hanger—a monkey I'm guessing—again wearing my sunglasses. We open the balcony door wide, inviting in the crisp salt air and soothing sea sounds. To bed.

Soon I hear the rhythmic breathing of Linda sleeping. I marvel that we found each other and are so happy. After Ruth died, I couldn't conceive of another relationship. The thought of being with someone else was abhorrent. Now, my feelings are all wrapped around Linda. Memories of Ruth have less and less emotional charge. I think of all I learned, of our shared spirituality sparked by the book *A Course in Miracles*, and of our travels in Europe.

When I moved to St. Louis, Ruth was the star and I her companion. Everywhere we went people greeted her and thanked her for the positive influence she had on their lives. Then, my star ascended as I became known in the labyrinth world, traveling to build labyrinths, give lectures, or lead pilgrimages.

When Ruth came along with the groups I took to France, she was like the mother hen taking care of her brood—literally. Usually, on about the third day, group members would develop colds, due to change of time, lack of sleep, different diet, and other stresses on the body. So Ruth would go down the aisle of the bus with a bottle of echinacea and put drops into the rows of upturned mouths, like a bird feeding its young.

At Ruth's memorial service, I projected photographs highlighting her life, starting when she was seven years old in rural Indiana, holding her pet chicken, Brownie. Now, other photos follow in my mind, as if doing the show again on the ceiling—grade school with her curls and plaid skirt, high school prom, college at Valparaiso, trip around the world, first marriage to Salim, us standing by a flowering bush in Tower Grove Park, operating One Heart spiritual resource center, ending with pictures of her rapid aging as the cancer devastated her body, her long blond hair replaced by short white hair and then just stubble.

I didn't take a photo of her in death, lying in her bed in the living room, looking like my grandmother. I knew she would never want anyone to see her like that. Nor did I want to remember her like that, but that last shocking image burned indelibly into my mind. I carried Ruth like that in my memory for years. Then, while cleaning through her things in St. Louis, I came upon two snapshots taken in our bedroom. She was standing near the closet, frontal nude, making a funny pose. I was reminded of her fullness, rather than her wasting away. I saw her frivolity, not her desperation. The photos reminded me of the real, vivacious, attractive Ruth. They replaced the distorted memory of her corpse, with its mouth gaping open.

Then I threw the photos away. My life is with Linda now. It wouldn't be appropriate to keep photos of that nature. My loyalties are not divided. Lying here next to Linda, the situation has changed. I have feelings only for her. I can't imagine how it was to be with anyone else. The previous marriages are just stories, history, memories. Only this new life with Linda is alive, thriving, affirming.

I match my breathing to Linda's, breath by breath. Soon, I join her in sleep land, smiling, happy.

Shipboard

Day 5, October 30, 2011

Linda sleeps on the balcony side of the bed. Against the ambient light from outside, I can see her silhouette when she gets up in the night. She sits up for a minute, perhaps listening to the sea or checking to see if the sky is starting to brighten yet. I reach over and touch her back or shoulder, an unspoken assurance that I'm still here. She feels so soft and warm, I'm never in a hurry to stop touching.

Several ancient geometric paradigms set proportions for the human body. One, from Egypt, assigns two proportions, one for the hips and another for the shoulders. For men, the lesser number delineates the hips, the larger number the broad shoulders. For women, the same two proportions pertain, but are reversed, with wider hips and narrower shoulders.

I really like shoulders, especially Linda's. She reminds me of Audrey Hepburn, whose petite shoulders I found attractive (not through personal contact, alas).

My thoughts about Linda stir remembrances of Ruth. Sex killed Ruth. That's a rather blunt statement, I realize, but that's how she thought of it. To stay sexually active, she took hormones which, she believes, led to her breast cancer, which ultimately caused her death.

Later in our marriage, sex with Ruth wasn't much fun. She was very directive, as in "Don't touch me there, touch me over *here*," as she would move my hand to the desired place. Our time in bed became so choreographed as to be mechanical, and not very satisfying, which, in turn, led to ever longer periods of inactivity. Essentially, her hormone therapy was for naught, intended for an active sex life we never had. After her mastectomy, Ruth felt embarrassed and maimed. She dressed facing away from me, and never really wanted me to see her or touch her in that condition. Eventually, her illness made sex impossible.

How great the difference between those poignant memories of Ruth and the tenderness Linda and I share. On *Voyager,* ours was a cruise filled with newness and excitement. We had never been physically intimate before, even in non-sexual ways. Everything on that voyage was our first: our first kiss, our first snuggle, our first shower, our first dancing. During that period of physical familiarity, I worried that all the skeletons in my closet would come tumbling out. What a relief to find that everything unfolded casually and easily, with no prearranged script or expectations. We succeeded in our purpose, to be together, skin touching skin, free to love with impunity. The wonder of it all continues unabated even now. Add the gentle sway from the ship, ocean sounds coming through the door, and a star-filled sky, and it becomes clear why cruising suits lovers.

Now, pushing seventy, falling in love differs from those youthful romances fraught with developing ego and raging testosterone. In reality, I never was promiscuous. One night stands didn't interest me (possibly a rationalization based on religious teachings and the fact that I wasn't good at meeting or seducing women). Then, sex focused on performance and endurance and orgasm at the expense of real intimacy. Once those shallow goals were reached (or not), the event ended, whether well or poorly, in either case, ultimately unfulfilling.

Now, being physical isn't so driven or fraught with performance expectations. We honor each other's sensitivities, maximizing our pleasure and intimacy with each other. That our bodies have aged matters little. I don't think I have ever before enjoyed skin time this much. One supreme reason stands out for why I like Linda's body so much—because she's in it! I love Linda first and then I appreciate the packaging.

Today we begin our fifth day of cruising. Many short cruises would be over already. Whew. Twelve more days to go. I expect to be a bit more active now that my cold is gone and I feel much better.

From our balcony I can see white wisps of exhaust, puffing out from the funnel. Beyond, I see the Great Bear (Ursa Major) constellation, also called the Big Dipper, which reminds me of the folk song about following the drinking gourd, an instruction for escaped slaves to follow a route northward to safety. The last two stars, opposite the "handle," point toward Polaris, the North Star. This relationship was certainly the mainstay of ancient mariners in determining their direction. But what about cloudy days?

Onboard, I've examined an astrolabe ensconced in a glass case, dating back several hundred years. There are little lenses and mirrors and angle adjustments. These were used to locate the position of the sun and stars in the sky. The original astrolabe was much more simple. More basic yet was the quadrant. Picture a pie-shaped object equal to a quarter of a circle (hence the name). Hold the bottom edge horizontal, with the second edge pointing straight up. In between these two sides is a quarter of a circle, representing ninety degrees of arc. This was used to find the angle to Polaris. This allowed you to fix your latitude north of the Equator. Various charts would provide the latitude of your destination. Once you were at the right latitude, you sailed east or west along that latitude until reaching your destination.

My first round of editing this chapter took place in Suva, Fiji, in the South Pacific, in April of 2012. Being in that area reminded me of the true story of Captain William Bligh, who was put off his ship, *HMAV Bounty*, along with eighteen of his crew, into the South Pacific by mutineers. Bligh and his men had only a few days' rations; they had no charts or compass, but they did have a sextant and a pocket watch. Their twenty-three foot boat had a sail and oars.

Far from the overweight, aging tyrant pictured in the movies, Bligh was thirty-four years old and in excellent physical condition. He decided to navigate to Batavia (modern day Jakarta, Indonesia), some 4,800 miles distant. As he passed through this area, he made drawings, charting some of the islands of Fiji. Fierce natives patrolling in war canoes assured that they didn't land. In an amazingly skilled example of seamanship, Bligh and his crew arrived after forty-seven days at sea in Coupang, Timor, from which they reached Batavia, and then returned to England. Bligh had a long and illustrious career in the Royal Navy. The authorities tracked down the mutineers one by one, and brought them to justice.

Like Bligh, Linda and I are charting our way through our new lives together. Apparently not all retired folks welcome such an opportunity. Linda and I give seminars on the spiritual aspects of retiring and growing older. Retirement is a time to do the things you never got around to when you were busy getting educated, developing a career, raising children, or starting a business. We both consider this the best time of our lives.

Yet, we hear about people who fear going into retirement, as if it means boredom and awaiting death. In one instance, a wife was horrified that, in retirement, her husband would be home every day, all day. What was she going to do with him, she wondered. Her home had been her own little enclave. Now, her husband was going to invade it. That's not the case with us. We don't like to be apart, frequently reminding ourselves how lucky we are, what wonderful lives we live.

That being said, I must admit that I couldn't sleep at all last night. I was obsessing about a troublesome business deal back home, involving an unethical contractor trying to avoid making full payment for work that my company performed. I just couldn't get it out of my head, so I finally got up and sat in the bathroom (where the light wouldn't bother Linda) and wrote for an hour.

At 5:00 a.m., *Mariner* passed through the Straits of Gibraltar. Our sense of geography is terrible. On Day 2, the mysterious island on our port side turned out to be Sardinia. Now we are again uncertain, this time about Gibraltar. As always, the solution lies with Google and Wikipedia.

Looking at the map, I'm surprised to see that the geography isn't what I expected. I have always thought that the Rock of Gibraltar stuck out into the Strait of Gibraltar at the narrowest point. Not so. The southern coast of Spain fills that role, where the strait is nine miles wide. Gibraltar is a peninsula to the northeast of the narrowest point. I can see, with the Rock and all, how it would be a very defensible and strategic position and thus desirable.

An overseas self-ruled British protectorate, Gibraltar recognizes the Queen of England as head of state. Resident Gibraltarians are full British citizens. Spain also claims this 2,642 square mile area, which was originally theirs, but was lost in 1704 during the War of Spanish Succession. In 1713 Gibraltar was peacefully ceded to Britain. Not long ago, residents held a referendum and overwhelmingly rejected becoming Spanish. The United Kingdom handles defense, foreign relations, and the like, having successfully kept Spain at bay for several centuries. In *Innocents Abroad*, Mark Twain recounts his voyage to Europe in 1867, including his description of Gibraltar as bristling with cannon and weaponry, with extensive underground bunkers.

To this day, Spain remains irked by the English presence in Gibraltar, yet due south, across twelve miles of strait lies Ceuta, a Spanish exclave adjacent to Morocco. It has been part of Spain since 1668. In 1956, when Morocco received its independence, Ceuta remained a Spanish possession, which irks the Moroccans.

Knowing that it would be dark when we passed, we didn't see any reason to set an alarm. Nevertheless, Linda reports seeing distant lights along the shore during a period of sleeplessness. That would have been Africa. I suspect shipping is rather congested here, which might make for good ship watching.

For breakfast, we go to the dining room for table service. There, we sit at a table with ten people. Conversations often prove to be interesting, as passengers represent a wide range of professions and skills. Today, we meet a space technology engineer and amateur astronomer who talks about the immensity of the universe. He says that one of his classes has access to the Hubble telescope, which is in orbit in outer space, avoiding the distortion of Earth's atmosphere. They train the telescope on one tiny spot that is dark to earthbound telescopes, like looking through a straw at one tiny part of the sky. When the pictures are studied, they can identify ten thousand galaxies. Not stars, but *galaxies*. Amazing.

Referencing his upcoming enrichment lecture, he makes an analogy. When Portugal stopped their sea explorations, they stopped being a sea power. Spain and England took over while Portugal faded away. Today, the U.S. has given up on space exploration. He thinks that as a result, we will become has-beens regarding our influence upon space.

Who hasn't looked up at the sky and been moved by its immensity and our seeming insignificance. The sea, too, boggles the mind with its size and presence. Margaret Silf, in *At Sea with God*, points out that *Ocean* and *God* are both experienced as fearful and awesome. Both beckon us beyond ourselves. She suggests that we let life draw us beyond our known (and comfortable?) horizons, like ancient mariners, to explore ourselves. Silf sees life as a voyage of heart and soul. "See what there is to discover." Humorously, she points out that the ark was built by amateurs, whereas the *Titanic* by professionals. We have an incredible journey in these little boats, our bodies, on the sea of life. How can we look out at the endless expanse of sea and escape important existential considerations?

In *The Book of Awakening*, author Mark Nepo makes a similar analogy when he says, "Each of us is like a great, untamed sea." Our lives are an interaction between waves and depths, the shallow and the deep. The depths are unaffected by passing storms on the surface. The deeper the draft of a ship, the less it is tossed by surface features. All of this fits together as, symbolically, water represents spirit. Cruising evokes profundity and mystery and power in a way that land travel doesn't.

As a labyrinth maker, I'm often interviewed by journalists. I first make the point that a labyrinth differs from a maze in that it has a single path walked slowly and meditatively. There are no intersections or choices to make. No dead ends or false passageways. In walking a labyrinth, success in reaching the center is assured. The purpose is more about the journey than the destination.

"What do labyrinths signify?" I am asked. "What explains their popularity?" I try to respond in concise sound bites. The labyrinth represents our path through life—circuitous, yet directional. If we proceed diligently, we will reach our goal. I tell the journalists that modern life is shallow and unfulfilling to the soul. It engages us almost exclusively at the level of appearances, fashion, fads, status, and so on: surface things, tossed around at the mercy of life's storms and circumstances.

Labyrinths can take people within, to a deeper place, a healing place, where we learn more about our authentic selves. Deep within, we are safe from the storm and not beholden to external expectations. Labyrinths have become popular because we need them as a source of depth in a shallow world. Why shouldn't long cruises offer the same benefits as walking a labyrinth? Why can't we find depth here, aboard a cruise ship?

We can, of course, if that is our intention. That potential exists. The quality of our lives is up to us to determine. But usually that is not the case. No cruise company is going to advertise "come on a cruise and discover yourself." For good reason. Most people come on a cruise to be distracted from business (life) as usual. That is the emphasis of most cruise marketing campaigns. To give you an idea of the magnitude of the distractions, the following list represents a typical day's schedule on a sea day, both official events and our personal activities.

7:00 a.m. Vitality stretch, fitness center.

9:00 a.m. Boot camp, fitness center (an extra charge).

9:15 a.m. Enrichment lecture, "Portuguese Ancient Sea Kings."

9:30 a.m. A lecture, "Arthritis Solutions with Acupuncture." Presentations like this are often little more than infomercials offered by the spa staff to entice us to buy their services.

9:30 a.m. Chat with the cruise director at the Promenade Cafe. I show up for this public forum to discuss the problem with the daily sudoku puzzles put out in the library. The only one I have managed to finish so far had two answers, a strict no-no in sudoku. What fun are these puzzles for anyone? I think the cruise director needs to be aware that the puzzles have been problematic. However, at the appointed hour, he isn't there. Some urgent business apparently called him away.

10:00 a.m. Movie: *Kung Fu Panda 2*. There are also movies on the TV, including pay-per-view, but watching them would simply be killing time. I have nothing against time, I have no desire to do it any harm.

10:00 a.m. Bridge lecture. Bridge appears to be very popular among cruisers. I wouldn't mind learning it some day and playing when cruising. Having a logical mind, I do well at cards. In blackjack, I learned systems for counting cards. In hearts, I shoot the moon most hands. When I see twenty-somethings earning millions at Texas Hold'em poker tournaments, I feel like I could do that, too. But it would take more time and dedication than I can give right now.

10:00 a.m. Progressive Team Trivia, Round 2.

10:30 a.m. Programs, offered by the spa, on facial fun (??) and on how to get a flat stomach. For the latter, they offer treatments that presumably increase metabolism, which helps reduce your stomach fat. Here's my (better) idea: Don't eat meat.

10:45 a.m. Ballroom dance class: The Tango. I think I was taking a rare morning nap at this time. Darn, we would like to have attended.

10:45 a.m. Arts and crafts: Make a gift box. The craft events tend to be on the simple side, yet they are very well attended.

11:00 a.m. Destination talk, "The Italian Diaspora: Why Millions Left Italy."

11:00 a.m. Classical guitar played by Jedidiah. This guy can really play, but he is painfully shy. He rarely looks up at his audience, and a tip brings a meek, "Thank you." He's well worth listening to.

11:30 a.m. Wrinkle Remedies with Dr. Ulises. Now you can get cosmetic procedures on board, such as teeth whitening and Botox injections. Oh, Lordy. Does the sea support such vanity? Well, in the days of ocean liners it certainly did.

11:30 a.m. Ship building. I presume these are small model ships. It seems like cruise directors are really open to folks with special skills or knowledge proposing lectures or demonstrations. I may do that someday, for labyrinths, sudoku, Gothic cathedrals, sacred geometry, and self-publishing. Linda gives a great seminar on creativity, plus there are programs we do together.

12:00 noon Ice sculpture demonstration.

12:30 p.m. Afternoon string melodies.

12:30 p.m. Superstar power hour: "The Rat Pack" with DJ Jorge.

12:30 p.m. Lunch. Of course, one can eat in many venues and at any time. Today we choose privacy and order from a limited room-service menu in our stateroom. I suspect they don't encourage room service, which must be a big hassle—individual orders and delivery to 1,500 rooms? Whew! We are on the sunny side of the ship, and today there is full sun. Our room is getting so warm that we're forced to close the curtains and turn on the air conditioning while we eat.

1:00 p.m. Royal slot tournament.

1:00 p.m. Movie: *Source Code*. The screening room has very plush seats, but has room for only sixty people. One of the features I really like on Princess ships is the outdoor movie screen on the upper deck, complete with free popcorn and warm blankets. Royal Caribbean is beginning to install outdoor screens on their ships. Indeed, *Mariner* itself got one during its refurbishment six months after this cruise.

1:00 p.m. Napkin artistry class.

1:30 p.m. Jewelry-making workshop, 2. Maybe I should attend one of these classes. In the 1970s, during my hippie years, I made my living selling wire jewelry on the streets of Austin. I did quite well, thank you. I had a sign that said: "Free roach clip with every purchase." Straight people would ask, "What's a roach clip?" to which I replied, "If you had roaches, you'd know." If that makes no sense to you, don't worry about it. You didn't miss much.

1:30 p.m. World's sexiest man competition.

2:00 p.m. Duplicate bridge play.

2:00 p.m. Cartoon trivia.

2:00 p.m. Blackjack tournament.

2:00 p.m. Seminar, "Beautiful Hands and Feet."

2:00 p.m. Classical string melodies with the Three Seasons.

2:30 p.m. Origami class: Halloween pecking crow. This class usually packs the largest lounge, the Lotus Lounge, which holds three hundred people. I guess people *want* to do origami. Ruth and I once folded one thousand origami cranes, two per evening for five hundred days, as part of her cancer journey.

3:00 p.m. Ice Show. This event is free, but requires advanced tickets. Studio B is an ice skating rink, a feature unique to Royal Caribbean ships. It has banked seats on three sides and bar areas up behind them. I was surprised to learn that it holds nine hundred people. Even then, they ran out of tickets and some people we left out. The ice rink has a retractable floor that can cover the ice. We took dance lessons there on *Voyager*. But here onboard *Mariner*, a new choreographed ice show is being developed. The new performers need practice time. So for these two weeks, Studio B will be used only for ice skating, and our dancing lessons will be held elsewhere.

3:00 p.m. MOB dance class). Held in the Dragon's Lair, a very dramatic and unique disco space on Deck 3, under the casino. The decor includes gargoyles and Gothic arches. During the day, it gets little use. If we didn't require window views, it would be a good place to hide away.

3:00 p.m. Search for the nations scavenger hunt.

3:00 p.m. Latin sounds with Mirage Trio.

3:00 p.m. I try to work out at this time at the fitness center. Usually, only half the treadmills are in use and few people are on the strength-training machines. The fitness center faces the front of the ship. Outside, on the Deck 11 walkway, a roof covers an area called the Peek-a-Boo Bridge, which allows passengers to look through small windows into the actual bridge (which is off limits, of course). Usually, there is little to see. Directly below one window is the main console, which may or may not be occupied. Surrounded by a low wall, it is cockpit-like, with two chairs facing monitors and unidentifiable electronics. Carpet covers the floor. Due to the steep angle of the view window, one cannot see out the front windows of the bridge or see any other activity there. A sign asks passengers not to knock on the windows.

Did you hear about the famous sea captain? Every day at the beginning of work, he went to the safe and took out a small piece of paper. Read it. Nodded his head in affirmation, put it back away, locked the safe up tight, and proceeded with his day. He did this every day of what turned out to be a very long and distinguished career. Upon his death, his crew was overcome by curiosity as to what might be on that piece of paper. So they drilled open the safe and took out the piece of paper. When they opened it up, this is what it said: "Port = left, starboard = right."

3:30 p.m. Line-dance class with Sarah. Linda and I go to line dancing every Thursday morning in San Antonio. I had intended to go to this, but I forgot to watch the clock and missed it.

4:00 p.m. Lafite Wine Experience, a.k.a., wine tasting.

4:00 p.m. Movie: *The Perfect Game*.

4:00 p.m. Book club.

4:00 p.m. Meet Linda at our favorite deck chairs, starboard side of Deck 4, the promenade deck. Today being a sea day (no ports of call), everyone remains on board. You would think the ship would feel more crowded. Not so. I don't know where everyone goes. We easily find available deck chairs and read our Kindles for a while.

4:15 p.m. Royal cash-prize bingo games begin.

4:30 p.m. Watch the sea slip past, stateroom balcony. When sitting inside the stateroom, the slice of ocean view amounts to only five degrees or so. I time how fast the water goes by, from first viewing on the right to when it disappears on the left. Answer: ten seconds. Every ten seconds we see a new ocean. We interrupt our reverie to get into our evening clothes.

5:00 p.m. Ice show (second seating), "Ice Under the Big Top."

5:15 p.m. Guitar melodies, with Jedidiah.

5:15 p.m. Reception with the captain for repeat customers. That doesn't limit the group very much, being about two thousand of the three thousand people on board. In the welcoming line, we each get to shake hands with the captain and say a word. Notoriously, captains we have met have been totally bored and disinterested. They offer a weak hand and say a disinterested and insincere "Welcome," while looking off into space, devoid of eye contact or personality.

Not so with Captain Flemming B. Nielsen. Young-looking with hair cropped in a kind of long crew cut; four gold stripes displaying his rank on his sleeves; he smiles and talks to us for a moment. I confuse him by saying, "We're two of the two thousand." Not knowing the statistic, he looks puzzled. It wasn't a language problem, just one of reference. Of Danish origins, Captain Nielsen's English is almost flawless, with just a little Scandinavian influence. So I explain that there are something close to two thousand return customers on board. He smiles, and says, "Well, I hope you will come back again."

Many people come to the reception (held in the theater, the largest venue on the ship) for the free hors d'oeuvres and champagne. Soon after we sit down and put our tall champagne glasses on the armrests, Linda drops a shrimp on the floor. Afraid someone would step on it and squash it into the carpet, I bend down to pick it up. In so doing, my right arm tips Linda's glass over, dumping the contents into her lap, getting her all wet.

5:35 p.m. Surprise unexpected event. We hustle back to the stateroom, where Linda washes her beautiful sequined top, her skirt and underwear, as well as herself.

6:00 p.m. Dinner, our favorite window-side table for two, number 730. Dressed anew, we skip the Captain's speech and head right to dinner. I have banana and orange cold soup, goat cheese and spinach pizza, pear tart, and hot lemon water (just slices of lemon in hot water—something we have each morning at home, a healthy alternative to coffee). As we eat, Valentin asks, "Would you like some pepper from my garden?" as he wields a large mill (a regular joke for him). Jude, his assistant, is more reserved and solemn, but he opens up a little sometimes. Every now and then we catch glimpses of their underlying fatigue, from working days on end with little break.

I almost ordered the Asian duck (an exception to my vegetarianism). Linda had breaded mushrooms, tilapia, and banana and chocolate strudel. We weren't pleased with either dessert. They seemed dry and tough. It won't be hard to give up desserts at this rate. In the guidebooks, Royal Caribbean rates only somewhere in the middle for its cuisine. I find it hard to remember the food on other cruises well enough to compare one company with another.

6:30 p.m. Conversation and contemplation at dinner table. Every night so far we have had dinner by ourselves at our table for two next to the window. We had intended to sit at larger tables once in a while, to meet interesting people, but two things thwart that impulse. First, the wonderful location of our table. Sometimes conversation stops and we find ourselves in silence, just looking out at the sea. The ship's heading is different today, so we can't see the sunset.

The second problem with large tables is my hearing, which is less than perfect. At a large table, I often can't follow the conversation. At a table of four or six people, I'm OK, but larger tables may seat ten or twelve people. Most of the conversation tends to be, "Where are you from?" "Oh, Houston? We're from College Station." "Oh, you're an architect? I teach at A&M." That sort of thing. Not a big loss if I miss some of it.

Then again, there's no assurance that we will enjoy the company we share. On one cruise, a man went off on a long tangent about his investment philosophy and all the money he had made and all of his solutions for our economic ailments. I felt like asking him why he was on a cruise if he didn't leave all of that behind. I hesitate to say I'm a labyrinth maker, as most people don't know what that is, so I just say I'm retired or an artist. Linda hesitates to say she's an Episcopal priest, lest it dampen the free conversation. It's just a lot easier to sit at our wonderful table for two and enjoy the romantic setting.

6:45 p.m. People watching. We notice Mr. and Mrs. Horror sitting a few tables over. During our previous dinner conversation, they were bemoaning the lack of good espresso, which they had enjoyed so much in Italy. We give them four packets of instant espresso that we had purchased in France, asking for an honest report. If they like them, I have more to give. They both seem overjoyed at the gift. Mr. Horror asks if I have an electronic reader of some kind. Yes, I assured him, we each have Kindles. He said he would send me a PDF of his book. So, I guess I will send him a PDF file of this book. All for a little instant espresso

7:00 p.m. Movie: *Love, Wedding, Marriage.*

7:30 p.m. Piano melodies with Sergio, Boleros Bar.

8:00 p.m. Swing-dance class, Dragon's Lair. We go for fifteen minutes, but the lesson is too slow and too basic, plus it's hot in the disco. So we go up to the Promenade Cafe until time for the evening entertainment.

8:45 p.m. Cocktail piano, Schooner Bar. Sergio again.

9:15 p.m. Showtime, Savoy Theater. The performer is David Mayer on the Xylosynth. This is a glorified xylophone with the electronics of a synthesizer, which produces many different sounds. It can sound like a piano or a violin or ... a xylophone. With the resident *Mariner* orchestra behind him, screens with images, fancy spotlighting, and his wife dancing, he gives us quite a spectacle.

He's an example of someone making it big by taking his talent to a level beyond everyone else. In the program we learn that as a kid he received a little toy xylophone as a gift. He stuck with it. In high school, if he practiced two hours a day, he could borrow his father's car. With two hammers in each hand, he plays like the wind. He does the "Dance of the Sugar Plum Fairies," he does pieces from

Carmen, he does Led Zeppelin songs, he does "Pachelbel's Canon." The audience deservedly gives him a standing ovation.

10:00 p.m. Movie: *Thor.* Did you hear that the god Thor decided to come down and have a little fun with a very attractive and curvaceous earthling? He took the form of an ordinary man, spending the night having sex. In the morning, he decided he should reveal who he is, so he announced, "I am Thor." She looked up from the bed, exhausted, and said, "Tho am I."

10:00 p.m. Abba music hour in Dragon's Lair.

10:00 p.m. Latin dance music, Boleros Bar.

10:00 p.m. "Piano Bar entertainment," Schooner Bar.

10:00 p.m. Guitar with Ned, Wig and Gavel Pub. Entertainers sign up for contracts, in Ned's case, four months at a time. They can take time off before the next contract. This is his twentieth contract!

10:00 p.m. Guitar melodies with Jedidiah, Ellington's. We go up to hear him, only to find the lounge reserved for a private party for the diamond-level members. When Jedidiah himself shows up, guitar in hand, the special event is news to him. He stays but we leave. Perhaps he plays for the event. Lowly gold-level members, we go elsewhere.

10:15 p.m. Bedtime. We go back to our cabin.

10:15 p.m. Majority Rules game show.

10:45 p.m. Second showing of David Mayer on the Xylosynth, Savoy Theater. He put out a tremendous amount of energy for the first show. Now, after only half an hour break, he does it all over.

11:00 p.m. Nightclub dancing, Dragon's Lair.

11:00 p.m. Dance music with Portofino Quartet, Lotus Lounge. This turns out to be our favorite danceable group, although not tonight. We prefer the earlier venues.

Midnight Paradise lotto draw, casino.

2:00 a.m. Guests seventeen or younger must vacate all public areas.

2:00 a.m. Turn your clock back one hour. Ah, an extra hour of sleep, one benefit of cruising westward.

So there you have one day's schedule. Of course, it varies from day to day. On port days they schedule fewer activities, but still enough to involve those who choose not to get off the ship. Just listing it makes me tired. You can see the variety. The activities that attract me the least seem to be the most popular.

Royal Caribbean deliberately entices passengers to overindulge, filling every minute with activity and food, hopefully involving booze, gambling, shore excursions, and shopping—to part us from our money as efficiently and painlessly as possible. In that regard, Linda and I are not ideal prospects. Our preferences are more modest, and we are less inclined to spend on extras. We happily take advantage of the bargains and free perks. In our favor, we are also great ambassadors for cruising and encourage all of our friends to try it.

While mostly economics, part of our resistance is philosophical: Excess implies lack, as if saying, "We'd better grab what we can because we may never have a chance to do this again." Similarly, moderation actually expresses prosperity. You know you have enough of what you need, or can easily get it and afford it, so you have no reason to go overboard (an interesting metaphor, as literally going overboard is a fatal act).

Some people use a cruise to abandon their normal standards of propriety, figuring they will soon enough go back to their daily routine once they get home. I admit, there may be a rationale for escaping one's limitations occasionally. But most of the time, when I see someone with a plate piled high with greasy fried foods and sweet desserts, he or she tends to be unhealthy looking, indicating a pattern established long before arriving on the cruise. Are you really getting good value if overindulging takes a toll on your health?

Such excess is subtly encouraged, or at least deliberately enabled. Do cruises attract people for just this reason? Those with no inner or spiritual life, or unaccustomed to quiet, meditation, or contemplation, can find silence and inactivity boring and threatening. Every moment must be filled with loud music or amusement or drinking or other form of stimulation. Cruise companies cater to these tendencies.

One marketing expert typified the perfect cruise customer as a middle-class couple from the Midwest. Compared to life back home in Iowa, even a mediocre cruise experience can seem exotic. The great mass of uncritical and easily titillated passengers out there are to cruise companies today what immigrants were to ocean liners a century ago—plentiful and profitable. My disaffection with such ordinariness is no different from my alienation from the crass commercial nature of American culture generally.

Am I saying no place exists on a cruise for a disciplined, sophisticated cruiser? Not at all. They exist in abundance. There *is* something for everyone here. The easily amused can go to the belly flop contest while I can find a cozy corner in which to read my Kindle. The more experienced you are in cruising, the more sustainable your habits will become. Excess is an unsuccessful long-term strategy.

Or, perhaps we're just two curmudgeons. Maybe we need to buy the drink of the day, take a class in *napkin folding*, or join the ping pong tournament. Come on, Robert and Linda, get with it!

H-m-m-m, let's just go to bed.

Madeira

Day 6, October 31, 2011

The sky is dark, with one bright planet showing and several dim stars. Having gained an hour during the night—one of seven or eight hours that we gain going west—I get up early and go to Cafe Promenade for coffee and pastries. Located at the fore end of the Royal Promenade (near the entrance stairs to the Savoy Theater), the cafe stays open twenty-four hours a day. The display case holds a variety of sweet desserts, pastries, cookies, and the like—all free. Just say, "Two croissants please," and you get them. Light sandwiches, salads, fruit—all free for the choosing. I especially like the huge serve-yourself coffee machine that has several spigots and holds gallons of coffee. The spigots that deliver the coffee are half an inch in diameter, filling a mug in two or three seconds. It's busy every time I pass by, indicating how much coffee is consumed.

This morning, I try again for the scheduled informal conversation with the cruise director's staff, but again, no one shows up. That's twice in a row. I go to guest services and ask how to interview an entertainer, such as David Mayor who performed last night. She calls and leaves a message on his phone to call my stateroom to make direct arrangements. I go back to the cafe.

While I sit at my small, round table, little snippets of conversation waft by. The subjects are largely predictable. Introductions establish place of residence, number of grandchildren, or former professions. Then the topic turns to number of previous voyages, favorite cruise lines, stories of places visited or strange things that happened. Someone always brings up the topic of people who live aboard cruise ships, rather than forking out exorbitant sums to live in a retirement center. Good food, medical care, a variety of people to meet, regular entertainment—what's not to like?

Living permanently on a cruise ship you couldn't establish any lasting friendships, except with the staff, and even they change ships regularly. So, you would live in a shallow world of constant, insipid pleasantries. Of course, that wouldn't be true if you lived on a cruise ship with your sweetie, as I would do. Nor would it be true if everyone else also lived on the ship, in which case the friendships would last longer, more like being neighbors.

Such is the case with *World of ResidenSea*, a ship known as *The World*, a 644-foot ship in which each stateroom is privately owned, essentially condominiums. Linda and I once saw this ship docked in Aruba. That something is different about the ship is apparent at first sight: the huge size of the balconies and their limited number. The 165 condo cabins range in cost from $1.4 million (studio, around 290 square feet) to $6 or 7 million (two- and three-bedroom units from 1,400 square feet to 2,000 square feet). Someone told me that the annual condo maintenance fee is $300 per square foot. For a two-bedroom unit, that would be $420,000 per year! *The World* circumnavigates the globe at a leisurely pace every two years or so, taking special excursions and onboard luxury to new levels. Their motto is "Travel the world without leaving home."

Linda doesn't find such a world of wealth, luxury, and privilege to be very attractive. To visit, maybe, for a week or two, but not as a permanent lifestyle. I suppose it wouldn't take much to hold a position that such extravagance is excessive and even immoral. Yet, I'm attracted to it. When I really want to daydream, I visit www.aboardtheworld.com and check out the units currently for sale. The sales pitch is certainly enticing:

Launched in 2002, The World *is the largest privately owned, residential yacht on earth with 165 luxury Residences. A diverse group of Residents from 19 countries own the homes onboard and share interests in world cultures, history and adventure, and exploring fascinating destinations. They circumnavigate the globe every two to three years following an extraordinary itinerary that they select. In-depth expeditions and one-of-a-kind experiences are complemented by world-class amenities and impeccable service.*

Meanwhile, back in the real world, I arrive back to our humble stateroom just as Linda hangs up the telephone, having talked with someone on the PR staff who set up an interview for me on November 2. Apparently my requests for information have at last come to some fruition. We'll see.

Madeira is now visible on the starboard side. We will have only a short afternoon to visit the area, from noon to 5:30 p.m. However, at 4:00 p.m. a sudoku challenge will be held in the library. I'd like to go and see exactly what takes place and who is organizing it.

An orange sun peeks through the ranks of clouds as we sit down to breakfast in the stern of the ship. Weather prediction: 76 degrees and partly cloudy. As I got dressed this morning, I discovered I had left my long-sleeved travel shirt, which I use as a jacket in case the air conditioning is too cool, in the cafe last night. We go to guest services and, happily retrieve one of my favorite wardrobe items. I'm glad not to have lost it. Thanks to someone for turning it in, and to those who kept it safe for me.

I worry that during the hours I spend writing Linda feels neglected. She says she's enjoying reading, either from the ship's library or on her Kindle. True, at home we don't get to read as much as we would like to. Equally true, I would like to have a little more free time, so I too can read. This morning, in the stateroom, Linda did a little watercolor painting. I was glad to see that. Of course, at the end of the day, sitting at our table in the dining room, looking out at the sea, we both acknowledge how wonderful our lives are right now. So, I guess I shouldn't worry. Linda can speak up if she needs something.

While in port, the crew performs maintenance on the exterior of the ship. They sometimes use boats (or once, a barge) to pull alongside. Other times the crew will stand on the dock and paint with long poles. When the ship is not moving, workers can hang down in harnesses to work on hard-to-reach areas. The average cruise ship dedicates sixteen crew members to do nothing but paint, night and day, at sea or in port: paint, paint, paint! They consume as much as eighty gallons every week. Rather like the Golden Gate Bridge, when they finish painting, they go to the other end and start over.

The problem is the salt. People who live on coasts know that sea air corrodes automobiles. Even more so a ship in the water. Here again we have a love/hate relationship with the sea. It supports the ship and provides a surface on which to travel, yet at the same time, left unchecked, it would create lethal rot and rust. Many ships at sea, such as freighters and tankers, hide deplorable conditions under a coat of paint. That may fool the inspectors, but heavy seas can cause a poorly maintained hull to break apart and be lost—an event that happens many times every year.

You can read *The Outlaw Sea: A World of Freedom, Chaos, and Crime* by William Langewiesche to get a picture of how dire a problem this is. Another interesting book is *Super Ship* by Noel Mostert, written in 1974 about tankers. Dozens of tankers break up every year, spilling their contents into the ocean and onto shores. We've been told that cruise ships are the largest man-made objects that move, but tankers are actually larger. A cruise ship is 10 percent below water and 90 percent above, whereas tankers are just the opposite. The hugest ones have such a deep draught that they can't go near the shore, or into the English Channel or the Black Sea. Compare the largest cruise ship *Allure of the Seas* with *Knock Nevis* (better known as *Seawise Giant*), which was at one time the largest tanker.

	Allure	*Knock Nevis*
Length	1,181 feet	1,504 feet
Beam	184 feet	236 feet
Draft	31 feet	97 feet
GRT (enclosed area)	225,282 tons	236,710 tons
DWT (cargo)	19,750 tons	564,650 tons
Speed	22.6 knots	13.6 knots
Displacement	100,000 tons	647,951 tons

The deck surface of the *Knock Nevis* stretches to almost ten acres. Picture five football fields end to end, with five more alongside. The two ships share a similar volume (GRT), but *Allure* contains mostly air inside, whereas the tanker carries 4.1 million barrels of crude oil. Being mostly a submarine, the tanker is much slower and far less maneuverable. The *Knock Nevis* was put out of service because it couldn't fit through the Suez Canal—it had to take the long route. The last I heard, it was being used as a floating storage tank.

While the crew begins their painting, we head to lunch. At the buffet I pile on sweet potato slices with brown sugar, fish balls (I didn't know that fish ... oh, never mind), Burmese coconut fish soup, and chocolate mousse.

We go down and stand in line to be among the first to get off the ship. We wait perhaps ten or twelve minutes, scan our ID cards, file over to the shuttle bus, and ride into Funchal to the base of the cable-car lift. On our last visit, on *Voyager*, we took a tour that rambled through banana groves and vineyards, all terraced on the sides of the steep hills. We went to the top of the highest sea cliff in Europe, Cabo Girão, more than 1,700 feet above the sea (a different source said 1,930 feet). Then we visited a hotel and vineyard for a wine tasting. They served cheese and bread with the wine. It wasn't the legendary fortified Madeira wine, however, just normal table wine. The cheese was wonderful. Everyone kept asking about buying the cheese. The irritated hosts kept saying, "The cheese *isn't* for sale, this is about the *wine*."

During the period of sea exploration, Madeira and the Canary Islands were the furthest west stepping off points, before heading into the unknown. Madeira wine was fortified with spirits distilled from grapes so that it would travel longer and give more of a punch for its volume. Hence the song, "Have some Madeira, m'dear, you have nothing to fear ..." Other fortified wines are spiked with brandy. They are excellent for cooking and last quite a while after opening.

Home of the world's first sugar plantation, Madeira produces bananas as its main crop. The bananas here are smaller (but sweeter and tastier) than those found on trees in Central America. Each plant produces a single red flower which becomes a large bunch of bananas. I thought that meant only one banana crop per year, after which the plant is destroyed, until I learned that the plants are hermaphrodite, which means they are self-reproducing. During the growing process, they send off shoots which will become other individual plants.

The hills are very steep and terraced. Left undirected, rain water would just rush down the hill, so beginning in the sixteenth century, residents have built many miles of irrigation ditches, called *levadas*, that cut into the hills horizontally. About two feet wide and deep, they usually have a path beside them, which creates a perfect network for hiking.

We think Madeira is a paradise, rightly called the Pearl of the Atlantic. One writer said the whole island is like one big botanical garden, brimming with hydrangeas, bougainvilleas, geraniums, and more. Last visit, I took a photo of Linda standing by some brilliantly red sword aloe vera plants. I remember the purple jacaranda and various types of frangipani growing everywhere. The air is fragrant with the smell of blossoms, a floating garden in an azure sea.

We recently read that mudslides here had done some damage and taken some lives. Given how steep the hills are, I guess heavy rains would cause a dangerous situation. There aren't good beaches here, either. For that, you must go to another of the Madeira Islands, Porto Santo.

This is a marvelous city for walking. We start in the Old Town which, as you would expect, has narrow streets. They are lined with restaurants, each with tables spread in the street, all decorated to look very inviting. The owners or employees stand out next to the menu and invite us to take a look. We had just eaten on the ship, so we weren't interested, but we exchanged pleasantries as we moved down the street.

One side street was clearly for locals, with dark nameless bars filled with workers. The newer part of town has numerous pedestrianized streets or wide sidewalks, many of which have decorative designs in the pavement made from black and white chips of a slate-like stone. Some have checkerboard patterns, others spirals or geometric designs. Laid one piece at a time, the walkways represent miles of mosaic—quite a feat. We've also discovered similar pavement designs in Lisbon and the Azores, which like Madeira, are part of Portugal.

We seek our usual destination, a place with Internet access. We end up in a bar, thanks to an attractive young woman who engaged us in conversation as we passed, inviting us in. I have a fruit cup and Linda a beer as we casually spend an hour answering our emails. On the ship, the tab would have been more than $30.

Linda has been asked to do a memorial service for a former parishioner up in Massachusetts, to which she will fly immediately upon our return to San Antonio. She's working out the details for airfare, lodging, and transportation.

I have emails requesting information about making labyrinths, mostly do-it-yourselfers seeking technical advice, or, in one case, an Eagle Scout project. I promise everyone that I will reply in more length when we get back to Texas.

Continuing our walk, we end up on a street with a forty-foot-wide patterned sidewalk. Numerous benches entice us to sit, while attractive cafes also beckon. We buy a day-old *International Herald Tribune*—today's edition doesn't arrive until late afternoon—one of the disadvantages of living on a distant island. We notice signs indicating that this whole street is a hot spot for Internet access. Sitting on a bench, Linda opens the iPad, and sure enough, she gets online. None of our friends are currently on Skype, because of the time difference. It's about 7:00 a.m. back home. Usually during our travels, when we reach someone, we hold up the camera and show them our surroundings, but not onboard ship. The bandwidth is so minimal that Skype might not even work. Signs ask people *not* to Skype onboard.

The prices in Funchal, at both restaurants and stores, are less than we found in Italy and France. Madeira is located off the coast of Morocco, close to Africa. After our second visit, we are now even more convinced that we would like to return here for a longer stay. We have seen online affordable hotels in wonderful scenic locations (60 euros a night, that sort of thing). October seems like the perfect time to visit. Linda says she doesn't want to fly here. ("No small planes for me, thank you very much.") I guess we could take a ship from Portugal.

People fill the streets. The Aida ship *Sol* is also in port. A few of the stores have signs in the windows indicating that they are officially approved by the cruise lines as being reputable and honest. Of course, Royal Caribbean gets a kickback for that recommendation. Signs in one window indicate special prices for "*Mariner of the Seas* crew." Did they really mean only those who work on the ship, and not passengers? Perhaps they mean "cruisers."

I'm quite impressed by the extent to which the rest of the world speaks English. Still, I think it's incumbent for travelers to learn at least a few polite phrases in the local language. I say *bom-dia* (good day), enjoying the smooth way it slides off the tongue. I tried to learn a little Portuguese when I went to Brazil with Ruth, but I don't remember much now. Later I learn that my greeting is particularly Brazilian and looked down on in Madeira. Oh well, I tried.

With this profusion of pedestrian streets, we expected to find many street performers. Look at *Las Ramblas* in Barcelona, for goodness sake. Today we see only one, a young woman playing a kind of hammered dulcimer, using a flat pick and her fingers. Dark and lithe, she has a pile of CDs for sale. We don't buy one.

When we feel we've seen enough, we walk back to the ship, getting there around 3:00 p.m., well ahead of the deadline. Earlier, when we were dropped off at the foot of the cable cars, we saw open-topped buses offering ninety-minute tours, with the option to hop on and off as desired. We were tempted. They cost 12 euros, the same price we each paid for the one-mile mandatory shuttle ride from the ship. Just at the entrance to the dock, we notice taxis that will take several people to the center of town for 7 euros. The shuttle bus wasn't such a good deal. We would rather have a choice than be told what to do. I'm sure the taxi drivers would appreciate that, too.

Cruise ships have been stopping in Madeira for more than a century. In *A Trip to the Orient: Story of a Mediterranean Cruise*, Robert Urie Jacob writes a detailed account of a cruise in 1907 on Hamburg America's *Moltke*. Hamburg America developed pleasure cruises and around-the-world voyages decades ahead of its time. Jacob's now-dated descriptions of the places he visited are quite a hoot.

He had two qualms about going on the cruise: 1) Would seventy days be enough to adequately cover the 14,000-mile trip, and 2) Would the five hundred passengers constitute a crowd? He overcame those objections and took the journey. He calls his fellow passengers "tourists," as do the official publications, which he quotes. They are awakened each morning by "Reveille" played on a bugle, followed by the steward tapping on each door. Wrapped in blankets out in their assigned deck chairs, the passengers looked forward to hot tea and bouillon brought by the stewards.

Seven days after their departure from New York, they arrived at the first stop, Funchal, Madeira. Think of it—only seven days to cross the Atlantic more than a century ago. Arriving late at night, the only places open were bars and casinos, which were glad to see the arrival of dollars. Throughout the year, Jacob points out, the temperature of Madeira is like May in England.

The tourists were tendered into shore the next morning, after which the following happened:

> *There, in place of cabs, a hundred low sleds with canopy tops and cushioned seats were in readiness to convey us on a sight-seeing excursion through the city. This ride in ox-drags was a novel experience. Each sled was dragged by two bullocks, driven without reins by loud-voiced natives who, with frequent yelling and prodding sticks, urged on their teams. The drivers carried bunches of greasy rags which they occasionally threw underneath the sled-runners as a lubricant to diminish the friction of their movement over the stone-paved streets.*

Think of that. A hundred sleds would have been pulled by two hundred bullocks. Think of the noise of the drivers and the sleds dragging on the ground, not to mention that they would drag through piles the bullocks deposited onto the street as they passed. Quite a different scene than today. He complained that the residents seemed disinterested in the visitors, barely giving them a glance. Clearly not the highly developed tourist economy of modern Madeira.

A group of tourists from his ship went up a cogwheel railway to the top of the hill and then rode down on sleds, just as they still do today. Rowboats gathered around his ship, with peddlers selling their wares. Others went right on board and set up on the decks. Residents could come out and visit the ship. Not the kind of security we have today.

As was the custom of the time, passengers got together to form their own entertainment, games, lectures, and so on. They spoke highly of their "cozy" staterooms. Wouldn't they have been surprised to see the developments of the subsequent century of cruising?

Of course, people have been traveling the globe for millennia. Historically, world travel has brought with it many dangers. The plague, which devastated Europe in the Middle Ages, began when a Genoese ship brought an infected person from the Black Sea to Sicily in 1347.

Similarly, a major cholera pandemic from 1899 to 1923 began in India, where it killed more than 800,000 people (that's not a typo), and spread by ship passengers to the Middle East, North Africa, Eastern Europe, and Russia. The last cholera outbreak in the United States was in 1910–1911 when *Moltke,* the same steamship that took Robert Jacob to Madeira brought infected people to New York City from Naples. They were quarantined on Swinburne Island, which contained the spread of the disease, although eleven travelers and one health worker died.

We take our afternoon naps, and then I go down to the library for the 4:00 p.m. Sudoku Challenge. I wait fifteen minutes and nothing happens. The only three people there argue vociferously about politics, decrying the state of the world. So I go back to the room. We look at the schedule and discover the venue for the Sudoku Challenge is the Schooner Bar, not the library. I had remembered it wrong. I rush down, only to find the person in charge packing up, the event over. Four people had showed up, she tells me. They raced to see who could finish a particular puzzle the quickest. Darn, I missed it. She gives me the puzzle, which I sit down and complete in about two minutes. I think I could'a been a contender. I don't bother to explain to the crew member the problems with their daily sudokus.

Suppose you had a moment in your day, towards evening, which brought everything into focus, that assured a comforting continuity, that acted as a gyroscope, giving stability to your activities, becoming a time to anticipate and to remember. We have exactly such a moment in our day: our dinner, sitting at our table for two next to the window, looking out at the passing sea. Somehow, everything feels right. The movement of the sea adds a consistent, almost relentless normalcy. Sure, if the sea were raging against us, it would be a different situation. Without exception, the sea has been the element that touches us both the most deeply.

Deciding to attend the 7:00 p.m. entertainment, we go to dinner at the earliest time, 5:30 p.m. Seated next to us are two ladies from Texas who are outlandishly snobbish, we're-better-than-you, unfriendly, condescending. That's quite a rarity. Most folks are laid back and friendly. A snippet of our conversation with them:

Linda: Where are you from?
Snob: Texas
Linda: Where in Texas?
Snob: Texas
Linda: What part?
Snob: Brownsville, do you know where *that* is?

I could have answered, "Oh yeah, Brownsville, don't they call that Little Mexico, riddled with drug crime and violence?" I bite my tongue—we may sit next to them again before the journey is over.

On the last cruise, we sat at tables for six or eight every night, usually with completely different people. For fun I thought I would create entirely fictitious personalities. One evening I could say I was a neurosurgeon, the next I could pick a different profession. I could claim to live in very desirable places and to have cruised virtually everywhere. My fiction would be a live version of the virtual identities that people sometimes create for themselves on the Internet. In the end, though, I didn't have the guts to do it. I think it would have made Linda uncomfortable. Yet, if she didn't want to reveal her status as an Episcopal priest, she too could make up an alter ego of some kind.

At dinner, Linda overhears someone complaining, "How come they always get that table?" We have no explanation for our good fortune. My dinner this evening is simple but delicious and includes, cold guava and banana soup with lychee, pan-fried basa filet (a type of catfish, often from Vietnam, for which the Latin name is Pangasius bocourti) fixed Portuguese style, mixed vegetables, and fat-free mango mousse.

Linda has the salmon filet. We end with hot lemon water, which is warm and refreshing at the same time. As we were having dinner, the ship left port and turned south, heading for the Canary Islands. The sun sets right in the middle of the horizon during our meal. The clouds briefly turn colorful, but nothing spectacular.

The entertainment tonight is of a type frequently seen on cruise ships, namely, performers who never quite reached the top levels of fame and who are now starting to get a bit over the hill. Once, on a Princess ship, an older, overweight, singer had to stop singing. He told the audience he needed to catch his breath and wait for the black things swimming in his vision to go away. He gave a dialogue that was very crude, encouraging all of us to gorge ourselves with food to get our money's worth for the cruise. Maybe that's what he had done earlier. We were attending the second show, and I think he just ran out of energy. He managed to make it through, but it was quite sad.

I'm not familiar with tonight's entertainer, Britain's David McCain. (He could be a big star in England.) During his dialogue, he says that he went pro in 1972, making him at least seventy. He cracks on a few high notes, and his speaking voice comes out a bit gravelly, but he does quite well. He's clearly a seasoned and talented professional. Of course, many of the older ladies in the audience swoon. Still quite trim, he wears a simple gray suit and vest, removing the coat after the second song. He tells a few stories, but mostly he sings a variety of material. I think the Neil Diamond numbers go over the best. He jokes about his CD selling well *under* a million copies. At the end, people give him a standing ovation. He certainly worked hard for it. Later I search for him on the Internet, but I can't find him.

Our evening continues in the Lotus Lounge, where a band plays danceable music. We're capable of having a good time out on the floor, but I'm still rather self-conscious. Sometimes I'm so concentrated on trying to think of a variation for the step we are doing that Linda has to remind me to smile.

As often happens, two couples apparently have taken advanced Arthur Murray classes, and they want you to know it, swinging wildly over the floor with various dips and twists and kicks. Did you know that *Dancing with the Stars* claims more viewers than any other television program? Maybe these folks should try out. When the two showy couples are in action, we stay in the middle of the floor to let them zoom around the perimeter. I enjoy watching accomplished dancers, trying to remember some of their steps. However, we forget even the most basic steps and variations between cruises. It seems like we start over every time we get on another ship.

Linda now shows signs of developing a full-blown cold, so we head back to the room at about 9:15 p.m. In the Royal Promenade, we pass Mr. Horror, all dressed up for the Halloween costume parade. He is sitting in the pub, his bed sheet now a Roman toga. Later he reveals that he made his crown from folded gold foil butter wrappers, which the waiters saved for him. Back in our room, we conk out long before the parade even starts.

Canary Islands

Day 7, November 1, 2011

After breakfast we disembark the ship for a look around Santa Cruz in La Palma de Tenerife, Canary Islands (not to be confused with our earlier stop at Palma de Majorca or Santa Cruz de Madeira). The Aida ship *Sol* again docked right beside us. Both ships backed into the slips, to be able to leave by pulling straight out. Here, the Old Town is not unlike many others, with narrow streets made from stones and cobbles. They will never wear out, but they sure are rough. They remind me of my annual visits to Puerto Vallarta, Mexico, where the stone-paved streets cause taxi cabs to replace their shocks every few months, while the bone-jarring, rattle-trap buses dispense with shocks altogether.

Today being a bank holiday, all but the tourist stores and a few bars and cafes are closed. Such is the luck of a fixed itinerary. The streets are filled with cruisers, but most of the stores sit dark and shuttered. We are lucky to find a silver spiral pendant to go with Linda's spiral earrings, and I find an attractive, light blue T-shirt with illustrations of six types of sailing ships once built on this island. As we wander, I'm wearing a yellow T that I bought at the cathedral in Majorca. T-shirts are my favorite souvenirs. (In French, "*souvenir*" means to remember. When I wear these T-shirts, they really do jog my reminiscence of the places they depict.)

We get fruit juice at a cafe in order to use their Internet, but it doesn't work. After several tries, we give up. Frustratingly, another cruiser at the counter nearby taps away on her laptop without difficulty. During the next six consecutive sea days, there will be no alternative to paying the ship's Internet prices. They know they have captive customers, especially people like me who need to keep an eye on business.

After around ninety minutes of walking and minor shopping, back to the ship we go. Today is day seven of our cruise and our fourth port. Enough already! Time for our favorite pastime, actual cruising, across the wide Atlantic.

We sit on the deck for a while reading our Kindles. My white one is older, with just 3G, but Linda's black one, slightly smaller, has both 3G and wireless Internet capabilities. Getting restless, we go up to the buffet. When in doubt, eat. Down below, we can see the port far to our right. Straight ahead is a black-sand beach with quite a few people on it. A small red-and-white-painted cafe with umbrellaed tables serves the beach goers. Here on the ship, I have small portions of chopped cucumber and tomatoes, Asian glazed duck (an exception to my vegetarianism, and probably left over from being on the dining room menu two days ago), poached salmon, channa masala (a very tasty chickpea dish), stir fried vegetables, and for dessert, a coconut semolina pudding.

After the usual long blast on the fog horn, *Mariner* makes its way out of the harbor. Soon, we pass by several of the other islands, one with a huge, cone-shaped mountain. These islands originated through volcanic action, of course, a process that continues in the present.

Here in the Canary Islands (but out of our sight), the eruptions of a volcano currently threaten one of the smaller islands, El Hierro. For several months the volcano has been heating up. Unlike earthquakes, seismologists can predict volcanic eruptions due to many warning signs. Just a couple of weeks before our arrival, the six hundred residents of the small town of La Restinga were evacuated as vibrations from the volcanic movement were causing huge rocks to dislodge from the mountain that towers over the town, crashing down into populated areas.

News reports tell that the surface of the ocean has become covered with a vast greenish stain, produced by sulfur thrown out by the volcano. This stain kills fish and sea plants. The area of the stain surpasses the size of the island itself. As the eruption takes place just 150 meters below the sea surface, physical material will likely be blown into the air, further threatening the island. The precautions have not been without controversy, however. Displaced residents claim the volcano is quieting down. They want to go home. Loss of income from tourism may amount to tens of millions of dollars.

Just a week after we passed by, the volcanic eruptions caused a 4.3 magnitude earthquake and thousands of tremors, followed by visible eruptions of magma, flung into the air. The appearance of a new island spurred officials to consider what to name it. If it grows large enough, it could join onto the land mass of El Hierro. A year later, as I worked to compile my notes into this book, hundreds of small earthquakes still took place daily, measuring up to 1.0 in magnitude. Hotel occupancy for 2012 reached only 33.5 percent—probably mostly scientists.

The Canary Islands have the clearest skies in the world, with good weather and no pollution. Due to such favorable conditions, numerous important telescopic observatories have been located in the Canary Islands, with an attendant community of astronomers. This clarity was my experience early this morning, looking out at the amazing star-studded, pre-dawn sky.

A trivia question for you. What nationality were the immigrants who founded San Antonio, Texas, where Linda and I live? Spanish? Nope. Although a predominant influence now, and in the past, through the missions. Germans? No, despite the numerous German towns surrounding us.

Give up? San Antonio was founded by people from the Canary Islands. Really! Every year, at the big fiesta in April, these origins are remembered and honored. So, here we are, among the people who had the foresight to come to Texas and found our fair city, now the seventh largest in the United States. (Houston is the fourth largest and Dallas the ninth, so Texas has three cities in the top ten. First is New York City, of course, followed by Los Angeles and Chicago.)

It's now official, Linda has a bad cold. She's sneezing and blowing. Although neither of us has verbalized it, chances are that she caught it from me. For almost a week in Cortona and Civitavecchia and the first few days aboard, I was the one taking it easy, getting extra sleep and curtailing strenuous activities. Now comes Linda's turn. So again we take after-lunch naps. Then, on a kick, we indulge ourselves, ordering spinach and artichoke dip with tortilla chips from room service, accompanied by two glasses of lemonade and two cookies which I have retrieved from the buffet.

At 3:30, I go to the fitness center and Linda goes to the Internet point. I increase the weights a bit today, trying to make progress without hurting myself. On some of the machines, I do the exercises one arm at a time, to protect against stressing my sore shoulders. I may have discovered a worthwhile technique, as there is no need to rest between sets—each arm rests as the other one works the exercise. My method increases the aerobic quality of the whole exercise.

A couple of bulky guys lift fairly heavy weights, which I notice with some envy. It seems unlikely that I will ever attain that kind of strength. I don't think my body will tolerate it. Yes, the muscles can get stronger, but the tendons and ligaments and joints can't keep up and would get damaged. So, I must be satisfied with a maintenance level that keeps me flexible and toned.

Looking in the mirror, I'm shocked to see how much my stomach bulges, complete with new side handles. Shoot. I'm gaining weight. (This, after being critical of others who heedlessly pig out and overeat.) Today was certainly over the top, with our snack and all. I don't think I can work out long or hard enough to burn off all the calories I'm eating. Perhaps I should cut out desserts. I see a change coming.

So, when we go to dinner, I get a second appetizer in place of the main course. First comes another cold fruit soup, this time chilled tropical mango. Then, I have grilled goat cheese polenta with tomato and white bean tapenade. Linda has the same soup and zucchini piccata, which turns out to be three slices of fried zucchini, with spaghetti and tomato sauce. Not what she expected. She skips dessert, but despite my new best intentions, I indulge in a slice of Boston cream pie, which is excellent—plenty of cream and not too much sponge cake.

It looks as if we may be permanently installed at our window table for the duration of the cruise. Wouldn't that be wonderful? As the sun sets and it gets dark outside, the windows become reflective. Rather than looking out at the sea, we see ourselves and what is be behind us in the dining room. The water is gone, replaced by crystal chandeliers and ornate decoration. Upon leaving, we give Mr. Horror and his wife the rest of our instant espresso packets. They called them "jet fuel."

Mr. Horror writes fiction. Fantasy. That's fitting on board a cruise, as fantasy is the main tack taken by almost all cruise marketing. A cruise may be listed for a certain number of days, but in many ways it exists outside of time and space. We have escaped our landed lives. For that reason, a cruise lends itself to establishing a sort of alternate reality. Most people find this kind of escape desirable. Cruise marketing plays to that predilection.

In the excellent book *Cruise: Identity, Design, and Culture*, authors Peter Quartermaine and Bruce Peter make these observations:

> *Aboard a cruise ship, passengers can assume different identities and move easily between contrasting experiences, secure in the knowledge that reality is hours, days or weeks away—back on land. Time assumes a different pace, and through drinking, dancing, eating, gambling and romance, multi-sensory experiences are heightened in a novel ambiance whose decor and lighting encourage just such shift.*

Where else do we readily experience fantasy? At the movies. Cruise lines often pick up the theme of Hollywood. The Disney ship *Fantasy* (4,000 passengers), promises "animation magic." Not to be left out, Royal Caribbean has made a deal to bring Shrek and his friends to sea. *Oceania Cruises Riviera* (1,250 passengers) touts one thousand thread-count sheets and an "Art Deco lobby that borrows from a 1920s Hollywood movie set." Fantasy twice removed.

Costa Fascinosa (3,800 passengers) creates "cinematic glamour with soaring ceilings and opulent details ... inspired by great films and grand theaters around the world." Cunard's tag line is "Feel famous." You're not really famous, of course, but you can pretend to be like those glamorous figures portrayed in ocean liner lore.

Fantasy fulfillment is not a bad thing. I'm not complaining. It might be just the right sort of escape. What do pipe dreams do best but fulfill our every desire? A Crystal Cruises brochure declares, "From the moment you step aboard one of Crystal's luxurious, impeccably appointed ships, the world is transformed to fulfill your every wish." Most cruise lines promise the same thing. As ships constitute a very contained and controlled environment, artificiality can be easily achieved. One advertisement called cruising "a journey beyond imagination." Hm-m-m-m-m-m. Holland America gives us a little more credit, including us in the process. Under the subhead "indulgences abound" it invites passengers to "design the day of your dreams." These are not empty promises.

Along with our new made-up world and identities comes the loosening of our normal inhibitions. Far removed from our workaday world, we experience great release and freedom. In my case, it gives a chance for reading and writing, free from the distractions encountered at home, but cruise lines would prefer it to take the form of partying, drinking, and shopping. The payment system assures that you never see the transfer of money, just hand over your room card. A sign in the casino informs us that we can charge up to $2,000 a day on our account.

I'll admit that I buy into a certain degree of pretense myself. All dressed up, having a drink before dinner, I know that a 15 percent tip is included in the price. Yet, at the bottom of the slip is a line for additional gratuity. It seems almost obligatory for me to tack on another symbolic dollar or two, as if to assure both the waiter and myself that I have the wherewithal to be generous, that I'm not a total fraud.

Recipient of all this service and luxury, it's not hard to start playing the role of someone who lives with it all the time and has unlimited means. I can feel myself doing it, and I don't resist or object. Of course, passengers can check at any time to see their current account balance, but most people wait until the end of the cruise, where they sometimes receive a shock that brings them back to reality. Fantasy over. Pay up. Come back again.

I don't fault the cruise lines for offering us fantasy. In some ways, passengers impose their insatiable desires on the industry and not the other way around. I think there's a sociological paper waiting to happen: to study these temporary sea-bound communities, some the size of small towns, that form and then dissipate within the space of a few days or weeks.

Peter Quartermaine and Bruce Peter offer this mouthful about cruise ships:

> ... *they are important cultural phenomena: mobile, self-contained, self-selecting, and inherently transient communities that exemplify the rootlessness and conspicuous consumption so characteristic of globalized mass culture in the twenty-first century.*

Sure, that's what I meant to say.

Ports of call, in some ways, continue the fantasy, projecting images of happy natives in fairy-tale settings, whisking people off in air conditioned buses, far from poverty or the reality of daily life. Rarely are port visits about trying to understand or interact with the authentic indigenous culture (except for specialized small-ship educational tours). At best, port tours parade among historic buildings and relics—interesting, but unlikely to challenge (or enlarge) our view of the world.

So why visit a real country at all? Why not just a movie set, a Disneyland construct? Why let the messiness of real life interfere? Why indeed? Now many cruise lines have their own Caribbean Island developments, so they can control even the shore excursions—Half Moon Cay (Holland America), Princess Cay (Princess), Great Stirrup Cay (Norwegian), Castaway Cay (Disney), and Coco Cay (Royal Caribbean, which also has Labadee on the shore of Haiti). Perhaps cruise companies will eventually have their own towns, or countries, so we can all travel in fantasyland without danger from the unknown, the different, or the unexpected.

Rod Serling wrote an episode of *The Twilight Zone* in which he portrayed life after death as perfection. When the protagonist played pool, all the balls went into the pockets. When he ate, he didn't get full or fat. When he played poker, he was dealt royal flushes. Beautiful women were friendly and available for pleasure. Finally, bored with his flawless existence, the protagonist exclaims in frustration, "I hate it here in heaven." A cynical voice replies, "What makes you think this is heaven?"

Cruises risk making everything so easy and perfect that they lose their meaning. There needs to be hardship to appreciate ease, overwork to appreciate leisure, deprivation to enjoy indulgence. When a cruise constitutes a week's break from such hardship, overwork, and deprivation, it comes as a welcomed relief. But what about persistent cruisers, such as ourselves? Will we lose touch with the world? Well, we can certainly try!

We were going to skip the entertainment this evening by the ship's musicians: the resident band, Darren from the Schooner Bar, and Ned from the Wig and Gavel Pub. At the last moment, we decide to go. Both of these guys are better at relating to the audience and being showy than in exhibiting depth of talent. Darren, especially, is young and seems almost to be pretending. On the stage, they start out doing three songs together, Ned sings and plays guitar, Darren accompanies him on the piano. Apparently, they have been building up quite a following, as the audience responds very positively toward them. The extreme amplification makes their rather weak voices seem full.

The first song is *"Country Roads,"* and the audience sings along vigorously to the chorus. I remember all the words, of course. We also sing along with *"On a Jet Plane"* which Ned plays in a strangely low register, rather than the high John Denver tenor to which I am accustomed. I'm a big John Denver fan. (Thanks to arthritis in my fingers, my Martin guitar stands forlorn in the closet, my folk singing at a standstill.) In one verse, Ned changes the words from jet plane to cruise ship.

Darren leaves the stage and Ned does a song with the house band, perhaps the best performance of the evening, a rocking version of "Mustang Sally." Someone was good at planning this. I thought the band would do some numbers on their own, but they just play a supporting role. Then Darren comes back, not as a piano player but as a singer. He has tons of energy, roaming the stage and even comes down into the aisles among the audience. Back at the piano, he reminds me of a young Elton John. Indeed, at the end, he does an Elton John song. After thunderous applause, they do an encore, a song, from Queen. The cruise director comes out and thanks them, ready to give the final announcements, but the audience is on its feet, chanting, "More, more, more …"

We are already past the appointed ending time. The cruise director asks, "Really?" He goes over to talk to the band leader, who shakes his head no. That was all they had been prepared to play. The audience chants even louder. The band director and cruise director looked at each other, as if to say, "What do we do?" when Ned and Darren come back out to save the day. They do one last, somewhat strange song, but it seems to please the ravenous crowd. The crowd again chants for even more, but the cruise director squelches the movement, even though he's clearly impressed and delighted by the audience's enthusiasm.

"This is the first time we've done this," he confesses. I think a surprise snow storm in New England grounded planes and kept one or more of the scheduled entertainers from reaching the ship in the Canary Islands. Maybe that was good, as I seem to remember the airport there being deemed the most dangerous in the world. So, the cruise director put together this impromptu program instead. "Maybe we need to do this every cruise," he exclaims. It would save them the expense of hiring outside talent.

We go back to our room to rest, but the evening is not yet over. We await the 10:15 special bingo game, a single game, the prize for which is a one-week Caribbean cruise for two. Several hundred people show up, although not as many as I expected. For $22, we receive a card that has six 5x5 bingo grids on it. Up front on stage sits the usual professional bingo set up, with a device that randomly selects balls that are flying around in a chamber, and a large electronic board that displays the numbers. A crew member from Jamaica, Colin, serves as an energetic MC. The game is "Big X," which means the winner must have two diagonal lines, corner to corner. The center space is always free, so it takes eight numbers to form the X and win the game.

I think winning a cruise would be a perfect addition to this book. Sure enough, the first number, B-12, turns out to be a corner number in one of my grids. Second comes G-51, also on the diagonal of the second of our six grids. After ten or twelve numbers, two of our grids need only two remaining numbers. When you get down to needing only one number, you stand up. At that point, the audience boos, as they don't want you be the one to win. A man on the far side of the room stands up. "We have a stander," announces the MC, to the dismay and boos of the crowd (us included).

After the next number, a woman behind us said, "Bingo." She hadn't even been standing. She takes her card down to the front, but it turns out she has done only one arm of the X. There is still hope for us. I-28, O-64, B-6, or G-58 would make me a stander. Someone else meekly says, "Bingo," barely audible. Another false alarm. When I get bingo, no one will have trouble hearing me. Two more numbers to go, but several pass which aren't useful. Not good. Our hopes dim. Then, the man standing yells, "BINGO!" Indeed, he has won. Darn, we were so close. I make a calculation. If three hundred people paid $22 (some bought more than one ticket), that adds up to $6,600—several times the cost of the prize. Plus, the retail value doesn't reflect the actual cost to Royal Caribbean, although I guess they would be deprived of that income by giving away the stateroom. Nor did they indicate what kind of stateroom. Probably not the Owner's Suite. More likely an inside cabin, with the possibility to pay more to upgrade. It would have been fun to win, but I guess it's no big loss, either.

We go back to our stateroom. The last of the Canary Islands have long since passed out of sight. In ancient times, this was unknown territory. Charts said things like, "Here there be monsters." Contrary to rumor, I don't think many people thought the earth was flat. The ancient Greeks knew the earth was round. Certainly sailors saw ships sink out of sight slowly, with their masts descending into the curved horizon. Still, heading out to a distant horizon with no idea of what lay beyond, or how long they would be at sea, or if they had enough provisions, in a ship that was tiny by today's standards, must have been both exhilarating and worrisome.

Christopher Columbus's ship would easily fit inside *Mariner*'s main dining room. Of course, some explorers never made it home. Those days were certainly a far cry from this luxurious floating palace, the location of which is pinpointed at every instant, and the arrival time, 3,200 nautical miles away, is estimated down to the minute.

We get into our 'jamies and crawl into bed, our favorite moment of the day—not as a precursor to intimate activity, but rather, because it's evidence that we are together. This aspect of appreciation is a much stronger part of this relationship than any of my previous ones, perhaps because finding each other was so miraculous.

We talk about our day, and then I read from *The Hungry Ocean*, the Linda Greenlaw book that we are reading out loud at bedtime. We have read several of her other books (*Lobster Chronicles, Seaworthy, All Fishermen are Liars*), as well as several by Bill Bryson (*A Walk in the Woods, In a Sunburned Country, Notes from a Small Island, A Really Short History of Nearly Everything*). Bryson travels and then writes about it in a very readable style. He includes opinions and stories and history. In a way, he stands as a model for my writing. Maybe I will become the Bill Bryson of the seas. Alas, Linda showed me an article announcing that Bill Bryson was to be the featured presenter on a Seabourn cruise. Hm-m-m-m. Maybe *he* will be the Bill Bryson of the seas.

I intend to be much *less* like Brian Bruns, however, whose accounts of working on cruise ships (*Cruise Confidential, Ship for Brains*) are filled with hyperbole and exaggeration. Yet, he's honest and direct and fun to read. Like mine, his is also a love story that takes place at sea (if at a distance). His latest book (*Unsinkable Mr. Brown*) describes how his love affair took place over the seven seas, from Transylvania to, well, just about everywhere. I read that he was recently on a Norwegian cruise doing book signings and readings. Hm-m-m-m-m. Wouldn't I like doing that someday, with this or subsequent books!

I can see stars twinkling out in the night. Linda has dozed off, so I tiptoe out onto the balcony. It's about midnight. I hear a few noises from up on Deck 11, site of a late night buffet and dancing under the stars from 11:30 p.m. to 1:00 a.m. The music is audible. Indeed, they are under a sky brilliant with stars. Off in the horizon sets the quarter moon. The atmosphere magnifies it, turning it into an orange bonfire lighting up the clouds. Quite dramatic. The moon will be getting increasingly full during the second half of our trip.

Back in bed, sleep eludes me. I ponder how I had ended up here, on this ship, writing this book, with a life now filled with leisure time and love.

My first marriage, to Merle, was my "hippie" marriage. I had just been released from the military prison in Fort Leavenworth where I was incarcerated for reverse murder, that is, *refusing* to kill people.

That's frowned upon when you're in the military. As an officer and radar operator, I had refused orders to go to Southeast Asia. At that time, B-52 bombers took off from Guam with very little fuel, so they could carry more bombs. Once in the air, they met up with a tanker and fueled up, after which they headed for North Vietnam. It would have been my job to direct those refuelings. I don't think so! I had gone through ROTC wanting to serve my country, but not in that way.

Upon my release, I became a full time Vietnam War resistor. Merle and I worked together in The Resistance, in Rochester, New York. Once married, we went to Columbia, South Carolina, to join the staff of the UFO, an antiwar coffeehouse. There, we were all arrested and sentenced on trumped up charges to six years in prison.

During the trial, Jane Fonda came to work with the women (specifically excluding the men). Once the women were properly liberated, they all wanted divorces—including Merle, who was pregnant at the time. So, I have the weird distinction of claiming that Jane Fonda, bless her heart, broke up my marriage—not that there was any assurance that it would have lasted. Our child was stillborn. Merle and I went our separate ways, never to see each other again. As far as I know, that baby girl was the only child I ever fathered. Ironically, we were married on April Fool's Day and divorced on Valentine's Day. On appeal out sentence was reduced to time served. I was a free man.

That marriage lasted one year, whereas my second marriage lasted ten. It was also unusual, in that I was married to my first cousin, Susan Ferré, a world-class concert organist. My uncle became my father-in-law and my cousins became my brothers- and sisters-in-law. Susan and I traveled in Europe, with me serving as roadie, turning pages and pulling stops. We certainly had some memorable times, such as practicing the organ in Notre Dame in Paris at midnight. Spooky. After a decade with me, Susan met the person with whom she was really meant to spend the rest of her life. We divorced, and she is, indeed, still with Charley, more than thirty years later. My brothers-in-law reverted again to my cousins, my father-in-law back to my uncle, right back where we started.

Ruth and I were together for twenty years. Counting the time with Linda, I can say I have been married for more than 33 years—it just wasn't to the same person. Clearly I have nothing against marriage.

Apparently I'm not going to sleep soon. So, why not check out the dancing under (not with) the stars. I slip on pants and a jacket over my pajamas and sneak out into the hallway. My watch says 12:15 a.m. As I walk down the narrow hallway, I hear the walls creaking from the ship's movement. Intending to walk down the center of the hallway, I wander a bit. Nothing severe. I'm easy on myself and take the elevator to Deck 11, rather than walking up the stairs.

As I walk out onto the deck, I encounter a group of crew members pushing rolling carts with empty stainless steel buffet pans. I have missed the food entirely. There is, however, still a table with drinks in blinking blue glasses. I'm not swearing, they really do blink. Linda and I got two of them on *Voyager*. By pushing a button on the bottom of the plastic glass, you can turn on a blue blinking light hidden there. Presumably, that makes it easy to find where you left your drink at a party. Of course, if everyone else has the same glass, then you are still left guessing which is yours, as they would all be blinking. Our worker and house sitter in my home in Saint Louis, Mark, always seemed to pick that glass to drink from, but he didn't know about the light. One evening, I turned it on, to his amazement. Yes, I gave it to him.

I haven't missed the music, either. Everywhere I've gone during this cruise, I've noted that the average age of cruisers is well into white-hair range. When I see a young couple, I wonder what they are doing here. Perhaps they are part of a larger, multigenerational family gathering. Well, now I know where the younger folks hang out. After us old folks have gone to bed, they come out to boogie. There are a few white-hairs dancing under the stars, but for once they are in the minority. The band has cranked up the decibels. In front of the band are four crew members, two men and two women, facing the dance floor, demonstrating movements. The dancers are not in couples, but a mass group facing the band (about ten feet away), mimicking the crew members.

The steps are generally to the side, front and back, with an occasional turn, pointing, or throwing the arms into the air. The movements are easy to follow, even with a drink in one's hand. Most of the dancers are women, perhaps some of them traveling together as roommates. This type of dance includes everyone, which is perfect for singles. Around the perimeter, a few men hover at cocktail tables and by the poolside bar. I would say there are perhaps sixty people here, fifty-five of whom are female. Others may have left when the food ran out. These die-hards look like they have imbibed enough to feel no pain.

On deck I can't see the stars that were so visible from my balcony. The lighting blots them out. They're all still dancing under the stars, of course, but not visible ones. With little to keep me here, I go up to Deck 14 to Ellington's Bar, only to find it closing down, too. It would have been a good place to look down through the slanted windows and watch the dancers below.

My wandering takes me next to the Grand Promenade. With the stores closed, the only people around are cleaners and polishers, caring for the acres of glass on this ship. Most of the stairs have panels of glass under the hand rail. They look very sleek and modern, but what a headache to maintain. Some crew members do nothing but clean glass.

I pass the entrance to the disco, but don't go in it. I'm sure it's also filled with people still far from retirement age. At the end of the promenade, I come to the always-open cafe. Some fifteen people, mostly couples, sit at tables or in booths. One of the flashy dance couples is here, perhaps recovering from another night of kicking up their heels. It occurs to me to interview them, but they look tired. So I don't.

Cunard and Holland America still provide dance hosts, older men who are good at dancing, made available to dance with the many older, single women. Our friend Shirley, in San Antonio, was once a dance instructor, along with her husband. Wonderfully light on her feet, she periodically gives Linda and me a few pointers. Since her husband passed away, she books cruises that have dance hosts. I'm sure they enjoy dancing with her. She floats so effortlessly it seems that her feet don't touch the ground.

I sip a decaf coffee and write in my notebook for a while. Two tables of people are talking loudly. What do people have to say to each other at this hour and at such volume? I can imagine myself sitting here in the cafe and typing into my iPad late into the night.

Not tonight, however. It's almost one. The music on Deck 11 will stop shortly. I go back to good old cabin 8598 and slip the card into the stateroom door, slowly opening it, being as quiet as I can, only to find Linda with the light on, reading. We go back to bed. She asks if I want to read more from our book, as we are in an exciting part about catching swordfish. I say sure, but by the time I get the book out, Linda has dozed off, so I turn off the light.

A Learning Process

For seventeen years I had a side business called One Heart Tours, in which I took small groups to pilgrimage sites in France. There were times when I left home for ten weeks or more at a time. Ruth couldn't come along, because she had clients to see. So we were apart. I also have to admit that even when I was home, I often worked so many hours that my schedule amounted to abandonment, even though I was in the next room.

Ruth and I once had a psychic describe to us some of our past lives together. In almost every one, I was the male and I abandoned Ruth. Once, I came home from war terribly injured. After Ruth nursed me back to health, I went back to battle, never to return. Another time, I was a ship builder. Finally, I realized my dream of having my own ship. Ruth didn't want me to go, but I sailed away, only to be killed by pirates who wanted my beautiful, fast boat.

Linda's first husband was a pilot in the Air Force, often away from home on temporary duty assignments. Most military wives experience that. Linda's son, Mike, as a Navy pilot, must face parting with his wife and two children for weeks or months at a time when duty calls. Linda experienced abandonment in the worst way when her husband left with no word or warning.

Happily, these absences do not apply to us. When we're not together, the tension mounts until we remedy the situation. Is this healthy? Maybe not. Maybe we're too dependent, too entangled, too needy, but I don't think so. This doesn't feel like desperation, it feels like connection. It's comfortable and fun. Our compatibility makes us great travel partners, and cruises, it turns out, particularly suit our style.

I bring to the relationship some important lessons learned the hard way. In 1985, I was in the bookstore in Findhorn Community in Scotland. Someone handed me a book and said, "Read this book, it will change your life." It was a thick green paperback in the Arkana spiritual literature series. What a strange title, I thought: *A Course in Miracles*. I bought it, and it did, indeed, completely change my life. It presented the perennial wisdom in an intellectual format that fit my sensitivities. I found it gripping, from the first page.

Subsequently, I lived in the Pyrenees Mountains in France (in Ariège, east of Foix) where I worked on restoring an old stone house. Beginning with *A Course in Miracles,* a channeled work, Christian in language, I began reading spiritual literature, all of which was a great leap from my original Christian upbringing. My second book was *Cutting Through Spiritual Materialism* by Chögyam Trungpa (Buddhist), followed by the autobiography of Swami Muktananda (Hindu—this was somewhat familiar, as I had attended events in South Fallsburg, New York, with his successor in the line of Siddha yoga masters, Gurumayi Chidvilasananda). Finally, I read *The Nature of Personal Reality* (a Seth book, channeled by Jane Roberts with no religious affiliation). After two years of re-education, I saw myself and the world completely differently. How had I evaded such important knowledge for the first forty years of my life?

When I returned to the U.S. in 1987, I worked for a summer at Omega Institute in Rhinebeck, New York, extending my self-education into New Age directions. Driving through St. Louis, Missouri, in 1988, I met Ruth Hanna, who headed the Miracles Resource Center, subsequently called One Heart. Within six months, I had moved to St. Louis. Our relationship and marriage became a mutual spiritual exercise, based on *A Course in Miracles.* As I learned forgiveness towards myself and others, the world loosed its grip on me. Our love involved full, open, and sometimes poignant communication.

That wasn't easy for me at first. I didn't know how to get out of my head and into my heart. I thought discussions just meant an examination of the facts in a logical and rational way. Wrong. One night, I was completely flummoxed by Ruth's expectations of me. She cried, saying, "All you are offering me are words." Well, of course I was using words. We were having a discussion, for God's sake. In frustration, I got up to go outside for a walk. Ruth saw my movement toward the door. Knowing my proclivity to run away when the communicating got tough, she pleaded with the most heart-rending desperation, "You can't leave me." I understood. I returned to the couch, and we cried and hugged and connected in ways that the rational mind doesn't grasp.

That was a huge opening for me. I learned that when a voice inside my head said, "Come on Ruth, get over it, the facts are obvious," I was still in my intellect, not my heart. Facts, I would learn, are not the highest form of truth. Love and happiness are. A relationship involves connecting at the heart level, not arguing from the head. It's not about being right (or wrong).

Now that Linda and I have found each other, my intention is to establish the same kind of communication, with no exceptions, sparing no embarrassment. Complete openness and honesty. This represents new territory for Linda, to have the man in her life so available and accepting. At first, she hesitated to open up, not feeling safe. Developing protective measures had been necessary for her. As a priest, her personal life and opinions were carefully shielded from view. I think having a lover and confidant like me has taken some getting used to. Reaching such compatibility is a process that goes on for one's entire lifetime.

Interview

Day 8, November 2, 2011

We sleep until the sky is light, with red-tinged puffy clouds against a blue background. Linda feels worse and intends to stay in bed. Perhaps it's dehydration on top of the cold. "When you pinch the skin on your hand, it's supposed to pop right back. If it doesn't, you may be dehydrated," Linda tells me. She pinches the back of her hand, and it stays raised up. I pinch my skin, and quicker than I can move my fingers to take a look, it returns to flat flesh. Apparently I'm properly hydrated.

I go to breakfast alone, bringing Linda back a little fresh fruit and some stewed prunes. We have been slowing down for more than a week now, with one or the other of us under the weather. Still, if you're going to feel poorly, this is definitely the place to do it, with the curtains pulled apart and the ocean in full view, room service available, a flat-screen TV, and a comfortable bed. I look forward to taking cruises even when I am old and feeble, pushing my walker slowly down the corridor, staying in bed until noon.

Having kept our passports for security reasons, this is the time Royal Caribbean wants to give them back. They have assigned a time to come and pick them up. The line is ridiculously long. I'm not going to stand there for hours. Instead, I go to the Promenade Cafe and have a decaf coffee while listening to the classical guitar player. Displayed on the bar is the drink of the day. Here is the recipe.

KETEL ONE COOLER
Ketel One Vodka
Disaronno Origionale Amaretto
Orange juice
Sweet and sour mix
Splash of Grenadine (for color, no doubt)

Cost: $6.95, and you can keep the decorative glass. Just think, at the end of the voyage you could have a collection of seventeen glasses. Try packing those in your overstuffed suitcase!

I bring Linda more water. She still doesn't feel like eating, so I go up to the lunch buffet alone, to Jade again. I dish myself three delicious fish cakes, plus the usual vegetables. No dessert. I fix a plate of things that I think Linda might like, which includes a roll and butter, a piece of pizza, some fruit salad, and some French fries (my idea of comfort food). I cover it with another plate, grab two glasses of water, and head back to the room.

I zip down the stairs rather than taking the elevator. I feel good about being able to do that. Walking has not always been this easy and carefree for me. I have a long history of foot issues and shoes and problems walking. On my left foot, the toes are bent and curled (hammer toes). Arthritis has frozen the joints so that none of the toes move, except for the big toe. The bent joints stick up quite high, making it difficult to wear many kinds of shoes. The saga continues. On my next transatlantic cruise, sore knees compelled me to take the elevator, even for short distances.

At 1:45 p.m. I go down to the Champagne Bar to interview one of the officers. The Champagne Bar features highly padded chairs and banquettes. At the entrance stand two glass cylinders filled with liquid, with bubbles rising up from the bottom—obviously imitating champagne. Only two of the tables are occupied, and there is no bartender on duty.

An officer approaches, his white suit visible at some distance. He comes into the bar to my table and introduces himself, Mirko Taraba. He has a noticeable Eastern European accent but speaks English fluidly. His hair is cropped very close to his head, his build tall and athletic looking. The title on his business card is Marketing and Revenue Manager. On his shoulders are epaulets with three gold stripes.

I'm impressed. Three stripes is a high rank on a cruise ship, equaled by the head of hotel services and the medical doctor. Only the captain (master), staff captain (second in charge on the bridge), and the chief engineer have four stripes. The first officer, for example, has two and one-half stripes, and the second officer two.

I start by asking him to describe his duties. He supervises all sources of revenue, from the casino to the stores to the tours and the bars. This strikes me as a very important post. Yes, the captain must keep the ship on course and amuse the suite passengers, the chief engineer must keep everything working, and the purser must keep the passengers happy, but in the end, everything revolves around income and profit. The bottom line rules.

Taraba is the manager of the managers, with 250 people under him, twenty percent of the crew. He's as much in the dark about me as I am about him, unsure who I am or what I want. So I explain that I'm writing this book. He tells me that in most instances, journalists receive their credentials from the main office in Miami, and then instructions are sent to the ship to accommodate them. I tell him I had sent two emails, but neither received a response. He expresses surprise. I guess they went to the wrong people.

Before this position, to which he has recently been promoted, Taraba served in other capacities during his eighteen years at sea. He started out as a fitness director and moved up through the ranks to explorations director, which handles all of the tours and events. In that capacity, he would often receive visitors, such as writers from *National Geographic* or the chief honcho from a big tour company. He would show them around the ship, introduce the captain, and otherwise spend time with them.

I comment about the public persona of Royal Caribbean's claim "We're here to serve you," versus the private, behind-the-scenes company which, in my opinion, would not blink an eye in inconveniencing passengers for reasons of profit. I used the passports as an example. They required three thousand people to stand in line for hours to retrieve their passports, all of which have the stateroom number clearly marked on a sticker on the front. Why not just have the stewards put them in our rooms? I answer my own question, noting that it only took a dozen people to run the stand-in-line operation, as opposed to scores of stewards. Taraba confirms that they just don't have the staff to do it any differently.

I express a desire to go on the *Oasis of the Seas* sometime, the behemoth that holds 5,400 passengers. Taraba perks right up, giving (at some length) a glowing account of *Oasis*, on which he has traveled on two previous occasions, once with his family, including his five-year-old daughter, who loved it and still talks about it. His family lives in Slovakia. His contract is four months of work followed by two months off. During each contract, his family can visit for up to two weeks. Thus, he can see them five months of the year.

"Royal Caribbean," Taraba brags, "is the only company to do this." I have no way to really check that out. He continues about *Oasis of the Seas.*

"You know, they guarantee no longer than fifteen minutes for boarding, and luggage is in the stateroom within two hours." I mention that I had heard that before. I tell him how impressed I am with the design of Royal Caribbean's ships. For decades, each of their new ships, at the time of launching, was the largest then at sea. Then he says something I have already noticed on *Mariner.*

"You know, *Oasis* is usually empty," he adds.

"Empty?"

"Yes, when you walk around, you say to yourself, 'where is everyone?' There are never any crowds." This is an important statement, as many non-cruisers think it must be crowded all the time. Here on *Mariner,* there is a million and a half square feet of deck space. That's the size of a large regional shopping mall. *Oasis,* being more than 50 percent larger, would have significantly more than that. I ask about efficiencies of scale and whether ships that large are profitable.

"It was the best decision Royal Caribbean ever made," he assures me, and he's the guy who should know about profit figures. So, it seems a little inconsistent that the next class of ships to be built, already under way, will be much smaller than the *Oasis* class. Is the market getting too overbuilt with gigantic ships? On the *USA Today* cruise blog, I read that Richard Fain, CEO of Royal Caribbean, had demurred when financial analysts asked him to predict next year's numbers.

"Predicting and preparing for the coming year is the most important assurance of a successful year," Taraba declares. "So right now, with the recession in the U.S., the euro crisis in Europe, Greece near default, and inflation in China, who can predict?" Who indeed?

"I have noticed that Royal Caribbean keeps changing its itineraries," I tell him. "*Independence of the Seas* will be leaving its home port of Southampton. Royal Caribbean is now increasing its presence in Australia. I presume all of this is to find the best market." Perhaps they hope that Europe and Asia will break the stranglehold American passengers have on the cruise industry.

"Right now," he says, "Royal Caribbean is looking for crew members who speak Japanese, Korean, and Chinese. That is the direction they are headed."

"Two-thirds of the passengers onboard have previously been on a Royal Caribbean cruise. The other one-third have cruised before, as well, but with other cruise lines, coming to Royal Caribbean for the first time. What do you do to try to entice or steal customers away from your competition?"

"It's not a matter of stealing anyone away," he says. "Every cruise line has a personality and something that it does best. People just need to discover which one fits them best."

"What do you think are the most important considerations in making that choice?"

"First, is the ship itself. That is really important. And secondly, the itinerary. If you get either of these wrong, you won't have a very good vacation."

"I notice that Royal Caribbean doesn't have any marketing directed toward retirement-age people, like me. I guess the marketers assume that older people will come, regardless of advertising. Your ads always seem to emphasize adventure, which isn't the main draw for older people."

"Sometimes, the itinerary makes a difference," Taraba explains. "The Fiords in Norway, Alaska, the Panama Canal, and longer cruises, tend to have an older clientele. But it's true, our focus is on families. We believe we have something for every age group, which makes us ideal for families."

"My impression is that Royal Caribbean is trying to position itself at the top of the bell curve, where there are the most customers. They aren't the most expensive, nor the least. The food is great, but less than superb. The entertainment is second tier but enjoyable. Everything is meant to satisfy the needs of the average person. If you want fancier food, or better service, go with one of the pricier lines. If you just want drinks and sun, go with Carnival and have fun."

"Yes, I think you have stated it right. We do have an upscale product, as Royal Caribbean owns Azamara Club Cruises."

"Tell me about Richard Fain, the CEO. Have you met him?"

"Several times."

"Fain is generally recognized as being an astute guiding force. At the same time, there is a lawsuit by investors who are unhappy that he gave a rosy report of anticipated earnings in January, while, at the same time, selling millions of dollars of his own stock while it was at its high of $45 a share. In July, he revised the financial prediction downward, due to so-called 'accounting errors,' causing the stock to fall to $30. The investors think he knew something he didn't share with them."

"I don't know about the stock. I found Richard Fain to be a pleasant man, very bright. I can't say that he knows my name, but we have talked about business matters and he is very sharp."

"We have been barred from several venues because there were events for diamond or higher ranked passengers. What are the requirements for diamond status?" Taraba takes out a small notebook from his pocket and shows me a chart. Status is determined either by the number of cruises, if they are short, or total number of days at sea. For diamond status, you need at least eighty days at sea.

"Our previous cruise was fourteen days, and this is seventeen, so we will have thirty-one days at sea. What level is that?"

"You will be Emerald level, the one before diamond. Three more of these cruises, and you will reach diamond." That doesn't seem so impossible. In fact, it seems downright likely.

I tell Taraba that I feel this is the platinum age of cruising, that never before in history, has travel on the ocean been so easy, so safe, so comfortable, so entertaining. He says that it hasn't always been that way. He has seen many changes over the past eighteen years. Now there are cameras everywhere, there are programs for a healthy and safe environment, things are much better now than they were even in the relatively recent past.

During that transition, he has been working his way through the ranks. The only higher position available to him is hotel manager. When I ask if he has his sights on that he says no. "My focus is on learning to do the best job possible. Everything else will take care of itself." I believe it will go well for him.

On that note, we say our good-byes. He pops up and strides away. At that moment, he seems busy and ready to go back to work, but not once during the interview did he look at his watch or in any way indicate impatience or disinterest.

I wish now I had asked him some tougher questions. Like why there are no Laundromats on Royal Caribbean. That makes it very inconvenient. Are they just trying to gain another profit center by making us pay for laundry service? I think they have let down the passengers in that regard, especially since in my experience the laundry service has done a poor job.

Next, I shower, put on my formal clothes, and head for Studio B, the ice skating rink, for a program. We have two tickets, but Linda wants to take it easy. She decides to meet me in the dining room after the show. I get to the skating rink early enough to claim a good seat at the end of the second row. The venue has a stage at one end and high-banked seats on the other three sides. My information sheet says that it holds nine hundred people, but I can't see nearly that many seats. That must include the bar area.

The ceiling has a large conglomeration of girders and spotlights. I expected it to be cold in here, but it isn't. I was at Guest Services a few days ago when someone asked about the free tickets and was told they were all given out. Fortunately, we obtained ours right away. Yet, there are two areas roped off for VIP passengers that are going unused, sitting empty, perhaps seventy seats total. Too bad.

The ten skaters do a variety of group numbers in various colorful costumes. Additionally, each performer has the spotlight for an individual routine. One guy seems to be the star, landing one triple something but falling down on another. The ship is rocking a bit, so maybe when he came down, the ice was not where he expected to find it. The audience claps and oohs and ahs with every move. It's engaging, although I fail to see how devoting this much space to ice skating rinks at sea (a Royal Caribbean exclusive) is enough of a draw to be the highest and best use for the space. Apparently so.

The costumes are quite elaborate. In one routine, they imitated Russian Cossacks in brilliant red. In another, they wore large hoops under their costumes, making themselves appear bigger-than-life. One skater with gymnastic skills did a routine involving a trapeze bar and a hoop. The lights and movement of the ropes and other devices are all timed and computer operated (although there is a manual override if needed by the engineer in the control booth). Everyone must do everything right on cue or things will go awry.

In one skit, the mini-Zamboni machine, usually used for resurfacing the ice, was covered so that it looked like a train engine, which pulled several cars around the ice. All told, the show provided constant variety, color, and creative choreography.

As the last piece finishes, I become one of those people who pop up and leave early to beat the crowd. Was there an encore piece? I don't know. Now past 5:30, I want to get to our table by the window to see if Linda feels better. I enter the dining room and give my room number. The maître d' says, "Your wife is already there."

I walk through the dining room, turn the corner, and my heart does a double flip. Linda is sitting at the table, with no one else near her. She has on her long black dress and a colorful scarf with the image of a peacock. Her hair is pulled back, with bangs in front. She's looking out the window, where the sea is gray and dramatic, with swells and whitecaps, the horizon lost in misty fog.

What a vision! I'm overwhelmed with love for this woman. How do I deserve this good fortune? Throughout the meal, I express this sentiment a dozen times. If I didn't already know Linda, she would be the one in the whole room most likely to capture my attention, like in the movies when everyone else goes out of focus.

Every evening we have shown up at approximately the same time, and every evening Jeffry has assigned us this table for two beside the window. It has really added another dimension to our cruise, making dinner a special event. Little could we have predicted the completely different circumstances on our subsequent cruise, in April of 2012—we were seated in the middle of the room next to the noisy waiter's work station. In the end, it all balances out.

I appreciate professional waiters, having been one myself years ago. Clearly the staff have been trained in the proper way to place or remove dishes and other details. When serving bread, the waiter reaches over and removes the lid on the stainless steel container that holds the individually wrapped pats of butter (President brand, which is French, from Normandy). When we order hot water and lemon, he places the pot and cups to the right of the table setting, and reaches over to remove the lid of the container holding the sugar packets, to make them available. While we manage to exchange small pleasantries, they need to keep moving to serve everyone. Linda finds that the food is not as hot as she would like it. She prefers it piping. I find the food a suitable eating temperature. When I take the ship's tour, I will look to see if there's an explanation. Perhaps the waiters have a long distance from plating to delivery.

For dinner I have a seafood salad and vegetarian moussaka. Linda has roasted peach soup and New England bay scallops. My portions are mercifully small, in keeping with my new diet. Then comes dessert. Valentin recommends the sugar-free tart, but I choose the cherries jubilee and Linda the sampler of three small chocolate items. "You don't trust me," Valentin objects light heartedly. "Oh yes we do." When he brings the desserts, he also brings an extra one, the sugar-free tart, which turns out to be the best of the three. Linda eats part of hers, while I eat all of mine plus most of the tart. There goes my diet again.

The couple at the next table are speaking French. I notice the husband does the ordering and the talking, so I presume that the wife doesn't comfortably speak English. When I say something to her in French, she perks right up, happy to hold a bit of conversation. She tells me they live near Bordeaux. Were my French better, I would tell her my Saint Émilion story (a wine village near Bordeaux). Maybe another time.

Here on board, there is a French presence, as I have frequently heard the language in use. According to the cruise director, the passengers come from thirty different countries. I have also heard quite a bit of Spanish, a little German, something Eastern European, and several Asian languages. Still, Americans make up the vast majority of passengers, many of them with inelegant drawls.

The night's entertainment is comedian George Kanter, flown in from Phoenix to the Canary Islands on short notice as apparently the planned entertainers cancelled at the last minute. Kanter has some very funny segments. No spring chicken, his last bit is about his heart attack, pacemaker, and defibrillator. "That was a $200,000 joke," he quips. The audience understands. The seas have become higher, reaching swells of around twenty feet.

When the ship crashes into the side of a wave, it makes a huge banging sound. At the level of Deck 3 at the front of the ship, the stage receives the full brunt of these crashes. Some happen to take place directly after his punch lines, to which he turns and responds with some comment.

We head to our room (and bed) as soon as the program ends. The ship rocks just the way we like. People walking down the hallway together drift left and right in unison, according to the ship's movement, as if we were all following a choreographed script. I suppose under these circumstances drunk people walk in a straight line.

Foot Problems

Before the toe issues, I had problems with my right heel, which required a cast for a while. Not being flexed or used, the foot then developed painful plantar fasciitis. All of these foot problems started in 2001, when Ruth and I went to Brazil to see the healer named João Teixeira de Faria (in English known as John of God), hoping to eliminate Ruth's breast cancer. John of God is a trance channel who does unexplainable things with the help of discarnate entities. We reached his center in Abadiânia, *Casa de Dom Ignacio*, by flying to Brasilia and then taking a two-hour bus trip into the wilderness.

I use John of God in some of my lectures to illustrate how little science knows about spiritual things and how the immaterial can affect the physical. Atheists and myopic scientists go berserk over spiritual healing, claiming it must be fraudulent, psychological, or hysterical. John of God invites skeptical Western doctors to stand next to him while he does his work. Often they say, "I saw it with my own eyes, but I still don't believe it." He takes no credit, saying it's God working through him. Not only does he not charge for his work, he provides free lunch. Hundreds come every day, some of them indigent people bussed in from all over Brazil, but mostly the visitors are foreigners. Everyone is requested to wear white clothing.

It isn't drive-through healing for anyone that shows up. John teaches the necessity of a moral lifestyle and of giving selflessly to help others. Sometimes healing takes years. Sometimes it never happens. John represents a tradition in Brazil called Spiritism, which began in the nineteenth century. The spirits of those who have died continue, after death, their own programs of self-development. They benefit from helping those of us who inhabit the physical world. Not all spirits are positive, however, so one must be careful to invoke only the compassionate spirits. When John of God is in trance, these spirits work through him.

We wanted the cancer to go away. The spirits promised, "We will handle it," but we didn't know in what form. Ruth enjoyed a period of five years in which the cancer was held at bay. Perhaps that was our gift. It was on that first trip to Brazil (Ruth subsequently took a second trip) that my right foot started hurting. In that case, it was retrocalcaneal bursitis. My ability to walk paralleled Ruth's illness. As she got worse, I became more crippled.

Another parallel was our pine tree. Outside our home in Webster Groves near Saint Louis was a towering white pine tree, easily fifty feet tall, with long fluffy needles. When we were looking for a home in 1998, Ruth had had a dream about sitting under a huge pine, seeing her psychotherapy patients. When we first saw the house, she exclaimed, "This is the tree in my dream." We bought the house, which we loved dearly. As Ruth's illness progressed, not only did my own health slowly deteriorate, the tree also became ill. The needles became more sparse and started turning brown, dropping in ever-increasing numbers. In 2006, for the first time, it bore no pine cones. By fall, it was totally brown. We brought professionals out to cut it down. Three months later, Ruth died at home, no more than thirty feet from the remaining stump of her beloved tree.

Who could have predicted then, my business neglected, my health tenuous, my feet crippled, feeling emotionally and spiritually devastated, that slightly less than five years later, I would be writing this book about the love Linda and I have found—in each other and in cruising—and that I would be walking easily, restored of health, and looking forward to the future. It's all quite amazing. Linda and I constantly appreciate the wondrous lives that we are living.

One of the elements of my recovery was foot comfort. I discovered Z-Coils, a brand of shoes that calls itself "pain relief footwear." They are weird-looking shoes that have a large coil on the heel that serves as a shock absorber, softening the impact of contact with the ground. I wear my Zs almost every day. When I switch to normal shoes, it seems like my feet are pounding the ground needlessly. Now that my feet have recovered, I sometimes wear Brooks running shoes and sometimes Finn Comforts. The latter have an unusually shaped and roomy toe box, giving plenty of space for my hammer toes. They serve as my dressiest shoe—none of those slim pointed Italian fashions for me.

Saint Emillion

In November 1988, Ruth and I took our honeymoon in France, four months before being married in March of 1989. (Why get married first, only to discover on your honeymoon that you made a mistake?) We took a moment in Chartres Cathedral to privately exchange our intentions of being a permanent couple. Then we drove to Saint Émilion, a long day's drive, arriving around 10:00 p.m. Entering a small hotel, I rang the night bell. The owner came out and said that she had a room available with two single beds. I asked for "un grand lit" (one large bed). "Non," she replied aloofly, "impossible." I looked dejected and lied to her, "Oh, what a shame. We were just *married* this morning. In *Chartres*." Her eyes grew big and she rushed back to talk to her husband. I could hear bits and pieces "married ... Chartres ..."

Being the slow season, they had closed a second building for lack of demand. She came out with a large set of keys, took us across the street, opened the door, and showed us to a wonderful room with a huge bed and a luxurious bathroom. The entire building was ours alone. (Perhaps she thought we might make too much noise.) We felt a little guilty, although we discussed using the same ruse again someday if needed; after all, couples often return again to the site of their honeymoon. It's good for business.

Health and Safety

Peace and quiet are sometimes hard to find on sea days, which are filled with onboard activities lest people get bored with the prospect of being alone with themselves or their loved ones. A teaching that I respect suggests that the purpose of the physical world is to distract us from the true spiritual journey to ourselves. This seems to be the philosophy of cruise ships. Sea days are apparently considered necessary inconveniences that must be crammed with distractions so people won't notice how boring they are. We don't agree.

We go first to a quiet bar on the second deck, but it's reserved for a private event. So we go to the other bar that is usually empty during the day, but it is host to a trivia game. So we go to the library, but it's next to a bar being used for cha cha lessons. Really. Perhaps out by the pool. Nope. The DJ is on the mike, conducting some kind of participation event. So we go to the other pool, only to find loud music. Of course there is our stateroom, but we need to be gone long enough for the steward to clean.

We end up in the only designated morning quiet place, the Crow's Nest (yet another bar) on Deck 14. The panorama extends 270 degrees, really giving a feeling of being out on the vast blue ocean, horizon to horizon, nothing but water. For us, this remoteness is a novelty, but think of the crews sailing on small ships, navigating up and down the swells. The prospect of endless ocean might not be quite so thrilling.

As this area is designated in the daily schedule as a quiet space, everyone is sitting and reading—except for four people who arrived just after we get here. They have no books nor anything to do, other than to talk loudly. Apparently there are no signs, nor anyone on the staff, to enforce silence or to suggest that there are many other venues at which to hold a loud conversation.

Unable to avoid listening to the inane conversation, Linda goes for a walk. I put one finger in my ear and try to keep reading. At one point, the talkers were considering going to the 11th deck, which I would have strongly favored. On the far side of the room, another foursome is noisying up that space, so moving would be to no avail. The people say something about "seven more minutes to go." The bartender begins setting up the bar. They hail him from afar, clearly acquainted with him. Finally, 11:00 comes. Now perhaps I will be rid of them. Wrong. They move from their table to bar stools. It seems that the bar opens at 11. That's what they were waiting for. Assuredly, as they drink, they will get louder still.

I look out the slanted windows at the activity below. A raised walkway rises above the Lido Deck, at the level of Deck 12, extending between the fore and aft structures, crossing in the middle to make a huge infinity sign. A steady flow of walkers, most wearing jackets or sweatshirts, brave the thirty-knot wind (including the ship's speed). The walkway doesn't have the protective glass walls found on the Lido Deck, thus making it more exposed to nature. We prefer to walk on Deck 4, which joins via stairs to Deck 5, allowing a complete circumambulation of the ship that is more protected from the wind and elements.

The pools have been emptied, as the rocking of the ship would cause the water to splash out. A net covers each pool for safety purposes. The bar is open, of course, at the site of the dancing under the stars party the other night. Around to the side, a machine dispenses free soft-serve ice cream to anyone looking for a treat.

Some of our friends avoid cruising because they fear getting seasick. There are methods to combat motion sickness, from pills to patches to devices that you wear on your wrist. But we don't need them, finding the ship's movement enjoyable. The captain calls it the "motion of the ocean," telling us that *Voyager*, currently crossing the Atlantic further north, was forced to change course and come further south toward us, to avoid extremely rough seas. Ah, they get all the fun.

Periodically, one reads about a cruise ship being hit by a rogue wave, an unexpectedly large wave that takes them by surprise. Damage can be extensive when a broadside blow causes a ship to roll at a steep angle. I remember seeing a video on YouTube showing people clinging to posts as the furniture slides back and forth. Of course, some things, like pianos, get chained down or otherwise permanently affixed to avoid being damaged or causing injury. Our movement today may reach two or three degrees. Six would seem quite extreme, with more than that causing special precautions.

During the (seemingly endless) writing and editing of this book, in June 2012, Linda and I browsed in The Barrow, a used bookstore in Concord, Massachusetts. I went right to the maritime section where I took down from the shelf a book on ocean liners by William Miller. Tucked inside the pages, I found a newspaper clipping from Saturday, September 16, 1995. The headline read: "A bit of white-knuckle time" with the subtitle, "Ocean liner rides out giant wave off Canada."

The article described an event involving *Queen Elizabeth 2* in the North Atlantic while passing through the remnants of Hurricane Luis. Captain Ronald Warwick had slowed the ship to five knots and ordered all passengers to stay below deck.

At 2:10 a.m., a ninety-five-foot wave approached the ship, equal in height with the bridge, causing the captain to report "It looked as if we were going right into the White Cliffs of Dover." During his thirty-eight years at sea, Captain Warwick had never seen a wave of this magnitude. (The largest recorded wave was in the Pacific, marked by the *US Ramapo* in 1937 at 112 feet.) "A bit of a white knuckle time," said the captain, which was quoted for the title of the article.

Fortunately, the wave hit straight on rather than broadside, which might have resulted in a more tragic story. It washed tons of water over the superstructure and bent some of the railings in the process. Dipping into the following trough, the ship then took a second wave over the bow. The forward whistle mast was lost, and several windows stove in, causing minor flooding in some lounges. Since it happened at night, most people were in bed and unaware anything had happened. No passengers or crew were injured.

Captain Warwick, whose father had also been master of *QE2*, had high praise for the ship. Unable to avoid the hurricane due to its size, he was confident she could handle it, and so she did. His only regret was that due to slowing their speed, they arrived in New York eight hours late. A diagram in the article showed that once waves begin to grow, they offer more surface for the wind to push, thereby growing even further.

For centuries, stories of monster killer-waves were considered myths and exaggerations. In the modern era, however, telemetry from sea buoys and satellite photos affirm their existence. A buoy near the site of the *Queen Elizabeth 2* incident registered a wave over one hundred feet tall. Unusual, with unpredictable frequency, rogue waves result from some kind of random multiplying effect of smaller waves and current, especially in a confused sea, when swells and wind waves are coming from several directions. This phenomenon differs from a tsunami, an event in which an earthquake displaces mass on the ocean floor, causing a huge wave to form. Tsunamis are no problem for ships in deep water—their passing would hardly be noticed. Only when the waves reach shore does their mass come into play. During the 2004 Asian tsunami, the only ships lost were in port.

During our honeymoon on *Queen Mary 2*, a ship purposefully built to handle the rough North Atlantic weather, Linda and I hoped for rough seas, just to see what she could do. Unfortunately, the seas remained calm the entire trip. On a Princess ship tour I once asked the captain the maximum roll his ship could sustain and still right itself. He said 60 degrees. On a different ship, the captain said 42 degrees (after which, the deck railings would be under water). I remember an account of the original *Queen Elizabeth* being hit by a wave that rolled it to 21 degrees. Thousands of dishes and bottles of wine and pieces of furniture were destroyed and hundreds of people injured, but the ship righted itself, with no danger of sinking.

To sink, you need to give a ship a little help. Two months from our current cruise, on Friday, January 13, 2012, the Costa *Concordia*—the same ship we saw in Civitavecchia—left that port around 6:00 p.m., only to rip a 160-foot-long hole in the hull a few hours later after hitting rocks off the island of Giglio. Costa caters to a mostly European audience, so U.S. cruisers might have been unfamiliar with the ship and that island. Built at a cost of $569 million in 2006, *Concordia* carried 4,200 passengers and crew. The crew had *not* performed an adequate lifeboat drill before departure. Reports later revealed that the so-called safety drill was used to tout products and services for sale onboard.

Authorities posit that Captain Francesco Schettino was hot-dogging it, trying to get close to the shore, having received a letter from dignitaries on the island thanking him for a previous close pass. Tragically, 32 people were killed—trapped in staterooms when the ship rolled to its side in shallow water. Misinformation caused mass confusion for both crew and passengers. The angle at which the ship listed made it difficult to use lifeboats from either side. Some passengers swam to shore. Others held on until rescued by helicopters. Schettino was arrested for abandoning the ship before the passengers were rescued, manslaughter, and shipwreck.

Photos in newspapers around the world showed the ship lying on its side in two-hundred feet of water, a few hundred feet from shore. There are stories of both loss and heroism. One crew member from the Philippines lost six months of wages, paid in cash, stored in his locker. Chief purser Manrico Gianpedroni, fell in the act of aiding passengers, breaking his leg. He was rescued from deep inside the ship thirty-six hours later. Erika Fani Soriamolina, in an act reminiscent of tales from *Titanic*, gave her life preserver to an elderly man who safely escaped, but she did not—one of five crew members who perished.

The captain has frequently changed the story of what happened, now saying he was distracted by talking on the telephone and that another officer was at the wheel. Apparently a problem exists with the black boxes, which are supposed to record all relevant data. Costa places the blame on the captain. According to reports, Chief Executive Officer Pier Luigi Foschi said Mr. Schettino changed a preprogrammed route to make a maneuver that was "unauthorized, unapproved and unknown to Costa."

Costa Cruises is owned by Carnival, a Miami company. Besides losing a ship costing more than half a billion dollars, salvaging/scrapping operations are expected to cost more than the original price to build the ship. As of this updating, in November, 2013, the cost has surpassed $600 million. I have watched with fascination the progress in righting the ship (a process called parbuckling). See for yourself at http://www.theparbucklingproject.com.

Costa first offered $14,000 in compensation for each surviving passenger to cover lost luggage, laptops, clothing, passports, and personal items. Eventually the amount offered reached $35,000. Some 80% of the crew and passengers accepted the settlement. In the first civil suit, six of the remaining passengers asked for $450 million. They filled the claim in Florida, the home state of Carnival. However, the small print in the tickets unambiguously specifies that Italy shall be the jurisdiction for litigation. On April 15, 2013, a hearing was held in Italy that was attended by so many attorneys suing Costa that the court proceedings had to be moved to a theater to accommodate them all. One lawyer said he was asking for one million dollars per passenger. What a headache for Carnival, victimized by the egregious actions and poor judgment of the captain and some of the crew.

In July 2013, four crew members and a company official were sentenced to between 18 and 34 months in jail as part of a plea bargain in which they pleaded guilty. Jail time is likely to be suspended in favor of house arrest or community service, a common practice in the Italian judicial service. There was widespread outrage by victims of the cruise at such leniency. Captain Schettino requested a plea bargain limiting his sentence to three years five months, but it was rejected. As this book goes to print, the trial is in progress in Italy.

This incident does not scare me. The chances of an accident such as this are infinitesimal compared to the number of cruises and passengers. According to one industry report, in 2013 some 283 cruise ships, holding a capacity for 438,595 passengers, will carry a total of 20.9 million passengers. Disasters are almost always caused by the convergence of numerous disadvantageous circumstances which in aggregate result in the problem. While the chance of such events happening is not zero, it is extremely low.

Procedures and policies on cruise ships are intended to both prevent and prepare for emergencies. On port days, while most of the passengers are off the ship, the crew practices mandatory fire or safety drills, enacting hypothetical scenarios such as an onboard fire or collision. I have personally seen on *Mariner* posters prominently displayed in crew areas that list every crew position on the ship and what that person's responsibilities are in case of emergency. Every lifeboat is launched and tested at least once a month.

There are fewer disasters today partly because of increased communication and navigational technologies. Ships divert for bad weather or radio if there's a problem. Captains can pinpoint their location. The greatest unknown, as in the Costa situation, is human fallibility. The *Titanic* officers fell victim to smug arrogance about the ship's abilities, ignoring the dangers that surrounded it. Rather than slow down in the presence of icebergs, they plowed ahead at an unsafe speed, as if, like some companies during the recent Great Recession, it was too big to fail. Or sink.

In response to the *Titanic* tragedy a century ago, the industry instigated many changes, including the founding of the International Maritime Organization and the Safety of Life at Sea (SOLAS) convention. New ships were subsequently designed with double hulls, to preserve the ship should the outer hull be breached. Waterproof bulkhead doors block off sections of the ship in the event of flooding. More lifeboats were added, enough for every passenger and crew.

In 1954, the organization that would become the International Maritime Organization was founded as part of the United Nations. It now monitors more than fifty international conventions. Recent additions to SOLAS include equipment and electrical requirements for preventing, detecting, and fighting fires, including mandatory fixed-sprinkler systems.

As a result of the *Concordia* incident, the Cruise Lines International Association (CLIA), the organization that represents the cruise industry, announced a list of new safety policies, effective immediately. First, members pledge to carry onboard more life jackets than required by law. Second, non-officers will be banned from the bridge during potentially dangerous times. Third, cruise-ship routes must be planned well in advance and shared with all members of the bridge team. That would prevent the hot-dogging of which the *Concordia* captain has been accused. Finally, emergency drills for all embarking passengers must take place before the ship leaves port.

I believe two things are in the mind of every cruiser, whether consciously or not. One is that they are part of a great romanticized tradition of sea travel. Just getting out onto the ocean is a thrilling experience. We all buy into that great adventurous and mysterious image. It isn't all peaches and cream, however. We know danger lurks. We have heard about shipwrecks or seen the movie *Titanic*. Hence the second belief, namely, that surviving the dangers of the sea, whether real or fictional, creates part of the thrill of ocean travel.

Ignorance is not bliss. Being aware of what happens during disastrous events can best prepare us should any such eventuality happen. As passengers, our duty is to attend the muster sessions, stay alert, and have a plan in case we ever hear those seven short and one long blasts.

A word commonly coupled with safety is "health." Ships contain a hull-bound group of people who interact and socialize in numerous ways. If one passenger carries an infectious disease, many more can get infected. The practice of health and safety, a high priority for cruise lines, addresses and prevents causes of injury and illness.

Sometimes safety and health work against each other. On rough days at sea, the captain urges everyone to grasp the railings when going up or down stairs or passing through hallways in order to be safe and avoid falling. Unfortunately, railings are a good place to pick up germs. Clinging to the rails is not a good choice from the point of sanitation. Linda and I avoid handrails assiduously.

Virtually all mass-market cruise lines have at one time or another reported outbreaks of disease onboard, according to the U.S. Centers for Disease Control (CDC). The most frequent culprit is the *norovirus*, a virus linked to gastroenteritis (the "stomach flu"). Norovirus infections spread quickly on a cruise ship due to the close quarters. According to the CDC, cruise ships participating in the Vessel Sanitation Program are required to report the total number of gastrointestinal (GI) illness cases (including zero cases) evaluated by the medical staff before the ship arrives at a U.S. port, when sailing from a foreign port.

A separate notification is required when the GI illness count exceeds 2 percent of the total number of passengers or crew onboard. Information of the CDC website about noroviruses is well worth reading.

While not life threatening, the symptoms include vomiting, diarrhea, stomach cramping, low-grade fever, chills, headache, muscle aches, nausea, and tiredness—which typically last a day or two.

Noroviruses are transmitted through direct contact, such as shaking hands or touching a surface formerly touched by an infected person. Food or drink can also be infected. Outbreaks happen on land but are rarely reported (often being misnamed "food poisoning").

Three things are very important on cruise ships. First, wash hands frequently. Before entering any food venue and at other places there are dispensers with hand cleaner. Not uncommonly, I see people walk right by without using them. Bad idea. Second, if you cough, cover your mouth, but not with your hand. If caught unprepared, cough into your sleeve. Third, report any cases of illness. Not wanting to curtail their vacation plans, people sometimes continuing their activities while sick, thereby putting others at risk. Better to stay in bed for a day.

To see the cruise ship inspections for a particular ship, visit the CDC Vessel Sanitation program website (www.cdc.gov) which posts inspection reports. I looked up *Mariner of the Seas* (score: a perfect 100) and *Rhapsody of the Seas* (score: 99) before booking.

On Holland American ships, for the first forty-eight hours, the staff serves the food in the buffet. After that, starting on the third day, it becomes self-service. During that first two days, any virus would likely show up and be addressed. I once asked a Royal Caribbean officer why they didn't do that. He said their approach was to replace the serving utensils every ten or fifteen minutes. I suppose that would help limit the spread, but it wouldn't do much for the next person to touch the spoon immediately after an infected person handled it. That only takes a few seconds.

Cruise ships take far more precautions than land-based establishments. One day, in the Windjammer buffet, we saw an officer inspecting for cleanliness by rubbing his white gloves across a surface and then shining a special UV light on his hand. This tests whether targeted surfaces have been properly cleaned. The special light also shows the presence of organic matter. I have seen similar lights available for travelers who want to check the cleanliness of hotel rooms and linens.

The fact that the officer made the inspection while passengers were present, rather than during some off period, was probably meant to impress us. I suspect they use other methods in the food preparation areas, such as meters that test surfaces for ATP, the energy molecule within all living cells. It's found in bacteria, mold, and fungus. I certainly wouldn't want to have the responsibility of keeping a ship free of germs.

Linda reminds me frequently not to touch my eyes or mouth with my hands, which gives germs entry points into the body. It's surprising how many times, without being conscious of it, my hands and fingers go back to my face. Over and over I find myself rubbing an eye or chewing on a fingernail. We wash our hands frequently with lots of soap and hot water for twenty seconds. I sometimes hum the tune "Happy Birthday," which is just about the right length of time.

After norovirus, a common ailment is respiratory infections. Twice I have come home from my cruise with a cough that lasted for two months. Wherever people are gathered, such as in the theater, you hear sniffling and coughing. I just consider this one of the risks one takes to cruise with several thousand other people. Given proper precautions, staying healthy should be no big deal.

Developing a serious illness carries another big risk on cruise ships, namely the standard cruise line policy of discharging passengers who have serious medical problems. The cruise lines don't really have a choice, as the ships are not equipped to offer specialized or lengthy care. Nor should they be held responsible for medical services not included in the cost of a passage. As an unfortunate result, passengers can be forced to leave the ship in distant foreign places, to obtain their own care and transportation home, at their own expense, which can be considerable. I have heard horror stories of frail or elderly people being left to fend for themselves. Because of that potential circumstance, Linda and I always purchase travel insurance that includes medical evacuation. If we should need it once, it will pay for all the insurance we have ever bought. If we never need it, that will be a good thing. It's a win-win situation. In the case of insurance, I want to waste my money.

Mid-afternoon, Linda and I go to the photo gallery, which also has a small store, to buy a mini-tripod. The sales person is from Eastern Europe. She reminds me of my visit to Budapest a few years ago. It may be a free country now, but they still miss some of the subtle components of capitalism, namely, friendliness and an inclination for customer service. In the days of Soviet domination, everything was by decree. The idea that the customer is always right hasn't yet sunk in. It's more of an attitude that implies "Hold your horses, I'll wait on you when I feel like it."

The girl at the camera store doesn't have a tripod unwrapped that I can examine. They are in impregnable plastic bubbles. So, I declare, "OK, I'll buy it, and if I don't like it, I'll return it for a full refund." She looks at me like I'm from Mars. "Huh?" Any good American entrepreneur would say, "Yeah, sure, no problem. How many do you want?" I repeat my intention, and she continues to frown. We complete the transaction, I open the package on the spot, the tripod fits just fine, and I go on my way. Linda goes to do her stretches while I head out to take movies of the ocean passing by.

Except I don't. Until now, with my new Sony camera, I have been taking still shots set on fully automatic. I change it to the movie setting, mount it to my tripod and train the camera on the rolling swells. I push the red button, and the camera blinks "recording." I hold onto the camera, wanting a good long feel of the ocean. However, the camera turns itself off, and the lens retracts. What? I turn it on and shoot another segment. It, too, stops on its own. I go on the elevator and shoot through the glass as I ascend and descend. Again it closes. When I go back to the stateroom and look at the clips, most are two seconds, with the longest achieving ten seconds.

Nothing got captured. I had walked down the deck thinking the camera was shooting, pointing out the lifeboats and carrying on an animated conversation. Not there. I guess I have to get out the instruction book again.

We have dinner again at our window table. This time we each order a glass of wine, a Rothschild Lafite Languedoc Cabernet Sauvignon. We both have the chilled fruit soup for the appetizer. I would like the potato gnocchi, but they put ham in the sauce, which I don't want. So I order roast turkey (another exception to my vegetarianism, so I might as well have accepted the ham) and Linda picks the seafood tempura.

Perhaps our standards have been raised after so many good meals, or perhaps, as the voyage continues, Royal Caribbean tries to slip in a few losers. In any case, the turkey has no appeal. Picture three huge slabs of white meat (far too much for one serving) and one piece of dark meat sliced from somewhere unrecognizable, riddled with gristle and inedible. The advertised bread stuffing forms a tiny dot the size of a quarter. The vegetables are good, but I leave half of the meal. Linda's tempura, on the other hand, is tasty, so I have a piece of her fish. I could order a different entree, but I don't bother.

Dessert offers two versions of key lime pie, one of which is sugar free. I take the real one, as I believe most sugar substitutes are far worse for you than is sugar. I have high standards for key lime pie, one of my favorites, of which I make a pretty mean version. This one avoids many of the pitfalls, making it decent but not spectacular—not like my homemade extra-thick, buttery graham-cracker crust and plenty of zest to make the lime taste really pop. But it was still good, especially considering the quantity they produce for the dining room.

Linda's wheat cake with apples flopped, however. So, on this night, when we finally spring for $9 glasses of wine (although we use a two-for-one coupon), the meal disappoints us. Some of our Texan neighbors just order a big piece of prime rib every night and couldn't be happier.

The three-tiered dining room and two special event rooms hold a total of 1,862 people. (What restaurant do you know on land with that capacity?) In two seatings, they can serve all the passengers. Of course, many people eat up at the Windjammer Buffet, which seats 796. On port days, the dining room remains closed at lunchtime, which sends everyone to the buffet. It would take four seatings to accommodate everyone, but of course, many people eat in town.

After dinner we go through an excruciating experience trying to access our email. The ship can't have broadband, or cable, or fiber optics as it's limited to some kind of satellite system. The ship's literature describes it thus:

> *Internet speed in optimal conditions is 128 kBs. Certain ship positions will affect satellite coverage and interrupt or slow down the service. Network has limited bandwidth, so large numbers of users using the network simultaneously (especially on sea days), might affect the Internet speed.*

Might affect! In other words, it works best when you're not using it. If you don't bring your own laptop (which we didn't), you must rely on one of the sixteen computers located one deck above the library (which we did). People could be online in other hot spots, such as Ellington's, the Solarium, Cafe Promenade, Wig and Gavel Pub, Schooner Bar, and the Conference Center. Besides being expensive, Internet access is unreliable. Linda fussed and fussed with it, spending twenty-four minutes just to glance at her email, at a cost of $12.

Considering it a necessary business expense, I just pay their price and move on. Linda needs to work out the details for the memorial service she will be conducting in Massachusetts immediately upon our return, whereas I'm tracking the progress in getting the payment for some work my crew did (installing four labyrinths at a new mental hospital in Worcester, Massachusetts). Hence, we are hostages to the cost and inconvenience.

When I type in the address of the email server at GoDaddy, it takes about thirty seconds to one minute just to open that page. Then, it takes another minute to load the passwords and open to the inbox. Anything more complicated than that takes even longer. We considered using our iPad, but there is this posted warning:

> *If you are unable to log off, please type 192.168.132.1/ekgnkm/icafe2.asp in Safari's address bar.*

That seems scary. If you can't log off, your expensive time would keep ticking way, adding up to a fortune. We should just enjoy the cruise and forget email. I see people on their cell phones, which is even more expensive, up to $15 per minute. Maybe we should consider a message in a bottle.

Tonight's entertainment features Maria Nellia, a violinist. She is quite short, a bit hefty, bent over, and old. Very old. She can hardly walk, a prospect made more difficult by the ship's movement. She's quite a character. Her style can be summed up in a single word: fast. She performed on the Ed Sullivan Show twenty-four times, beginning at the age of three. She has played for two presidents, etc., etc. Her violin, made in the seventeenth century by the master who taught Stradivarius, is valued at $300,000.

I have heard other violins played on cruise ships, some of them electronic versions that have just a neck and a hint of body. Once amplified, they were clear and audible. Here, she has an electric pickup attached to the violin. Perhaps the problem is with the mixer, but I find it hard to hear her over the band, which she has just met this afternoon. She plays nothing slow or melodic or soulful, just fast and frantic, which draws the audience to their feet several times. They fall for it. While impressive, her performance reminds me of the last energetic bursts of a supernova before it explodes. How can she keep this up? She definitely kept everyone's attention, despite the lack of variety.

We go to bed.

Immigration

Day 10, November 4, 2011

Here's Colin again. You can't miss that he hails from Jamaica. Tall and extroverted, he often acts as master of ceremonies at bingo and other events. His gleaming smile is infectious, and his *joie de vivre* apparent. He's been with Royal Caribbean for more than three years, including breaks between contracts, one of which was five months. Colin describes to me the process to become an entertainer on the ship. He points out that the entertainers do many tasks in addition to the shows in which they perform.

To get on the staff, he first applied to the agent in his country. Similar agents can be found all around the world, who help determine your language capability and the degree of talent you offer. If you pass that preliminary screening, you are then interviewed by the national office in Miami. Once accepted, you show up either to a ship or a training facility, as directed.

The applicant bears the cost of the whole process, including medical exam, visas, and plane ticket. I ask Colin if the same entertainment takes place on all their ships. He says no, that they are independent, which, if true, would be completely different from Princess, in which they spend up to a million dollars to put together production numbers that are then performed for several years on all of their ships. That way, entertainers can transfer between ships.

Once Colin returns to his duties, Linda joins me in Cafe Promenade. Few tables are free. The shops are open, leading people to stroll through the promenade. We're waiting to attend a lecture about the history of cruising. The title is, "The Great Transatlantic Migration: From Sailing Ship to Luxury Liner."

The couple at the next table seem to know just about everyone who goes by, greeting them by name. Perhaps they became acquainted at the many events for diamond-level cruisers. Or maybe they belong to a large group. Being that so many cruisers are from Texas, they often talk about going to the University of Texas or Texas A&M, or how their sports teams are doing, "Ain't the Cowboys doin' just awful?" Sitting here, we catch little snippets of conversation: "We bought a company that ..." "We built houses in the four hundred thousand dollar range ..." "Out at the ranch ..." "Once we retired, we sold our..."

We head for the lecture to discover a surprising number of people packing the theater. The speaker, Michael LeMay, PhD, a retired professor, specializes in human migration, both immigration and emigration. The author of several books on the subject, he speaks in an easy and personable way. He gives a lecture on every sea day, which makes ten lectures. Today, it involves ships, so I came. He starts with the push and pull factors of immigration. In some cases, such as the great potato famine in Ireland, people were driven out by external factors. In other ways, immigrants were drawn to new possibilities. Back home, they measured their tillable topsoil in inches, whereas in the New World we measure it in feet—nirvana for a farmer.

Skilled tradesmen from Germany and Europe had a good life awaiting them. Shockingly, as many as one-third of the immigrants to the U.S. went back home again. The early wave, until 1860, consisted mostly of Germans, French, and Irish. The second wave came from Eastern Europe, from Poland, from Greece. They were more impoverished. The relationship with ships was symbiotic. The more immigrants there were, the more ships were needed. Similarly, the larger the ships, the more opportunity for immigration. Most immigrants came to New York, crowding on the outer decks to catch their first glimpse of the Statue of Liberty, its flame burning brightly in the morning mist.

Emma Lazarus wrote her sonnet, "New Colossus," for a fund-raiser auction to raise money for the pedestal upon which the Statue of Liberty now sits. Not receiving much recognition, the poem was forgotten after the auction. In the early 1900s, after Lazarus' death, one of her friends began a campaign to memorialize Lazarus and her sonnet. The effort succeeded, and a plaque with the poem's text was mounted inside the pedestal of the statute. We all recognize the line:

> *"Give me your tired, your poor,*
> *Your huddled masses yearning to breathe free…"*

It is well worth reading the whole poem, which you will find at this link: http://www.libertystatepark.com/emma.htm.

Three-masted sailing boats took up to two months to get to America. The British government chartered private companies to carry packets of mail and other cargo throughout the empire. Hence, the origin of the term packet boats, which were built to carry cargo, not people. Samuel Cunard won such a charter to carry the mail to Halifax, Boston, and later, New York. Each voyage took on a few passengers. Cunard soon discovered that cargo takes two days to unload, whereas passengers just walk right off. Furthermore, they paid more money and took up less space. Slowly, ships' designs included more passengers and less cargo.

In the beginning, passengers brought and prepared their own food—for two months! During the day they sat in big rooms with bunks along the perimeter, three-high, dormitory-style, men and women separated. No privacy. A very smelly toilet situation. Cooking presented a constant fire hazard. Many ships carrying passengers (not Cunard's) never reached their destination. One author estimated that 9 percent of the passengers never made it, dying or being killed en route. Imagine! Former slave ships were sometimes used for immigrant transport. Travel was a daunting and dangerous task. There certainly must have been a strong push or pull for passengers to suffer such privation.

The nineteenth century should be called the Age of Mass Migration. Before that time, 98 percent of the population was born, lived, and died within a few miles of their family home. Family names became associated with geographical areas for that reason. My own name is an example. My Swedish grandfather changed his name from Anderson (too ordinary) to Ferré, a French name, complete with accent mark. In the mid-1980s, I lived in the Pyrenees Mountains in France for a couple of years. It turns out that's the region from which the name Ferré originates. I saw furniture stores ("Ferré: Monsieur Meuble") and hotels and restaurants with that name, rarely seen in other parts of the country. It spread into Spain and is common in Spanish. A former governor of Puerto Rico and a former mayor of Miami were named Ferré. France wasn't the place of my ancestors, yet my name ended up "home."

Everything changed in the nineteenth century, LeMay told us. During that time up to seventy million people came to the United States. Compared to the existing population, that represented a huge number. It started slowly, but as the ships increased their capacity, it became a flood, not curtailed until the restrictive immigration laws of 1921 and 1924.

Conditions in the 1800s in America encouraged immigration. In 1862, the Homestead Act promised free land out west to anyone claiming it. In 1848, the population of Chicago numbered five thousand people. Two years later it reached thirty thousand. By 1900, it climbed to 1,690,000. That growth rate equates to adding a medium size city every year! Think of all the workers and skilled trades needed for construction, services, and sales.

Today we see a different sort of immigration, namely, a quarter of a million workers, often from Third World countries, who work on cruise ships—a nationless floating state rather than a foreign destination. Like their previous counterparts, crew immigrants escape unfortunate circumstances back home to seek a better life.

The lecture over, we mosey over to the dining room, choosing table service rather than going up to the buffet for lunch. We sit with five others and have interesting conversation. I have seafood bisque and tempura catfish filets. Linda has mushroom soup and the catfish. Portions are large and we eat too much, finishing at around 1:30 p.m. Fortunately, the desserts don't seem too tempting.

We waddle back to our stateroom for nap time. We can't seem to get back out of bed, and why should we? Scattered puffy white clouds fill a blue sky. The sea turns the bluest we have seen. It's fifteen thousand feet deep right here—almost three miles. I find that statistic hard to comprehend. Snuggling in bed with the balcony door wide open, the sounds of the sea, and the joy of being together—these are the reasons we love cruising. Sure, we enjoy traveling on land, too, because our love extends wherever we go. Still, these circumstances remain our favorite. When I try to get out of bed, Linda pulls me back, and vice versa. Our nap stretches to two hours, some of which actually involves sleep.

Eventually I go out to take photos of the ship. On Deck 15, a small chapel sits unappreciated. Decorated with multicultural symbols, it's used only for occasional weddings as church services are held in the much roomier Lotus Lounge. A Catholic priest on board holds mass every morning, plus he leads an ecumenical service on Sundays. We once wondered if there would be a position for Linda, as an Episcopal priest, to lead some services or offer spiritual direction. Apparently, Royal Caribbean feels that one priest can handle everything.

The Cunard tradition always called for the Master, the captain of the ship, to conduct the Sunday morning non-denominational service. On *Queen Mary 2*, we saw commodore Bernard Warner (now retired) perform this function. He was perfunctory at best, dull and boring at worst. At the end, he essentially apologized, saying, "And now I'll get back to what I do best, commanding the ship." On one Princess voyage, the cruise director conducted the service. He had served as warden at an Anglican church in London, and he did a very credible job.

Aft of the Royal Viking Lounge are two outdoor smoking areas. Against the stern side of the funnel, on Deck 13, rises the well-publicized Royal Caribbean rock-climbing wall. Nearby, the rear deck houses various sporting facilities, including table tennis, a mini-golf course, and a strange track for inline skating. It's U-shaped, fifty or sixty feet long, narrow, and has three-foot high padded walls. Doesn't look like much fun. Yet, one man leaned on the wall, dressed in full crash gear.

From Deck 13 you can look down into the open area on Deck 12 that comprises an enclosed basketball/volleyball court. The most aft structure on the top deck houses Adventure Ocean, a space for children ranging in ages from small to teenage. Behind that a lounge space clearly indicates "Reserved for teens—nonalcoholic area." I note half a dozen adults sunbathing there. No teens in sight. Also aft, tucked along the starboard side, is Johnny Rockets, an old-fashioned diner with a juke box selection mechanism at each table.

Enough words about photos. Rather than try to imagine these, you can go to the website www.cruiseoftheheart.com to get a better view of things.

I had agreed to meet Linda on Deck 4, where she likes to sit and read. Past the cantilevered walkway, the deck widens, with room for chairs and shuffleboard. Just behind the bowed area is a little niche protected from the wind, out of the way of walkers. That's where I find Linda, reading a book. I get another chair and join her. With the ship cutting through twenty-foot swells, we can trace the movement by watching the relationship between the railing and the horizon.

We decide to play a game of shuffleboard. It takes a little practice, as the deck slants for drainage purposes, plus the ship keeps moving. Linda complains that twice I knock away her scoring disk by blasting it with one of mine.

"Why don't you just focus on your own score, rather than undoing mine," she grumbles.

"Strategy is all part of the game, Sweetie."

All's fair in love and shuffleboard. The score remains very close.

Once called shovelboard, the game we are playing dates back five hundred years or more. We know that King Henry VIII of England played it, as extant documents record the paying of losing wagers. For anyone not familiar with the game, allow me a quick description. Lines painted on the deck surface delineate the playing field. Officially, the measurements should be thirty-nine feet in length and six feet in width. Being long and narrow, it fits nicely on the decks of ships, where its presence has become quite traditional.

At each end of the court is a triangle divided into four horizontal scoring areas. The first is the tip of the triangle, worth ten points. The subsequent trapezoid decreases in value to eight points, and beyond that another trapezoid worth seven points. The final category, in the widest part of the triangle, is worth minus ten points, a penalty which reduces one's score. To qualify for points, the disk must be completely within the area and not touching any line.

Efficiently, with a triangle at each end of the court, play takes place in both directions. One game consists of ten round-trips. Of course, every sport has its own terminology: the disks are called *biscuits* and the push sticks are *tangs*. Shoving a disk toward the scoring area is known as "sending the biscuit." Sounds more like afternoon tea to me: "I say, would you mind sending me another biscuit?" Of course there is an International Shuffleboard Association, a hall of fame, and world tournaments. Mostly, shuffleboard brings to mind old folks like us on cruise ships or in retirement centers.

A few people walking around the deck pass by our game. Perhaps the morning hours are busier. I'm reminded of our stay in Italy. As part of our daily routine, in the late afternoon and early evening, we took a stroll along the walkway which bordered the Mediterranean. We weren't alone. Families and friends and people of all ages came out to socialize, filling park playgrounds and benches. How civilized. No fancy entertainment, no loud amplifiers, no electronic games, just people relating to each other. I wrote the following passage in my journal, describing Levanto, Italy.

> *The evening brings forth a phenomenon not seen back home in Texas. People come out for a walk in the cool of the day, just before sunset. Older people walk slowly in twos and threes, canes in hand, talking, stopping to sit on well-worn benches. Families push strollers, as kids ride bikes steadied with training wheels. The stone bench at the bottom of the wall fills with people. The scene resembles evening on the Malecon in Puerto Vallarta, also a walkway along the sea, also filled with families out for strolls. We don't do that in the U.S. We have no time. We're all out working and making money, too busy to have a life. Nor are there many public places to gather, as the inner cities are sparsely inhabited and the suburbs too spread out. Starbucks hopes to serve as the new village square, but it isn't the same. Here, in Levanto, children scream with delight as they play together in the park. Back in the U.S., kids sit around, exercising only their thumbs, texting friends.*

Primped and dressed for dinner, Linda wears the beautiful green sequined top that I previously doused with champagne. I'm wearing a high-necked black T-shirt. Because of the color and neckline, it looks dressy, yet is supremely comfortable. My slacks dress up the T-shirt even more. Although time for dinner, neither of us is hungry, having had a late and copious lunch. Yet, we worry that we will lose our advantageous situation in the dining room. So, we go down at the appointed time and tell Jeffry we are skipping only one night, assuring him we will return tomorrow night, as usual. We hope he appreciates our gesture and our proprietary interest in that table.

We go up to the buffet, discovering that it doesn't open for dinner until 6:30 p.m. That seems rather late. So, instead, we go to Cafe Promenade, where we have fruit salad, pizza, and chocolate cake, the dinner of champions. We finish early enough to attend the 7:00 p.m. evening show.

Tonight's performer is Martin Lewis, a magician from England whose father and grandfather had also been magicians. He does mostly sleight-of-hand things, skillful tricks, not Vegas-style illusions that make a Hummer disappear or appear to saw someone in half. He does a classic Chinese trick manipulating six steel rings that he hooks together and unhooks in various combinations, even though they seem completely solid.

At the end he performs a beautiful and elegant classic Japanese trick, magically producing snowflakes from his cupped hand, using a fan to waft them all over the stage. I had never seen that before. By the time he finishes, the whole stage is covered. His act has class.

We leave the theater to go to the Schooner Bar, get a beer, and eat some munchies. However, we encounter a huge crowd there, awaiting a game of naming tunes from the '80s, directed by Colin, the young man from Jamaica. So we go to the Royal Promenade, where we find two of the resident entertainers engaged in a "street" concert, loud, and not in a style we like. So we try Boleros Bar, arriving just as the band plays the song "YMCA." The dance floor is packed, so we join in miming the letters Y-M-C-A and then move on.

We end up back at the buffet on Deck 11. Linda has a baked potato and I have crackers and cheese. Then we sample a few items from the pasta bar. The dinner buffet offers more choices than at lunch, including tilapia, salmon, and halibut, fixed in different ways, and an extensive presentation of sushi and sashimi. We could eat well here, but we prefer our exclusive engagement in the dining room. Some people come here to circumvent formal evenings, as the buffet has no dress code.

We find a movie on the TV in our room, a melodrama about love and Rome. Outside, the sea continues to slide past relentlessly at twenty knots. Linda wafts off to sleep and soon I follow.

Water

The ocean outside our window forms rolling swells. To the average observer, it's not apparent how deep and powerful swells really are, nor how much mass they have, nor that their speed is twice that of the ship.

The water doesn't travel horizontally, even though it looks like it is moving. Rather, it goes up and down. The energy that creates the swell differs from the physical water that gives it visible form and expression. Consider the apparent movement of light around a theater marquee. The bulbs don't travel around in a circle, they stay in place. By turning them on and off in a certain sequence, the light appears to move.

Waves work in a similar way. By moving up and down in sequence, waves also seem to move. The actual molecules of water go in tiny circles as the wave or swell passes. The size and strength of waves are determined by wind speed, duration, and fetch (how far they are exposed over open water). As a rule of thumb, take half of the wind speed (in knots) to estimate the height of the waves (in feet). So forty knot winds produce twenty foot waves. As the swells get close to land, the ocean floor rises up, forcing the water into a shallower space. In that instance, the energy begins to push the water toward the shore. The resistance caused by the shallow bottom increases, causing the leading edge of the wave to slow down. The back part of the wave overtakes the front part, coming up over it in a crest which becomes a breaker.

In June of 2012, I wrote a poem in Maine that alludes to the technology of waves.

OGUNQUIT

just yesterday
we walked on the wide sand
scratched a quick labyrinth
with a bent stick
walked its crooked trail
imagined how it would be
to actually live near the sea

this morning the tide
reclaims our beach
the rain pelts the
metal roof above our bench
two determined children
play in the cold surf
their parents huddled
under large rainbow umbrellas

the energy forming these swells
travels thousands of miles
the ocean rising and falling
in uncountable repetitions
until the shallow shore
causes it to stumble up and
trip over itself as a white wave

a momentous event
so ordinary that only
we few morning observers
mark its passing until
our coffee is long cold and
we are finally tempted away
by blueberry pancakes

Swells and waves are related, of course. Waves reflect local conditions within a small area, whereas swells travel great distances. The winds that generated them are likely hundreds of miles away. Because they are not caused by local conditions, swells may appear even when the visible weather is calm. These phenomenon reflect the hydraulic nature of water. Specifically, water can't be compressed. If you push on it, it moves until something else stops it. The degree of pressure can be reflected in the periodicity of the swells, which is to say, how close they are together. So as we look down, we may be seeing swells that have traveled from Africa or even further.

Not only is the Earth's surface 80 percent water, our bodies are largely water as well. Some scientists believe that life once crawled out of the ocean and evolved into what we are today. No wonder we feel an affinity toward the sea. Now we can return to the sea, our original home, if only to swim and sunbathe and float on the surface.

Ruth

I have thought about writing a memoir, the subtitle of which would be, "Lessons, Joys, Regrets." I suppose it could be unproductive to focus on regrets, seeing the wonderful turn my life has now taken. But I do have regrets. I could have handled many things in my life better had I been more conscious and attentive.

One of my mistakes was working too hard. Workaholism rules our society while it ruins our lives. In some circles it's even admired. Yet it robs us of so many opportunities. It steals the lives we could have had. On my first cruise, I experienced cruiseaholism, avidly filling my days far too full, enamored as I was by the possibilities. It became quite stressful. Now, on *Mariner*, I go from activity to activity, but without pressure. If I miss out on something, no problem.

My work life before retiring commandeered sixty and seventy hours per week. At times, I was gone from home for so long that coming back required a reentry process. Ruth and I had to slowly reintroduce ourselves. Worst of all, I didn't make that much money. Had I slowed down, taken time to smell the roses, it wouldn't have been a huge financial imposition.

The moment Ruth was diagnosed with breast cancer, I should have closed up my business and spent the next five good years fulfilling our bucket list. She always wanted to go to Ireland. Why didn't we? I rationalize my choice to keep working by pointing out the cost of her treatment, which, being alternative, was not covered by insurance. I estimate those five years cost us $200,000 out of pocket. The only way we could afford that was for me to keep working.

That last year of Ruth's life, when I was the full-time caretaker, I finally put my business on hold. By that time, Ruth could no longer travel. For months she slept on the couch, all tucked in with pillows and blankets. Then we found a hospital bed on Craig's list, which we put in the living room. I did the cooking and the caring, assisted by an ever-present circle of her friends. In retrospect, I realized I could list all of my friends on one hand. I had never taken the time to stay in touch or to nourish friendships. Ruth, on the other hand, had an amazing group of women who came to her aid nonstop, giving her energy treatments, attending to her needs, reading, or conversing.

Two years earlier, Ruth and I had gone to my mother's bedside in the nursing home. Every day mom prayed to Jesus to take her home, sitting slumped in her wheelchair all day, her clothes in need of dry cleaning, her wig askew. We conducted a little service for her as she lay in bed, reading scripture and singing hymns. Although she seemed incommunicative, we told her it was OK to go to heaven, where my father would meet her. She had no obligation to stay here for us. That night, she died peacefully in her sleep.

I wanted to give the same permission to Ruth. Her endurance had been heroic, but we all knew she would lose the fight. Several of her friends and I were gathered by her bed, telling her, "Go to the light, Ruthie. Just let go." After doing this for several minutes, we heard a small voice in response. In a whisper, gathering all of her strength, Ruth responded, "I don't want to go." Ha! Good for you, Ruth. Rage, rage against the dying of the light. Hang in there until the end.

I'm sure Ruth didn't hang on because she feared death. Rabindareth Tagore said, "Death is not extinguishing the light. Rather, it is putting out the lamp, because the dawn has come." The channeled entity Emmanuel once said, "Death is like taking off a tight shoe." Ruth's shoe was very tight. Her ravaged body could no longer contain her beautiful spirit.

She was very particular, even demanding, in the way she wanted things. In life she had been a detail person, as if safety lay in her ability to control her environment and surroundings. As her illness progressed, the control became even tighter. She liked the bed and the pillows and the covers a certain way. Her friends, having changed the sheets, reassembled things incorrectly. In her exasperation, Ruth told them, "Ask Robert, he knows how they go." And so I did.

You see, the blue pillow went on the bottom, and then the two brown ones. More than that, Ruth showed a confidence in my being there and filling her needs. In that last year, I could show my love in action as well as words—a rare opportunity. She got the message.

Only a week before her death, we still held the hope that we could overcome the cancer and the treatment; that Ruth could slowly recover. When she had trouble breathing, we went to the emergency room. The x-rays showed that the cancer had spread and fully involved her lungs. Nothing could be done. The chemotherapy meant to fight the cancer had destroyed her immune system, giving the cancer free reign. The very treatment her doctors said would eliminate the cancer had, instead, made her defenseless against it.

Hospice helped that last week, providing equipment and, most of all, morphine. Ruth stopped eating. She waited to die until I had left her side to go into the kitchen. I have heard that is common. I returned to the room moments later, to silence. The labored breathing had stopped. I had never seen death before, so close.

Not so for Linda. She worked for a number of years as a hospice chaplain. She has held the hands of many dying people. She has conducted many funerals and counseled the bereaved. I don't think I fear death, although it looms as a huge mysterious uncertainty. All of nature is cyclical. Birth comes in the spring, the new lambs frolicking in the fields. Summer brings growth and activity. Death arrives in the fall, as leaves turn brown and fall to the ground, soon to be compost. Dormant winter follows, only to be revived by spring again. The cycle repeats. I don't think death is the end, just a change of form. I'll get a chance to find out, but first, I hope to have some more good years with Linda.

Ship's Tour

Day 11, November 5, 2011

Our days have gained a certain rhythm. Each of us starts the day writing, me on this book and Linda in her journal. Then we go for our power walk. The Promenade Deck doesn't circumambulate the entire Deck 4. Toward the stern, we must climb the stairs to Deck 5, which goes around the back of the ship and then back down again to Deck 4. Due to the ship's speed, the wind direction, and the waves, spray reaches the starboard side, making the deck wet and slippery. So, we walk back and forth on the port side.

In one place, amidships, the dining rooms extend outward, like a large bow window, all the way out to the hull, blocking the deck. The staterooms above and below follow suit. Even the interior hallway bows at that point.

To allow passage, a wooden walkway cantilevers out over the sea. I really like walking on this part, as it gives me a vantage point from which I can see the side of the ship, with the yellow lifeboats all tucked into their places. Because the walkway hangs out in space, often we can feel the spray rising from the water below.

The three deck levels of this bowed area comprise the floor-to-ceiling windows of the three dining rooms. Our favored table for two sits on the middle level, Deck 5, right in the center of this bowed area.

After twenty minutes of power walking, we sit in chairs for a moment to cool down and then go up to the buffet for breakfast. This time I skip the oatmeal and have waffles. I try the little cubed breakfast potatoes, hoping they will be good and crispy, the way I like them, but they are soft—clearly frozen and just warmed in the oven. Too bad.

Today, I will participate in a very special event, the behind-the-scenes tour of the ship. They conduct only two such tours during the cruise, limited to fifteen people each. Such privilege doesn't come free. It costs $150. I once did a similar tour, at the same cost, on the *Emerald Princess*. All participants sign lengthy waivers, releasing Royal Caribbean from any responsibility should we get hurt. The dress code specifies covered-toe shoes, long pants, and shoulder-covering shirts.

I arrive early, as usual. My birth pattern is to always be early, having been born seven weeks premature (10½ inches long, four pounds, incubator). Many times I have engaged in a process called "rebirthing," breathing in a circular pattern that leads me into an altered state that helps to heal emotional issues trapped in cellular memory. The process is called rebirthing because it can take you all the way back to re-experience the trauma of your birth. On two occasions while rebirthing, a blackness welled up and overtook me like an avalanche, cutting off my breathing. In each case, for a minute or more, I couldn't breathe, gasping for air. Something dramatic must have happened at my birth.

So, I asked my mother for details. To my surprise, I learned that I barely survived. She was rushed to the hospital, hemorrhaging, the placenta pulling away from the uterus wall. The doctor told my father, "We'll try to save your wife, but there's little chance for the baby." They did an emergency Caesarian, pulled me out, and discovered, lo and behold, I was alive. That darkness that I have experienced during rebirthing was likely that period during which I was disconnected from my mother.

Fascinated by the process, I studied and became a rebirther (as practitioners of rebirthing are called), conducting individual and group breathing sessions. I learned that as adults, we often reflect our birth patterns. For example, people who love to start projects but aren't so good at finishing them often had a Caesarian birth. That fits me, too. Early getting born, early as an adult; I hate to be late. I guess I just don't want to miss the action. If I'm only just on time, or, God forbid, actually late, I can feel the tension building up in me.

Accordingly, here I am, fifteen minutes early for the ship's tour. To pass the time, I sit down and write a poem. On some future cruise, I would like to turn my attention to writing poetry. I have written many poems, but without any training or understanding of technique. The advice I like the best comes from poet Mary Oliver, who suggests you write poetry every day at the same time, so that the muse knows where to find you. Perhaps that explains why my sporadic attempts seem so strained. Good advice for any writer.

Most of the tour participants have gathered on time. We give the crew members our waivers, don special badges on lanyards around our necks, and stand spread eagled while a security guard scans us with a wand and pats down our pant legs. They will repeat this procedure twice more during our tour, once before entering the Chief Engineer's control room, from which they monitor and control everything on the ship, and again before going onto the bridge to meet the captain.

Our group of fourteen includes three women and eleven men. They tell us that we can take photos but not videos or recordings. I fail to see how restricting videos enhances security. Maybe they don't want anyone else horning in on the tour business. Several people exclaim with dismay that they hadn't brought their cameras, thinking that even photos wouldn't be allowed. Nor does anyone carry a cellphone on the ship.

For the next four hours we walk around and see various parts of the ship. I'll cover far more details—literally the nuts and bolts—in the next volume. We end up on the bridge, where we spend more than half an hour. Captain Flemming B. Nielsen (generally called by his first name, Captain Flemming) is from Denmark, where he joined the Naval Academy as a cadet in 1983. He received his Master's license in 1992. As with every captain I have met, he started his career with cargo ships and container ships. Years of experience are required before being entrusted to carry passengers. He joined Royal Caribbean in 2000 and rose through the ranks until promoted to master of *Mariner of the Seas* in 2010. He represents a new breed of younger captains who are not so stuffy and aloof as in previous traditions. He's not the burly figure you might imagine for a sea captain, but is instead thin, with stubby hair and a ready smile.

They serve us champagne and sweets. We each receive a certificate of completion. We also have a chance to sit in the captain's chair at the main console and take our photo with the captain standing beside us. Those who haven't brought cameras are dismayed. I give my camera to someone to take a photo of me and the captain. Then I take one for someone else, promising to email it to him. Finally, we receive a canvas tote bag with a few goodies inside, including a key chain and an apron.

Frankly, this strikes me as being a bit chintzy. On the *Emerald Princess*, the tour also cost $150 and also lasted almost four foot-wearying hours. On *Emerald*, however, a staff photographer took pictures of us during the tour and at the end with the captain. We were each given a complete set of photos. Had Royal Caribbean done that, it would have relieved the distress of those who had no cameras. They could at least have taken a photo of each person receiving his or her certificate from the captain.

On Princess we received more significant gifts, including a chef's jacket, which I wear frequently in the kitchen at home, and a fluffy bathrobe. The value of these items in the ship's retail stores added up to the $150 that we had paid for the tour. The value of *Mariner's* gifts comes to around $40.

Another cruise company, on its $150 tour, includes an excellent lunch with paired wine for each course. Compared to such bonanzas, Royal Caribbean looks anemic. The best part of this tour was the time we got to spend with the captain. He must do this hundreds of times, yet he never flagged in energy or interest.

As we leave, Paul Rutter, the cruise director, shows up to greet us. I ask to interview him, so he writes down my stateroom number and promises to call with a time. One of the women in our group, Berit Liland, tall with a mild Scandinavian accent, heard me say that

I was working on a book. She tells me that she authored a four hundred page book on cruising the coast of Norway, written especially for the Hurtigruten line. Her book has been translated into four languages.

Later I look up Hurtigruten on the Internet. They have fourteen ships, carrying anywhere from 351 to 1,000 passengers (most are around 700) and a few hundred cars, built for plying the fjords of Norway. The MS *Trollfjord*, for example, looks like a very interesting ship. One photo shows it going through a fjord with barely any room on either side. I guess they don't have rocks there to worry about if they get too close to the shore. I find Liland's book on Amazon.com. It's called *Hurtigruten—Detailed 11 Day Voyage Guide: Nature, Culture, History, Legends*. Wow. No wonder it's four hundred pages. Reviewers have given it five stars. Amazingly, it costs $112, with a used copy available for $172! The dimensions of the book are 10 inches by 8.7 inches, which is a large format, plus at 1.3 inches thick, it weighs 3.1 pounds. Just the little pocket book every traveler needs.

Here's what reviewer Luce Beguin-Favre says about Liland's book.

> *You can either sit back in your cabin or take the guide up on the deck and learn about what you are seeing as the boat goes along. The author has skillfully inserted all the GPS waypoints and also time-to-go in case you wake up in the middle of the night (which would still be daylight in the summer) and you are not sure where you are. A general map of the area that one is about to discover is displayed at the beginning of every chapter, one per day. At the end of the book, more detailed maps are also available. The city maps are especially helpful for those who want to discover some of the surroundings on foot during the ship's numerous stops. Not only is this guide a very valuable source of information on local culture, history and legends, but it also has gorgeous pictures and its smart finish makes it a perfect coffee table book as well.*

So there you have it. I don't aspire to such detail and magnificence. This isn't a guidebook as much as a personal travel journal, diary, and memoir. Besides, it's a lot cheaper.

Returning to the stateroom, I find Linda there waiting. I had predicted that I would be back at 3:30 and it's almost 5:00. I'm pooped, and my feet hurt. I should have worn my Z-Coils, it would have been easier on my feet. I have a few minutes to ask Linda about her afternoon, and then I shower and get ready for dinner. When we show up at our usual table in the dining room, everyone says they missed us last night. We feel known and appreciated. I try to control myself, but I dominate our dinner conversation with details from the tour I have just taken. It's going to take hours to make sense of my scribbled notes.

I order the chilled cherry bisque and sole meunière, while Linda has lentil and root vegetable soup and Yukon gold potato pie. For dessert I have bread pudding, a big deal for me. I cover this confection in some considerable detail on my personal website, www.robertferre.com/breadpudding.html. A serious aficionado of bread pudding, I review ones that I have eaten, give recipes, and pontificate at some length on the subject. Since I became gluten free, I still manage to indulge in one of my favorite desserts, although I must make it for myself.

The menu describes this dessert as "dense." Dense suggests it will be bready, whereas I prefer custardy. Neither am I a fan of chocolate bread pudding. I consider chocolate a cheap trick to get people to like an otherwise ordinary dessert. Traditionally, real bread pudding has fruit and raisins and a nice sauce, such as vanilla or whiskey or bourbon.

Despite my apprehension, when the dessert shows up, I'm pleasantly surprised. It gets good marks for presentation—a round portion of pudding with a mint leaf and several berries on top for decoration, resting atop a small pool of chocolate sauce. If you're going to have chocolate, this is the best way to do it. As it turns out, the texture isn't dense at all. It has a soft and consistent texture, achieved by preparing it in a slightly nontraditional way.

Most recipes call for putting chunks of stale bread in a casserole dish and then pouring the custard liquid over it to be absorbed. When eating it, the pieces of bread are apparent, sometimes even a little crispy at the top. In this case, they blended the custard mixture and the bread in a food processor, basically making a heavy smooth custard (the "dense" refers to the custard, not the bread). The bread serves more like a thickener than a principal ingredient, not unlike how some soups (including a *ribollita* that we had in Italy) are thickened.

True, I have collected more than two hundred bread pudding recipes, but that's no record. I found someone on the Internet who claims to have *eight* hundred. How many ways can you disguise bread, milk, and eggs, you might wonder? Quite a few.

Later, back in our stateroom, we follow our now well-established routine of the three Rs. The first two are relaxing and reading before turning off the light. The weather has turned quite warm, with the days in the 80s. We've found for the past several nights the outside temperature is too warm and humid for us to enjoy leaving our balcony door open. With it closed, we can control the temperature of the room to a nice chilly sleeping temperature, but we still hear the rush of the water outside. If we were traveling somewhere that had weather this hot every day, it might make economic sense to have an ocean-view stateroom, with a window that doesn't open.

Turning off the reading lights, we roll onto our right sides in preparation for my favorite time, the third R, which is "rubbing." I rub Linda's back. Don't think of this as some altruistic self-sacrificing or obligatory husbandly duty. Oh, no. I consider it one of my most intimate and enjoyable moments. Linda's back couldn't be more perfect. First, she has just the perfect amount of flesh. Many thin people are bony and hard and angular, just skin stretched over bones. The other extreme would be a pillowy layer in which my fingers would feel nothing substantial. Linda resembles neither of those. She's just right—soft and firm at the same time.

In the dark, the first touch, with my right hand, establishes contact. We both sigh, making a little sound on the exhale, "Uh-h-h-h-h." That moment confirms that we're in bed together. That first touch says, "I'm here, Sweetie, right next to you."

We consider this ritual to be our gyroscope. No matter what has happened during the day, from restful to stressful, from curious to boring, from dragging luggage through crowded train stations to luxuriating on our balcony, from espresso to gelato, from amiability to grumpiness, once hand touches back, everything is as it should be. Even if we're in a new place and a strange room and a different bed (which usually means a sleepless night for Linda), this moment is one of familiarity. It reminds me of a piece I once wrote of hearing the train whistle from my house in Saint Louis, which I always interpreted as saying, "All is we-e-e-e-e-e-ell, all is we-e-e-e-e-e-ell." (I sound like Julian of Norwich.) So, in this moment of touching before we go to sleep, we acknowledge this same assurance, all is well.

To use two hands, I move away from Linda far enough to be able to stretch out my arms. Even then, lying on my side, I'm still restricted in using the "down" arm, which has limited range of motion. If we are snuggled closer together, then one hand works better, elbow bent alongside my body.

Two hands create symmetry. Two hands comprise a serious back rub, with opposing motions or karate chops or small opposing circles, appropriate for sore muscles after a hard day of getting older. Such vigorous action will more likely wake us up than make us drowsy. It's also more likely to elicit audible expressions of satisfaction and appreciation.

Most often, I favor the one-handed back rub. Sometimes I place my hand, fingers outstretched, in the middle of her back and then agitate slowly back and forth, like the motion of a washing machine. Or I place my thumb on her spine, with my fingers wrapping half way around the side of her rib cage. I drag the fingers toward the spine, move the thumb down one vertebra, and repeat. Other moves include making little circles up and down the spinal cord or spreading my hand flat and then bending my fingers, as if gripping a ball. Another is the windshield wiper, with the heel of my hand held in place while my fingers swing back and forth. A larger version is to plant my elbow and swing my whole forearm. I could go on, but you get the idea.

When I'm successful, the back rub helps Linda fall off to sleep. Sometimes, the back rub happens in the middle of a sleepless night, in which we are both tossing and turning, suffering the penalty of too late a nap or too much chai tea. Determined not to stop until I hear certain breathing patterns that indicate sleep, I sometimes rub for twenty or thirty minutes, although the average is closer to ten.

Toward the end of the back rub, I reap my reward. My thumb finds that little sliver of space between pajama top and bottom, just above the elastic band. Skin. Wonderful, soft, warm skin. I slide my hand to where the waist meets the curve of the hip—the essence of the female form. When Linda is lying on her side, that curve is exaggerated. It's one of my favorite spots (*e pluribus unum*).

I slip a couple of fingers under Linda's pajama top and finally, my whole hand. I move upward, fingers around the curve of the rib cage, thumb tracing the spine. Then, I cover the entire back, lightly, slowly, with the palm of my hand. Heaven. Love pours from my fingers.

Thinking Linda is asleep, I stop, only to find that frequently she rolls over and says, "Now let me rub your back." She's good, very good, with all the right moves and nuances. More often however, I fall asleep while rubbing Linda, my eyes close, my hand drops to the bed. I'm off to sleep land.

Poetry

This is the poem I wrote while waiting for the ship tour to start.

the endless sea

blue
blue
blue
calm
calm
calm
unrelenting
inconceivable depth
breadth
volume
we ourselves
are mostly
salt water

next of kin
to the sea
family
invited to
Sunday dinner
learning how
to swim

I feel intimidated, trying to capture a feeling about something as enormous as the sea. Samuel Taylor Coleridge (born 1772) wrote: "Alone, all, all alone; Alone on a wide wide sea." Such a phrase doesn't strike me as difficult to conceive. The words are simple and powerful. Yet, for me, words seem puny and inadequate, even in repetition. My poem seems a bit forced, except for the ending, which surprises me.

When I'm in poetry mode, I just write down what that little voice in my head dictates. Often, it starts with a single line and goes in unexpected directions. Usually, my poems are observations—where I am, what I see, how I feel. I don't generally work the poems over like, say, Hayden Carruth would. Then again, they don't have the same impact, either. Poets often say that they can't *not* write poetry. Nor would any other medium properly convey their message. I don't understand that ... yet.

I wrote poems to Linda, early on. Once, I decided to write a poem a day. It was more of a commitment than I could keep. Had I succeeded, in a short time I would have filled many books with poetry. Poetry and poets are essential to a sensible culture. Dana Gioia, in his book *Can Poetry Matter,* wants to wrest poetry away from academia and its incestuous practice of awards and publications and reviews, and return it to the people.

Poets use to herald a socially relevant message that was appreciated by the public, prophets, artists, critics. When Robert Service wrote his poems about life in Alaska in the early twentieth century, he made so much money that he retired to a chateau in France. People read poetry then.

In the early 1980s, in Dallas, I used to go to hear a poet whose work I enjoyed, Naomi Shihab Nye. Strangely, decades later, when Ruth and I looked into the family tree, we found that she and Naomi were distantly related. When Ruth and I were living in Saint

Louis, Naomi came there to speak to children at the public library and sing some of her folk songs ("Take a little rutabaga, put it in the pot, I'm gonna give it all the seasoning my little heart's got …").

Naomi told the story of her grade school teacher who required each student to read one poem a week. If written by someone else, the student had to explain why he or she liked it, but if it was the student's own poem, an explanation was not required. At the end of each semester, the students bound their poems into little books, to keep. Naomi came back from Chicago and shared this poem (I may be paraphrasing a bit, being from memory):

> *I went to Chicago*
> *There was lots to see*
> *Everything was very big*
> *Compared to me*

Her teacher liked it so much that she had Naomi read it to other classes. Afterward, one young girl came up and said, "I've been to Chicago, too, and I know just what you mean." At that moment, Naomi said to herself, "I'm going to be a poet." Two others from her class became poets and one a bookbinder. Think of the affect that one teacher had on those young lives. Scores, maybe hundreds, of other students probably grew up with a love of poetry.

Naomi grew up in Saint Louis, but now lives in San Antonio. Recently, she gave a reading at the public library which Linda and I attended. Prolific as a poet and editor, she is one of a very small number of people making a living as a poet while not relying on a teaching position.

After Ruth's death, we held a memorial service, during which I read a poem that pertains to ships. How many times have we seen a ship sailing away, wishing we were aboard, watching it disappear over the horizon. Vice versa, how many times have we sat on the shore and watched a ship arrive. In "Parable of Immortality" Henry Van Dyke (1852–1933) describes a ship leaving the shore, getting smaller and smaller until out of sight. It ends like this:

> *And just at the moment when someone at my side*
> *says,*
> *"There she goes!"*
> *there are other eyes watching her coming,*

169

and other voices ready to take up the glad shout:
'Here she comes!'

I'm surprised how close to the surface my memories of Ruth remain, and how this poem continues to touch me emotionally. At http://www.goingeasy.com/writeside_publishing/parable.html you can read the entire poem.

Ruth and I never went on a cruise together, but in many ways, she's on this one.

Priests and Pirates

Day 12, Sunday, November 6, 2011

Ho hum, another ordinary day at sea. Really? No! Princess captain Ivan Jerman, born and raised in a small fishing town of the South Coast of England, always knew he'd spend his life at sea. In an article about shipboard life he says, "... one of the most appealing aspects of this job is its diversity, as there is no such thing as an average day at sea." That's true for us.

We go to breakfast in the dining room rather than the buffet, which gives me a chance to ask if they can make me a smoked salmon (rather than Canadian bacon) eggs Benedict. They do, after a bit of a wait, with a reasonably good result, although I like my eggs a bit more runny. Linda goes to the self-service tables, getting a very nice mixture of dried cereals. It's not until we're leaving that she sees a second self-serve table with eggs, French toast, pancakes, and the like. We could have easily gone upstairs for an even more expansive buffet, but here the atmosphere is more quiet and dignified, with linen tablecloths and attentive waiters.

Our table-mates are rather taciturn at first, but then we asked where they were from (Ohio and Toronto), and they opened up a bit. I went to college in Ohio (Denison University) and went to the big Expo in Montreal in 1965. The wife of the couple really loved Holland, Michigan, when they lived there. I told them that I was born in Benton Harbor, not far away. The waiter brought the husband something that he must have ordered off the menu, namely, three huge, fat, *white*, grilled sausages. He added them to his plate, which already had bacon and small sausages on it. Ugh! It grosses me out. My brother David, however, would be in hog heaven.

On this morning, our second Sunday at sea, we go to the ecumenical, non-denominational church service, held in the Lotus Lounge. Yes, a church service in a bar, with people sitting at tables and in plush banquettes rather than hard pews. The waiters don't serve drinks, however. The Catholic priest, who held a mass earlier, conducts the service. He says he spent thirty years as a military chaplain. Now, he works at the seafarer center in Galveston, Texas, just a few blocks from the cruise port. The center offers services to those who work on freighters and cruise ships: email and telephone and other conveniences. And religion.

Informal in his style, the priest speaks to the assemblage as people gather. He tells us that there were four hundred people at the mass, earlier. I know from my information sheet that this room, while spacious, seats only 304. That would suggest there was standing room only. Now, I estimate we number around two hundred or so. If a total of six hundred people have attended church, that's 20 percent of the passengers. In the United States, polls estimate that 40 percent of the population goes to church regularly (although not necessarily every Sunday), while 8 percent say they never go. Interestingly, the numbers are different in Canada, where 20 percent go to church regularly and 38 percent never go.

We start by singing two verses of "Amazing Grace." I never wrote down his name, so I'll just keep calling him "the priest." He points out that Catholics don't sing much. Neither does this audience, singing a cappella, especially compared to what Linda and I are used to back home at St. Mark's in San Antonio. A printed bulletin shows the order of service, but the priest constantly interrupts the flow, commenting after each response on the significance of what we just read. He points out that Christians should be happy and are supposed to share their faith. I agree that everyone should be happy. He states categorically that Jesus was not just one of many significant historical prophets. Jesus is, he assures us, the only Son of God and the sole source of salvation.

That's when he lost me. I reject any religion that claims exclusivity. To me, all religions are attempts, within their cultural setting and within the context of their prophet's teachings, to dumb down the enormity of That Which We Can't Understand, to make it accessible to us. In so far as religion takes us into the silence and within ourselves and teaches us ways to tap into that unlimited power of Being, the essence of life itself, to the extent that religion empowers us and joins us in community and harmony; to that extent, I think religion is universal and relevant.

But when religion claims exclusivity, especially along the line of "believe our story or die," or "we are the only source of salvation and only our group will go to heaven," or "say the right words or suffer in hell for eternity," it caters to our egos and leads to discord and violence, division and conflict. Exclusivity, as good as it may feel to be among the select, leads to manipulation. The whole idea that "we are right and you are wrong" leads to tragedy, inquisition, and witch hunts, not to salvation.

The priest goes on about the "O" in the phrase, "O God" or "O Lord." What does the word "O" mean? Claiming the word can't be found in the dictionary, he went on a quest to define it. He concluded, that it calls for the attention of the one being addressed, so "O, Lord," would mean, "Here I am Lord, addressing you." After the service, I point out to him that we do have a contemporary equivalent in the word "yo"—as in, "Yo, home boy," which similarly means, "Hey, I'm talking to *you*."

My clever observation goes right over his head, as he says, "Or y'all." Huh? That's not the same at all.

I can't keep focused on the sermon, so I think about the opposite of religion, atheism. I'm interrupted in my thoughts by the ending of the service. We leave disappointed. Five months from now, in April 2012, on *Rhapsody of the Seas,* we encountered the same priest, and thus avoided all of the church services on that trip.

In an hour, we return to this lounge to learn the rhumba. I can never keep those Latin rhythms straight. The class is mobbed. The teacher does a great job by having people watch first, while she and her husband demonstrate the step, followed by a chance for everyone to practice. Not surprisingly, the rhumba calls for a classic box step, which is to say, a cadence of slow-quick-quick, slow-quick-quick, continuously. Then we learned a turn and a variation on that turn.

We have attended dance lessons on other cruises. On *Queen Mary 2,* the teachers were a Russian couple who were dance competition winners. They both had long, sleek bodies that moved in ways our bodies can't even imagine. They danced with the type of drama and showmanship that we find obnoxious in a cruise setting and hope to avoid. We have no interest in dancing to draw attention to ourselves.

On other cruises, teachers have been young dancers from the ship's troupe, who were rather rote and impatient. This couple on *Mariner* are older, and they do the steps simply, the way *we* would want to do them. This routine would never be sufficient for the two flashy couples we've bumped into (literally) on the dance floors here, but it works for us and the other 150 people who have shown up for class.

To finish out the morning, we go to another lecture by Dr. Michael LeMay. We previously attended the one on migration and ship design. This one covers the real pirates of the Caribbean, subtitled, "Not your everyday Disney cruise." He declares a pirate to be anyone who seizes ships for bounty by threat or force of arms. The audience numbers five hundred people or so, an indication of his growing following. He comes out wearing an eye patch and bandana and begins by saying, "Ar-r-r-r-r-gh."

Pirates come in several flavors, we learn. Privateers held a letter of mark, sanctioned by one country to raid ships of an enemy or competing country. Most privateers were British, hitting on Spanish ships. Some, like Sir Walter Raleigh and Sir Walter Drake, accumulated so much loot that they returned to England, were knighted, and finished their lives as aristocrats.

Given the dangerous nature of the trade, such longevity proved to be an exception. Many pirates lost their lives within a few years.

In some cases, the entire crew of a ship captured by pirates joined the trade, often for mutual benefit, as pirates made more money than a mere sailor in his country's service.

Buccaneers operated on the Spanish Main, an area claimed to be the possession of Spain, from Nicaragua south. Pirate ships did indeed fly the skull-and-crossbones flag, called the "Jolly Roger," as a means to create fear and intimidate merchant ships. Oddly, "buccaneer" comes from a French word that means to smoke meat. Perhaps for long voyages that was one of their main provisions. Why weren't they called dried cod? Who knows.

One theory holds that piracy rises as a result of a failed state that has no adequate authority over its territory. That would clearly be seen in Somalia today.

Has a cruise ship ever been hijacked by pirates? Well, the *Achille Lauro*, an Italian ship sailing from Alexandria, Egypt, to Port Said in 1985 was boarded by Palestinian terrorists who held the passengers hostage, demanding the release of fifty Palestinian prisoners. The hijacking was a response to an Israeli attack a few days earlier that killed sixty Palestinians. One wheelchair-bound Jewish man, Leon Klinghoffer, was killed when Syria refused to let the hijackers dock the ship there. The terrorists surrendered to Egyptian authorities after being assured of a safe flight to Tunisia. However, American fighter planes forced the airliner to land at a NATO base in Italy, resulting in the capture of the terrorists.

On November 5, 2005, Seabourn *Spirit*, a small, luxurious cruise ship carrying 151 passengers, was attacked by two pirate speedboats seventy miles off the Somalian coast. The ship was hit by machine-gun fire and rocket-propelled grenades. One crew member, Michael Groves, was slightly injured by shrapnel while operating an LRAD (long range acoustic device), which successfully warded off the attackers. *Spirit* ran over one of the speedboats and the other fled. Michael Groves and fellow crew member Som Bahadur Gurung (an ex-Gurkha) received awards for their bravery at Buckingham Palace by Queen Elizabeth II. After a brief stop in Port Victoria for repairs, *Spirit* returned to its normal itinerary.

Although the movies portray pirate boats as large, three-masted square riggers, they were actually much smaller, in order to be fast and maneuverable. One of the exceptions was Edward Thatch, also called Blackbeard, who captured a frigate, a Man-O-War military ship (although some accounts called it a 250-ton French slaver named *La Concorde*), onto which he mounted twenty-two guns and then renamed the ship *Queen Ann's Revenge*. He also had a two-masted brigantine. When the King of England offered pardons to pirates who would stop their activity, Blackbeard accepted. He settled down in North Carolina and married a local girl. Nevertheless, Alexander Spotswood, governor of Virginia, sent a naval detachment to North Carolina that killed Blackbeard at Ocracoke Island on November 22, 1718. So much for amnesty.

The life of legendary pirate Bartholomew Robert, known as Black Bart, also ended in capture and execution. A substantial professional hazard. Nassau and Jamaica served as headquarters for pirates, ships, and crews. The Caribbean was relatively lawless, being distant from the various colonial governments.

The Golden Age of piracy took place roughly from 1660 to 1720, with a brief flare-up in the early nineteenth century. As the world's biggest naval power, with far-flung colonies, Spanish ships were the choicest targets. Piracy dwindled after the United States became a naval power and when other countries saw the economic necessity of taking steps to thwart pirating. The major sea powers signed a treaty in Paris agreeing that no country would permit or encourage privateers.

After the lecture, I see in a guidebook that there's a pirate museum in Nassau. Maybe we'll take a look when we make port.

Whew! What a morning, full of priests and pirates. We take it easy in the afternoon. Until the formal tea, that is. We received an invitation for Gold and Platinum members to come to a tea service. We're pretty snobbish about high tea, having taken it many times on *Queen Mary 2,* where the waiters wore white gloves and served tea from silver pots every afternoon. After several days of eating scones with clotted cream and jam, plus assorted little pastries and canapés, we started putting on weight. Just too many calories. So we cut back, attending only every second or third day.

We once attended a disappointing tea on a Princess ship, with tea bags and wimpy scones. So, we're interested to see how Royal Caribbean will do. We sit down with another couple at a table for four, discovering three trays of goodies already on the table—one of small sandwiches and the other two of small pastries and cakes. A waiter appears and fills one of our cups with something that looks very dark.

"Is that tea?" asks Linda.

"No, it's coffee."

Hello? This is supposed to be a high *tea,* not a high coffee!

"Coffee!" responds Linda. "Do you have tea?"

"Would you like tea?"

Hello? This is supposed to be a high *tea*! Would we like tea at our high tea?

Linda shows admirable restraint. "Isn't that what we're here for?"

Hello? This is ... oh, never mind.

So the waiter brings a wooden box with a selection of tea bags, and shortly thereafter, a pot of hot water. Linda and I look at each other.

"Where are the scones?" she asks.

"Perhaps they will be serving them," I reply optimistically.

Nope. No scones. Just the goodies on the table. Maybe they're being reserved for the Diamond members. Not that we miss them. Several of the pastries tempt me and I relent, eating more than I should. The interesting couple sharing the table with us tells us about their extensive cruising. The head cook, the same man I had met on the ship's tour, welcomes everyone and introduces his staff, to generous applause. After about twenty minutes, we leave. We would have done better, calorie-wise, to have stayed away.

In the midst of my sugar high, I really don't feel like going up to the fitness center, but I do. I have been increasing the weight settings, which has left me with sore shoulders. Muscles naturally get sore after a vigorous workout. They develop small tears and rips, the healing of which makes them stronger. That's what causes the soreness. It's a good thing. At the same time, I want to avoid injury.

As the wave of baby boomers gets older (technically, I'm a few years ahead of them), orthopedic doctors and surgeons have reaped a bonanza, treating torn tendons and other injuries incurred trying to stay young and active. I do my usual fifteen-minute warm up, followed by a circuit on the strength-training machines. Then I return to the stateroom, shower, and dress for dinner.

They no longer lead us to our table, as we know our way. We greet the people around us—they have been consistent neighbors. Mr. Horror is here. I give him my email address so he can send me a copy of his book, as previously promised. (It never happened.)

Neither of us is very hungry, thanks to the low tea and pastries. With difficulty, we decline the bread and rolls. They're so good! Too often we fill up on bread before the meal even arrives. We each have the chilled carrot and apple soup. For my main course, I pick another appetizer, Mediterranean spinach pie. Linda orders the baked sea bass. Mine is good, hers a little soft and mushy. I'm not sure how you prevent that when you prepare frozen fish. I share some tales of yesterday's ship tour with the couple at the next table.

We also skip dessert, which means we're done by 6:35. Again, we make it to the early show with enough time to spare to play a few hands of cards. Our Phase 10 competition is tied, three wins to three wins. While quite evenly matched, our styles are completely different. I lay down my cards immediately when I have the required combination. I hope this messes up Linda, who then won't be able to discard any of those cards, thereby cluttering up her hand and leaving fewer cards with which to make her phase.

She, on the other hand, likes to retain the cards in her hand, so that she can go down and out suddenly, in a single *coup de grace*, leaving me with a handful of cards. If I go down first, she often goes down in her next turn. We don't buy any drinks from the waiters who are roaming the room, but they sometimes ask who's winning.

It's rare in glitzy Las Vegas for a solo pianist to have his own show, but entertainer Ryan Ahern's "Piano Las Vegas" is very highly regarded. As a traveling ambassador for the United States he has visited eighty countries over the past three years. Ahern won the Liberace International Piano Contest twice: the Amateur Division at age sixteen and the Professional Division at twenty-one.

On the Internet, I found a review of his playing by Sandy Zimmerman entitled "The Piano Keys Were on Fire!" and so they are. He physically plays more notes than any pianist I have ever heard, using a very active left hand in all the songs, with many arpeggios and much riffing of the keys. Amidst so many notes, with the band being proportionally louder than the piano, I sometimes can't make out the melody. He introduces one song as his recent piano arrangement of the theme from the movie *E.T. The Extra-Terrestrial*, which is going to be published soon. It's so complex I can't believe anyone could learn it from sheet music.

Ahern performs some animated boogie-woogie and ragtime pieces. During one piece he takes us by surprise, snatching up a harmonica from the piano and playing it very well. The audience loves it. So do I. Next spring, on *Rhapsody of the Seas*, we heard him again give essentially the same show.

As it is only a little after 8:00 p.m. when the program ends, we decide to go into the casino to use our coupons for one free try, each, on the big-prize slot machine. We give the coupons to Ashlee, the cashier, who gives each of us a large token for the machine. Neither of us wins anything. I notice Mr. Horror at a card table that has a wheel which the dealer spins to determine the value of something or other. I just can't seem to get interested in gambling on this trip. I'll have to ask him later how well he did.

We end the night in the Schooner Bar, where I get a nonalcoholic drink and Linda orders a Corona. We play more Phase 10, just as we did in the Schooner Bar on *Voyager*, when Ian West was playing. We eat our free snacks and sip our drinks and play our cards, but Sergio can't hold our attention. We drain our glasses and go up to bed. Linda says something about snuggling ...

Atheism

If you ask atheists their definition of God, they usually describe a limited and flawed God that I would never believe in either. If God were as they describe, I, too, would be an atheist. We are all atheists regarding some gods. Do you believe in Woden or Thor or Zeus? No? Then you are an atheist for those gods. We all pick which god(s) we want to believe in and which ones we dismiss.

Atheists generally describe a rather pathetic and impotent god. I don't blame them for rejecting such a god. But then they go after the institutional church, a target so easy and ripe for criticism that it's not a fair contest. I've read several books by atheists to understand their arguments. Take Richard Dawkins, for example. For such a brilliant scientist, I find his arguments against God disappointing. His faith in science and evolution is every bit as irrational and blind as any unthinking Christian whom he criticizes.

Most commonly, atheists claim they can't believe in a God who would allow evil to take place, such as children molested or people victimized by illness or crime. Often this belief comes after a tragedy or death that has personally affected them. Certainly a benevolent god would never let that happen, they suggest.

What are the options? If a mugger is about to hit me over the head, a hand comes from heaven and stops him? Some invisible force keeps me from stepping in front of a bus or a child from dying or stops a crashing airplane and puts it gently on the ground? How would life work without having to take responsibility for our actions? Without a law of cause and effect, how could we depend on anything? Life would be total chaos. There would be no place for morality or principles.

I once read the comments of an Islamic imam who believed that nothing happens without God's express direction. Even the Devil can do nothing without first getting permission from God. So all evil and suffering in the world, he taught, comes directly from the conscious control of God. Whew. Was your child abducted and raped? God allowed that. Did your country explode a nuclear weapon and kill hundreds of thousands of innocent people? God approved that. Did a suicidal jihadist explode his bomb in a crowded marketplace? It had God's seal of approval. I think *that* is the God Dawkins rejects. Who wouldn't? Line me up with the atheists for that god. Doesn't anyone get it? God isn't responsible for the bad things in this world, *we* are. We're doing this to ourselves (and each other).

The Other Side of Paradise

Cruise life is quite the rosy picture: gallivanting around the world in luxury, eating well, working out in the fitness center, dancing beneath the stars. For 99 percent of passengers, cruising is a fairytale kind of experience. However, that's not the whole picture. Behind the glittering facade exists a shabbier side to paradise. Rarely is it openly revealed. Nor has it been my direct experience, other than a few glimpses.

I slaved for weeks writing a chapter that tried to outline the dangers and abuses of cruising. My purpose was to be impartial, reporting on the negative as well as the positive, avoiding sugarcoating my cruise experience.

In the end, I was never satisfied with my account. My cruise experience *has* been sugarcoated. It's been glorious, with no glimpse of what lies behind those doors marked "Crew Only." Despite my extensive research, I feel unqualified to take a stand against the cruise industry. Criticism can be found in vociferous amounts on the Internet, most of it being quite old and dated.

The chapter that I wrote fits better in the second volume, where I have put it, but even the lighthearted, casual reader should at least be aware of the flip side to the cruise industry.

I've learned that, like many industrial lobbies, cruise companies have a strong political influence in the U.S. Congress, where they work to negate any laws that would affect their profits or freedom of action. This is especially true regarding the reporting of crime. Operating in international waters devoid of laws, cruise ships are an entity unto themselves. Legal jurisdiction is vague and confusing. Thousands of crimes, especially those involving sexual abuse (of both adults and children) and missing persons, go unreported, poorly investigated, and unsolved. If you are a victim of a crime onboard a cruise ship, justice is an unlikely result.

One American law requires reporting of robbery only if the amount of the theft is over $10,000. Huh? How about a laptop or camera or billfold? Are such thefts too plentiful to bother reporting or looking into?

In 2010, the International Cruise Victims Association (ICVA) finally saw a law passed in Congress called the Cruise Vessel Security and Safety Act. It required reporting of crime on a public website and other forms of transparency. Unknown to the supporters of the bill, one of the sponsors, John Kerry, made a change to the law just before it was passed.

The result was that only cases *completed* by the FBI would need to be reported. No reporting is required for cases handled only by the cruise lines, nor cases not completed by the FBI, nor cases left open and unsolved. Solved or unsolved, no matter who handled them, we would like to know how many crimes were reported. As a result of Kerry's gutting of the bill, in the following year, while it is certain there were hundreds of crimes, only sixteen were reported. The law helps the cruise industry to cover up criminal activity rather than making it more transparent.

After the Costa *Concordia* accident, pro-cruise industry Congressman John Mica from Florida held a hearing intending to determine the lessons learned from the *Concordia* disaster. In his book, *Abandoned Ship: An Intimate Account of the Costa Concordia Shipwreck*, Benji Smith details the harrowing escape by him and his wife, musician Emily Lau. His point in the book, made repeatedly to the point of being exhausting, is that after the wreck, no institutions functioned in a helpful way, including the Italian police, the American and Chinese embassies in Rome, or Costa itself. Even the news media wanted only to report the harrowing escape and not the failure of our institutions to serve and protect us.

When John Mica announced his hearings, Benji Smith called him and volunteered to come down from Boston to testify as to his experience. He was turned down. Instead, virtually everyone who testified worked for the cruise companies themselves or for the Cruise Lines International Association (CLIA), their public relations mouthpiece. The message they put out to the public was that everything is fine, and that such events are rare flukes. The single couple who reported their mistreatment at the hands of Costa was overwhelmed by the love-fest of cruise company insiders. Such manipulation does not give us an accurate picture.

Because of certain international agreements, cruise companies pay no taxes in any of the countries in which they operate, including the United States, even though they benefit from excellent facilities and Coast Guard security.

In volume two I will go into more depth on this subject. You can find more information at www.internationalcruisevictims.org. You can also review websites hosted by two rather visible maritime attorneys who advocate for cruise-ship passengers and crew: www.lipcon.com and www.cruiselaw.com.

Here's my best advice. Don't think that the isolation of a cruise ship at sea protects you from criminals. Some are likely to be among the passengers and crew members. Keep an eye on your children and grandchildren, as predators are learning the low risk of being caught and convicted on cruise ships. Finally, here is a link to the article "What Every Cruise Passenger Needs to Know" on the website of maritime attorneys Lipcon, Margulies, Alsina, & Winkleman, P.A.: http://www.lipcon.com/law_articles.php#9

Commodores and Casinos

Day 13, Monday, November 7, 2011

I 'm trying to share with Linda a passage from a book I have just finished, but I can't get it out. Emotion has choked off the words. My eyes are wet. How could anyone get so emotional just reading about a ship? I try again. "It ... it's just ... very touching when ... he first sees ..." I give up. I can't talk.

The book is *Captain of the Queens: The Autobiography of Captain Harry Grattidge.* He went to sea in 1906 at age fourteen and retired in 1953 as commodore of the Cunard fleet, having captained all of its great ships. But one was greater than the rest. Here are Grattidge's own words.

> In the spring of 1934 I had my first glimpse of my destiny. I happened to be on the Carinthia, returning from New York. As always, we called in at Greenock to land our Scottish passengers. Steaming up the Clyde, we saw her on our port bow, destined to be cherished and discussed as few ships have ever been. Project 534. The Queen Mary.

Within minutes the rails were jammed tight with passengers, crowded to watch her. She had been on her trials and was now proceeding to anchorage; already she had broken all records, with a speed of more than 29 knots against the fastest twenty six and a half. As she loomed above us, the great red funnels with the black bands standing out clear in the hazy afternoon, I was conscious of many emotions. The Queen Mary was the mightiest milestone in the history of British shipping.

From her clean classical stem to her bulging cruiser stern, she was a miracle of naval architecture. Her designer, Sir Stephen Pigott, had solved the problem of constructing a hull that would stand the unimaginable strains incurred as the sea washed under her 1020 feet, lifting her first by the bow, then amidships, then astern. To drive her four screws, each of them twenty feet across and weighing thirty-five tons, the engineers had harnessed the power of fifty locomotives. Beside her, the Carinthia seemed like a ferryboat.

Harry Grattidge had a distinguished career as captain and commodore. Leading dignitaries on the ship often dined at the captain's table, so his book overflows with stories about famous people. From his first days on a sailing ship to his final career on *Queen Elizabeth*, his career spanned forty-seven years.

Grattidge tells of leaving England under cover at midnight on *Lancastria*, along with *Franconia*, the day England declared war (World War II) against Germany. *Franconia* suffered serious damage and limped back to Liverpool for repairs. (I'll detail my family's personal interactions with *Franconia* in volume two.) Filled with troops and fleeing civilians, *Lancastria* was bombed and sunk near Saint-Nazaire with five thousand aboard, half of whom perished. Grattidge stayed on board until the end, literally stepping from the bridge into the sea and then swimming through the oil-covered water. For that and other heroic duties during the war, he received numerous medals.

In 1953, Grattidge arrived for the last time at Southampton as captain of Queen Elizabeth and commodore of the fleet. His biography ends:

> As we reached Southampton, and Elizabeth glided close to the docks, I knew what was to be mine forever: the silver path of the moon across the sea at night, the dazzling trail of the sun by day, the crisp unforgettable tang of salt water and the shouting of the wind …

Such poetry. One of the things you face, and hopefully find, at sea, is yourself. This inner quality permeates my experience of cruising. It's not *about* me, yet it *involves* me, awakens me, challenges me to simplify, simplify, simplify, while deepening my relationships with those things that count. The sea undermines pride, engenders humility. There seems so much of the sea and so little of me. Its expanse resembles the endless, expanding universe, in comparison to which I seem insignificant. No, I *am* insignificant. The magnitude of the sea makes me look at my priorities. It encourages me to ask deep questions that get ignored while living life only at surface level. The sea is deep, deep, deep, sometimes miles deep. But what about me? What are my values? How deep am I?

Most awesomely, the sea remains completely impersonal. Although sea tales often personify the sea as having intent (usually bent on destroying a ship or crew), I believe it completely ignores us, busy occupying itself with tides and winds, swells and storms, and utter calm. If I fell overboard, I would disappear beneath the waves and be gone. The sea wouldn't even notice. The same for whole ships or even cities destroyed by tsunamis. It ain't personal. The sea just is. We pollute it, abuse it, over-fish it, and disrespect it at our own peril, not because it may be vindictive, but simply because it can just shrug us off and we'll be gone.

In the past, cruise companies ignored the sea. Although cruises rely on the sea, of course, they typically make little reference to it, other than lifeboat drills and certain required and necessary safety procedures. A cruise rarely places emphasis on the sea that surrounds it. As ships have gotten larger and more advanced, they have become self-contained resorts that happen, as if only by chance, to have the same view from every window, deck, and porthole—the sea. It's an anonymous and unchanging background to the many events and activities that occupy most of the passengers most of the time. Only when storms and the resulting movement refuse to stay placidly in the background do some passengers notice the medium upon which they are sailing.

The cruise lines would much rather have us in the casino or a show lounge, spending money and buying drinks, than sitting watching the waves. Perhaps that explains why the decks seem to be getting narrower. The ideal passenger shops or goes on excursions in the ports of call. Very few advertisements invite passengers to just sit quietly and enjoy the beautiful sea. Rather, they are about rock-climbing walls, spa treatments, ballrooms, scrumptious food, excellent service and more—none of which relate to the sea.

The sea isn't my only reason for cruising, but it's first on the list. When I glance out the windows while working out in the fitness center or head for the buffet or sit in the cafe waiting for the Internet to come up, I notice the mood of the sea, as if nodding recognition to an old friend. Perched on some high deck, I peruse the 360 degree vista of nothing but water, in all directions, curved horizon to curved horizon. Our solitude, being alone in all of this water, excites and inspires me, which is a good thing for a writer.

Another phenomenon about cruising also fascinates me, namely, that the multiplication of small numbers can produce a large number. We are crossing three thousand miles of ocean at twenty-two knots. That's like driving from Seattle to Atlanta in second gear. Day and night, night and day, the ship relentlessly progresses toward our destination. On land, twenty-two knots would equal around twenty-five miles per hour. For a long trip, that would seem painfully slow. Even for ships, it's not fast.

Every time I have dinner—we are moving forward. All night while I sleep—moving forward. In the morning, working on this book—moving forward. In one day, we cover six hundred miles, a respectable distance. Driving at highway speeds, six hundred miles is more than I like to drive in a day. Do that five days in a row, and you have gone three thousand miles, across the entire Atlantic Ocean. Miraculously, it adds up.

Can this really be day thirteen of seventeen? Just four days left (Day 17 is only for debarking). Sheesh! How long does a cruise need to be before I feel it hasn't just flown by? Now it's 6:00 a.m. Linda and I are heading out for our morning power walk. Walking down to Deck 4, we find the door closed. Looking out, the deck seems dry. A crew member says to go out on the other side. That door is open, leading us out to a very wet deck that has just been washed. This is the door that should have been closed and the other opened. Their timing is off.

Feeling spry, I try jogging a short distance. I quickly remember why I gave up jogging. My knees. After walking the requisite twenty minutes, we head inside to Cafe Promenade to get some water. As we sit at our table, two Texas ladies join us, as all the other tables are full. They begin describing their cruise, which couldn't be more different from ours. Had they written this book, it would be unrecognizable as the same cruise. They enjoy the very things we choose to avoid. I guess the activities director would discontinue all unpopular activities. So their very existence is proof of their viability.

One of the women is close to winning a free cruise in the slot machine tournament. She tells us that she knows the people who won the free cruise at the big bingo game, in which we came so close. Apparently the winning couple has a housekeeper with cancer. They plan to give the cruise they won to her and her daughter. I guess I don't feel too bad about losing.

For breakfast, we go to the dining room again, but this time we sit at a table for two. I have a big bowl of mixed dry cereal, including muesli, granola, walnuts, and raisins, plus a selection of fresh fruit. Walking back to our room, we stop momentarily on Deck 4, at which point Linda suggests that I wait here, while she goes up to the stateroom to take her vitamins. She points to the bar just past the elevators. I ensconce myself at a table there and proceed to type into my iPad. Time passes. No sign of Linda. I look at my watch. Perhaps she fell asleep. After an hour, I know something's not right. I pack up my things and go back to the room. There, I find Linda sitting out on the balcony.

"Have you been here the whole time?" I ask.

Somewhat exasperated she asks, "Where were you? I looked everywhere."

"What do you mean? I went right where you pointed and stayed there the whole time."

"The Champagne Bar. I looked there and then went up and down the whole promenade. I couldn't find you anywhere."

"Sweetie, the bar you pointed to is on Deck 4. It isn't the Champagne Bar, which is on Deck 5. It's one deck lower. You were looking in the wrong place."

"I was so worried. I couldn't find you."

"Well, here I am."

I lie down on the bed. Linda joins me, and we hug. I reassure her that everything is OK. We hug a little more. One thing leads to another, but Linda won't let me describe the details. Her charms never fail to thrill me. The ship rolls noticeably. As it crashes into large swells, it thunders and rattles, shaking the whole ship. I find that impressive, as this is a very large ship. It feels like we're hitting potholes on a highway.

The ship's movement becomes an issue when we go to dance class to learn the meringue. With people lined up on the dance floor, the ship rolls to starboard, causing the whole line to stumble in that direction. The group emits an audible "o-o-o-o-o-oh" as everyone catches their balance.

Think of the time when you were unaware of a stair. You stepped forward, but where you expected to find floor, you met only air. As you plunged into unexpected territory, even if only a few inches, the surprise and added depth threw you forward, down to the level of the step. If you were lucky, you didn't wrench your back.

It works the same way when the ship moves, going uphill or downhill unexpectedly. Downhill throws us forward, stepping into space as the floor disappears, or uphill, when the floor comes up to meet us, causing us to stumble. Try learning a dance under such conditions. Everyone got into the spirit of it, though, and we all had a great time. We added new dance steps to our growing repertoire of soon-to-be-forgotten moves. What were the ones we learned yesterday? Something about Linda stepping back and behind with her right foot. Hm-m-m-m-m. I should write notes.

The teacher has the couples line up in a big oval with wives to the husband's right. Then she tells the men to dance with the woman to their left, a clever way to give people the experience of dancing with someone other than their usual partner. I partner with a large woman who seems very hesitant. Linda reports that the man she danced with was much better than I am in leading her. True, I'm a bit indecisive and sometimes too cerebral, rather than just getting into the music. When I get adventurous and try something spontaneous, it usually just confuses us.

We wander a bit. I think about the ship being a closed container. If we open our balcony door simultaneously with the door to the hallway, the wind rushes through like a wind tunnel. If we close the hall door but keep the balcony door open, the wind squeezes under the door and whistles loudly. Walking down the hall, I can always tell who has their balcony doors open, by the whistling sounds.

Linda goes to the casino and spends all of her quarters but wins more. She returns with a few dollars' profit. I still have some coupons that require matched play. I must bet $5 of my own money, plus the coupon. If I win, I win $10. The coupons are good only for even bets, like red or black in roulette. Passing through the casino earlier, I wrote down the sequence of roulette's winning numbers, shown electronically. I then took a few minutes to try out some of my betting patterns. Out of six betting patterns, five of them would have won, with only one loser.

In my experience, my favorite system wins 94 percent of the time, but in the remaining six percent loses so big that it wipes out all the winnings. The system wins slowly but loses quickly. I have thought of reversing it, to lose slowly and win quickly. Probably, I would just win back what I lost. Supposedly no system can consistently beat the odds. Curious? I'll explain some of my betting patterns in detail in volume two.

The day disappears. Suddenly it's dinner time again. I start with the chilled cranberry and mango soup, followed by penne pasta with a seafood sauce. The serving size is unreasonably huge (a pet peeve of mine), plus I eat two of those delicious pesto rolls. Linda has spinach and ricotta lasagna, a more reasonable portion. Of course, no one is holding a gun to my head and forcing me to clean my plate, but it's so good! I should skip dessert, but instead, I try the Magic Mango Parfait. Our waiter asks how my book is coming. I tell him he will be famous, so he jokingly demands part of the royalties. At least *I* took it as a joke. As already mentioned, his name is Valentin. That's V-A-L ... well, you get it.

Earlier in the cruise, in the Mediterranean, we watched the sun set from our wonderful dinner table by the window. Tonight, the sun has already set before we get to our table, even though we arrive at the usual time. In the dark, the window turns reflective, like a mirror, except when we look directly down, where we see the white water that is churning past the ship.

The window reminds me of an M. C. Escher painting called *Three Worlds,* which shows three aspects of water. The upper part shows the reflective nature of water, the middle shows the surface of the water itself, with leaves floating on it, while in the lower part of the picture you look into the water and see fish. Our window is both transparent and reflective, but we don't see any fish.

Finishing dinner by 6:50, we rush down to the theater and get seats for the 7:00 p.m. show. Tonight's program combines a production show by the resident singers and band with some of the other musicians from the ship, including performers in the Latin band and the string trio. Portions of the dancing are eliminated due to the movement of the ship. Similarly, the piano had been planned to go up and down on the center stage lift, as needed. However, the lift doesn't work well under these conditions, so they just leave the piano on the stage the whole time. Apparently the program was pieced together on short notice. When finished, the musicians seem pleased with themselves.

We walk through the promenade to see if we want to stay up a while longer. One bar features a contest to name that country-and-western tune. With so many passengers from Texas, it's standing room only. Another bar has a game show, and a third, karaoke. Finally we find a venue with dance music, but it's quite crowded, so we go off to bed, old fogies that we are.

Nassau

Day 14, November 8, 2011

Because we're arriving in the Islands of the Bahamas around 9:00 a.m., the breakfast buffet opens at 6:30 this morning, a time which we prefer. We're standing at the door when it opens. No land in sight. After our oatmeal and fruit, we pack our day items into my fancy high-security travel bag for our jaunt into Nassau. We were here two years ago on the *Voyager* trip. We are focused, as usual, on finding an Internet cafe plus buying a T-shirt for our granddaughter.

A spit of land protects the harbor at Nassau from the sea. As we slip past the entry buoy, the water takes on an unbelievable turquoise color, so impossibly green-blue that it doesn't seem to be natural. Certainly someone slipped some dye into the water. In reality, the color comes from the way water absorbs and/or scatters light. Air, for example, is colorless, yet the sky seems blue due to the refraction of the shortest visible frequency, blue, from sunlight. (Outside of our atmosphere, space is black.) Water, however, is not colorless. When we see a bottle of water, it looks clear only because of its small size. The larger (and deeper) the sample, the bluer it becomes.

Besides scattering light, water also absorbs the red end of the scale. Which wave lengths an object absorbs and which ones it reflects determines its color. Water, a blue liquid, also transmits green, which, in shallow water becomes more visible, thereby imparting the greenish-blue turquoise color. This unbelievably brilliant turquoise color only occurs in shallow water, such as in lagoons or near the shore. It is even brighter if the bottom is white sand. Deep water doesn't transmit blue very well and usually looks dark, almost black. The surface of still water can reflect ambient colors, but they are just reflections and not its own color. When water has waves, it loses its reflective quality and shows its true color.

Two other cruise ships have arrived ahead of us. We pull up to the left of them, side by side, perhaps one hundred feet apart. As we slowly inch our way into our berth, we tower over *Carnival Sensation*. They must have just arrived, as we can see people still onboard, lining the railing to watch us come in, just as we are lined up at our rails to look at them. *Sensation* has very few balcony rooms, whereas the whole side of our ship bristles with five decks' worth of balconies.

Many of the newest cruise ships contain as many as 80 percent outside cabins and balcony staterooms, giving a certain sameness to the look of ships. Long gone is the elegance of the old ocean liners, with their long, low, black hulls and raked funnels.

The ship next to *Sensation* has the telltale circular Viking Crown Lounge of a Royal Caribbean ship. Sure enough, it's *Majesty of the Seas*, which does three-day excursions from Fort Lauderdale, Florida. Three days! That's not even enough time to unpack. We hear the loudspeaker announcement from the Carnival ship saying they will leave at 5:30 a.m. tomorrow morning. So they have an overnight in Nassau. Some 70,000 GRT, *Sensation* was built in 1993 and holds 2,640 passengers. *Mariner* was built in 2003 and holds 3,114 passengers. While only 20 percent larger in passenger capacity, at 138,000 GRT, *Mariner* is twice the size of *Sensation*. We have a lot more open space. *Majesty* (1992, 74,000 tons, 2,744 passengers) is similar in size and capacity to *Sensation*. Of the 8,300 total passengers on these ships, perhaps six thousand are likely to go into town or on tours. A few weeks ago, due to a hurricane, several ships were diverted to Nassau, so that there were a record seven cruise ships in port at one time. Wow. Where did twenty thousand people go in the rain?

Meanwhile, the gangways are going to be on our side of the ship, so we look down and watch them roll out. We also watch the huge ropes being attached to the giant bollards along the quay.

When we hear the announcement that we have docked, we file off the ship, which takes no more than five minutes thanks to double lines on two gangways. The crew scans each person's room card to record who has left the ship. As we leave, we notice a man with a black suitcase talking with the security guards. We were told that one of the performers had missed the ship in La Palma, in the Canary Islands. Perhaps this is he, arriving plenty early. Indeed, he turns out to be Jonathan Clark, our entertainer for this evening.

As we walk down the quay, we notice a beautiful, sleek white yacht at the dock directly across from the bow of our ship. On the upper rear deck sits a helicopter. Rows of windows for two enclosed decks reveal statues and artwork inside the rooms. The upper level appears to be a lounge area and the lower a dining area. The bottom deck has smaller windows, probably staterooms, while portholes in the front of the ship indicate the crew quarters. The name on the front of the yacht says *Samar*. I'll have to look that up. It sure is a beautiful craft. I'm impressed.

The port walkway funnels everyone through a building filled with tour counters, taxi hawkers, food booths, and concessionaires. A musical group plays marimba-like instruments made from plastic bottles.

During our last visit, we wended our way through the narrow aisles of the famous Straw Market, which was massively overcrowded, suffocatingly hot and humid. Some vendors were fast asleep. It's a bit depressing, as all of them seem to have the same identical trinkets, each desperately trying to eek out a living. They must hate these rich people who stream past in huge numbers without buying anything.

A sign two years ago announced that the Straw Market would be replaced with a new building. As we turn right to walk up the quay, we see that the booths formerly in the market are now lined up three deep for two blocks along the edge of the water. The new Straw Market building looks finished but not yet in operation. I presume the vendors along the street will move there soon.

Last visit, like a sea-crazed sailor finally getting ashore and into a bar, I had my first chai Frappuccino at Starbucks after a month of deprivation. We sat out on the upstairs balcony, looking across the water at *Voyager*. To our dismay, Starbuck's is no longer there, replaced by a bar named Sharkeys or some such. So we walk on.

Along Bay Street, the crowded main shopping district, dozens of jewelry stores sidle up against the many T-shirt and souvenir shops. Men in suits stand in front of the jewelry stores, not really hawking their wares, just keeping an eye on things. The sun pokes out from behind puffy clouds as the temperature climbs toward its predicted 82 degrees. People pack the sidewalks, while white-uniformed policemen stand in the middle of the intersections to direct traffic and pedestrians.

Taxi drivers offer transportation to Atlantis Resort on Paradise Island. When getting off the ship, we noticed that a ferry ride to Paradise Island costs $4. I presume the taxis must be about the same. Walking down the street we spy two ladies conspicuously wearing fluorescent green vests that read, "Tourist Information." Clever idea. We stop them and ask what's so special about Atlantis. They point out that the hotel complex includes an aquarium, shopping centers, and restaurants. One of the women whispers to Linda that the stores there are very expensive. We could do better here, downtown, she advises us. We decide to stay put.

We walk several blocks looking for the library, which I remember as a yellow clapboard building on a street up the hill from Bay Street. We don't find it. Heading back downhill, we walk past a place we recognize from our last visit. It was very hot then, and we were looking to eat lunch. The tourist places, like the Iguana Cafe, were crowded and noisy. We ended up finding a little haven on Charlotte Street South called Van Breugel's Bistro and Bar. Just half a block from the main street, its front porch perches above the sidewalk and is reached by climbing eight or nine stairs.

I have a method to escape the teeming masses when traveling: go upscale. In this case, the bistro costs more than the tourist dives. It's also more classy, with white linen on the tables and fans cooling the air on the porch. Prior to our first visit, we had read about conch soup being a specialty of the region. Indeed, a man was selling huge conch shells on the street for $5, blowing on them to make a loud horn-like sound. At Van Breugel's, they served curried conch soup for around $13. We remember sitting out on the porch, enjoying a wonderful meal.

Now, here we are again. Same stairs, same porch, with a woman placing a "Wet Paint" sign on the railing. We ask if they have Wi-Fi, to which she answers affirmatively, but they don't open until 11:00 a.m., which is almost an hour away. So we go further down Charlotte Street, where we spy the familiar green Starbucks logo. Upon entering, we find the order counter on the left and stairs leading to tables and chairs on an upper level. Across from the counter is a single tiny table. Sitting at the table is a familiar figure, Mr. Horror. We greet him and learn that the Wi-Fi costs $3 for the day, a modest payment for a great convenience.

Chai Frappuccinos in hand, we climb the stairs to a somewhat claustrophobic, low-ceilinged space strewn with simple wooden tables and chairs. Balcony-like, it opens to the lower level. Only two other people are here. Our receipt has the necessary access code, so we whip out our iPad and get online. Linda goes first while I read her Kindle. She has quite a bit to do, so the first hour passes quickly. By then, the place is full of people, mostly cruisers with iPads or laptops, causing the connection to slow considerably.

After exactly one hour, the connection terminates. I hadn't asked how long we received for $3, as Mr. Horror told us all day. It turns out to be one hour. The space is hot and stuffy. We decide to walk around a while. As we leave, Mr. Horror's table lies vacant. Apparently he also ran out of connection time.

We walk around for a while, then return to Van Breugel's Bistro and Bar. We look at the menu and see they still serve curried conch soup, still pricey. We ask if buying a drink will get us a Wi-Fi connection. Yes! So we sit at the old-fashioned wooden bar, the only customers. I'm warm from walking. Above the bar a small air conditioner spews deliciously cool air. The amiable bartender asks what we want. "Is there a beer made in the Bahamas?" Linda asks. "Yes, Kalik. It's very popular."

Minutes later we are ensconced with our two ice cold Kaliks, served in tall frosty glasses, with a side dish of peanuts and a very fast Internet connection. Again, we have avoided the crowds just by paying a dollar more for our beers. I look through my email for anything critical. It can all wait a few more days. Today is Tuesday. We'll be home Friday. Can that be possible? A throb reminds me of the problem with my broken tooth.

Early in our trip (almost two months ago), I broke an upper tooth and lost the filling, which left a deep hole with a jagged ridge. Since that day in France, I have been careful to keep it clean. In Cortona, Italy, I went to see a dentist. I'll describe the full dental story at the end of the chapter.

After spending most of an hour enjoying our beers and checking my email, I decide to get a bowl of the curried conch soup served at the bar. It comes with a whole basket of bread, which I enjoy dipping into the tasty curried broth. The chowder contains a generous amount of conch meat. The tab for the two beers and soup is $20, a perfectly decent value for the quiet ambiance, fast Internet connection, hour of relaxation, refreshing air conditioning, and excellent soup. I think coming here may become a part of all future visits.

Walking down Bay Street, we find a cute T-shirt for our granddaughter at a sale table. Our grandson is not yet a year old. We can't find anything that small. We reject the T-shirt that says, "Someone who loves me very much went to the Bahamas and bought me this T-shirt." What a cliché. Most of the shirts have horribly touristic themes, like the beer police or obnoxious images. Still, there are some tasteful ones if you search. The one we buy for our granddaughter has some colorful fish and the words, "Schooling around." It's something she can wear to her Montessori school.

It starts to rain. Completely forgetting about the pirate museum I wanted to visit, we head back to the ship. Although there was blue sky when we left the ship, the forecast was for showers, so I threw an umbrella into my bag. Good move. But, it's too wet outside to take some of the photos I would have liked.

When we get back to the ship, I have a phone message from the cruise director, agreeing to let me interview him. I call him back.

"Can you meet me at the Guest Relations Desk in five minutes?"

"Sure."

I wash my face, grab my notebook, and head down to Deck 5.

While I wait, I notice the same man with the black suitcase, Jonathan Clark, whom we had seen when leaving the ship this morning. He tells a woman at the purser's desk that his assigned room already has someone in it. They seem to be slow in finding a solution. He excuses himself to go to the theater to find the production manager. It's already 2:00 p.m. When the cruise director appears, I point out to him Clark's problem. He takes a few minutes to help address the issue.

We go to the cruise director's office to talk, where we are interrupted several times. First someone assured him that they found a room for Clark. The second visit is the entertainer himself. He describes how he had waited for three hours on the dock, because no one in security knew that he was coming. His name wasn't on the embarkation list. He asks if he can get some shirts pressed. The cruise director says that he will have it done and takes the shirts. All in a day's work.

The cruise director, Paul Rutter, follows a routine I have experienced on other cruise ships. On stage, he gives a little greeting at the beginning of every evening's entertainment, saying "Hi, folks," to which the audience replies, "Hi, Paul." Then he summarizes the various offerings of entertainment around the ship, tells a joke, and introduces the evening's performers. Tall and thin, he interacts comfortably with the audience. It comes as no surprise that he was once a teacher and basketball coach.

As we talk, it becomes clear that he has a much higher estimation of the evening entertainment than I do. He takes exception to my theory that some of the entertainers are over the hill. Rather, he points out, on a longer cruise like this, the demographics lean toward an older crowd, more familiar with the music done by older performers than young ones. He also reminds me that many of the performers were young, a point which I grant him.

Paul assures me that the entertainment on Royal Caribbean has won many awards and has high ratings from travel organizations. Both Linda and I find it worth attending, but we still consider it inferior to Princess, Holland America, and especially, Cunard. Typically, the production shows cost a lot to organize, and thus, are used on all Royal Caribbean ships, although in varying combinations. Royal Caribbean produces everything in-house, with a facility in Florida for training. They have their own costume designers and choreographers. Shows can cost up to a million dollars to produce, so it makes sense to use them for several years.

I remember on a Princess ship when they introduced a brand-new production show based on the Beatles' music. Neither Linda nor I liked it very much, but it was fated to be around for several years. That's a risk they take.

The first lounge show on a cruise ship took place in 1978 on Carnival's *Festivale*. Referencing cavernous clubs that flourished between the wars that offered dining, dancing, music, and shows, Carnival named its lounge the *Copacabana*. They were looking for some of the mystique of that famous New York City nightclub. Carnival holds auditions in London, Sydney, and Moscow.

Entertainers on Cunard's *Queen Mary 2* impressed us greatly. Most hailed from Eastern Europe or former Soviet states. I think I read somewhere that Cunard pays its entertainers union wages. Whatever the case, the quality of the shows on *QM2* is superb, including plays, classes, and poetry readings by cast members from the Royal Academy of Dramatic Arts (RADA).

I ask the size of the theaters on *Oasis* and *Allure of the Seas*, Royal Caribbean's five-thousand passenger mega-ships. Paul says that those theaters hold only around 1,800 people, so not everyone can be accommodated in two shows. As a result, people make reservations for the shows, many of them by email before boarding. That sounds complicated. They also have shows in smaller venues that are repeated over and over so that more people can get to see them. We'll find out first hand, someday.

I ask about marketing for retired people. We seem to be invisible. All the marketing targets young people and families. Why not try to attract older people? Frankly, he tells me, the public image of cruises is that they are full of old folks. Retired people already know that image, as it dates from several decades ago. Royal Caribbean deliberately distances itself from that perception. It now concentrates on attracting intergenerational families. In that regard, Royal Caribbean has one of the top programs for children and teens.

He has a point. There is a standing joke that the passengers on Holland America are so old that they should paint a red cross on the side of the ship. That's not the image Royal Caribbean wants to encourage.

Paul turns out to be a part-time cruise director, retired from doing it full time. He fills in. If a cruise director has a four-month contract and then two months off before returning to the same ship for the next contract, someone like Paul comes and fills in for those two months. That way, he can work when he wants to, get in a few cruises, and then take a long break. Not a bad gig if you can get it.

I thank Paul for his time and go back to the stateroom. Linda and I have coupons for discounted milkshakes at Johnny Rockets, the diner-like burger dive on Deck 12. The shakes cost extra, specifically, $4.50. We get two very rich chocolate shakes. Before pouring in the shake, they dribble chocolate syrup on the inside of the parfait glass. Then they fill it with the shake and pile generous amounts of whipped cream on top. We sit in the outdoor booths, although it's rather chilly. The shakes are so rich they just about put us into a coma.

Not surprisingly, I'm not very hungry at dinner. For the first time, the cold soup isn't fruit, it's sweet red pepper, with just the right amount of spiciness. I order the onion and potato tart appetizer for the main course, which is thankfully quite small. Linda, on the other hand, follows her Caesar salad with a huge piece of baked cod on a bed of rice. She asked for a baked potato, so on the side is a baked potato along with a separate plate of vegetables. I don't think two of us could finish all of that. I should skip the chocolate marquise, but I don't. I have gained only about two pounds the whole cruise.

We don't finish dinner in time for the early show, so we have time on our hands. We go to one of our favorite sitting places, which is opposite a bar where they play dance music. I feel like a slug. I know I should ask Linda to dance. Most of the songs have Latin beats, and we just learned the rhumba and the meringue, and we already know the cha cha. I keep listening for a slow number, but it's fast one after fast one. One of the energetic couples who dance with such flourish are there. They seem to do essentially the same routine, regardless of the type of music. I guess that makes it easier.

I may have dozed off. Finally, it's time to claim our seats in the theater and play cards. I feel really awful for not having danced. It's fitting that Linda wins at Phase 10 and has pulled into the lead for the cruise, four games to three.

Jonathan Clark, whom we encountered several times today, sings and imitates other singers. Some of his comedy comes off a little weak, but other parts receive roars of laughter. He tells us he learned a song from a cassette recording that had been played thousands of times. His number starts out normal, then he makes noises like a tape slipping and stretching, while he skitters across the stage. I guess it loses something in the telling, but it was very funny.

In some of the songs, he holds out the microphone as a signal for the audience to sing that phrase. Toward the end, he does an imitation of the audience, singing way off key, and again, quite hilarious. He mentions having waited for three hours on the dock. This was his second show, so after his standing ovation, his long day is over.

On the way to the room we stop at the Internet station. I look up information about *Samar*, the yacht we saw in port. Gorgeous photos show large, beautifully decorated suites and other features. We had seen the helicopter on the upper rear deck, a Bell 407. Somewhere on board is also a Mini Cooper car and a boat garage. For the latter, the back part of the lower deck hinges upward, like a car ferry. Inside, is a 33-foot Chris-Craft with a six hundred horsepower inboard engine. Somewhere else, there are four tenders and four jet skis.

Linda says she wouldn't want to cruise on such a small boat. She isn't even tempted by some of the luxury cruise lines, like Seabourn, that have only a few hundred people. Their attraction is the high level of comfort and service, as well as amazing cuisine, with each meal prepared individually. I would like to try such a cruise one day, but perhaps not a transatlantic trip. The price of $800 to $1,000 per person per day is occasionally reduced to about $250 at the last moment. With tips and extras, perhaps it would cost us $600 a day, or $25 an hour. That's not a bad rate for dinner or entertainment, but what about sleeping? I wouldn't be able to afford to sleep a wink.

I show Linda photos of *Samar*. It boggles the mind how people can afford these things. A Kuwaiti oilman owns *Samar*, so I guess we know the answer. We think of the amazing yachts we saw in France, in the ports at Antibes and Monaco. Do they even get used? Many have full-time crews and stocked larders, ready to cruise at a moment's notice.

Samar measures 254 feet long, is made of steel and aluminum (no fiberglass in this baby), and was designed by Laurent Giles. Built in England in 2006, it's powered by a diesel-electric propulsion system consisting of three Wärtsilä 1,530-kW diesel generators and two 2,414-hp drive motors with twin fixed-pitch, five-bladed propellers. With a nautical range of six thousand miles, *Samar* cruises at a disappointing twelve knots—half of what *Mariner* can do. Amenities include ten-foot ceilings in the salon, a full gymnasium, Jacuzzi pool and open deck bar, movie theater, and more. Available for charter, *Samar* holds twelve guests, with a crew of twenty-six (twenty to run the ship and six to cook and wait on passengers).

Ready to book a charter for yourself and eleven good friends? *Samar* may be booked during its current stay in the Caribbean for a weekly cost of $350,000. At such a bargain rate ($50,000 a day), there must be some hidden fees. That calculates to approximately $4,300 per day per person, or around $185 per hour. If you wanted to go to Europe, it would take two weeks to cross the Atlantic—costing $700,000. What the heck, you could probably get three weeks for a cool million dollars. Hope you like sea days.

In comparison, our cruise price of under $100 a day ($4 per hour) looks pretty darn good. I guess relative to one's net worth, there are people for whom $4,500 per-day, per-person looks equally attractive. The proof lies in the fact that *Samar* even exists. Perhaps it would be a good place to be on the crew, especially one of the six people caring for twelve guests. Not like poor Michael, our overworked steward.

Perhaps this is what I will dream about tonight: unconscionable luxury onboard a yacht, as a huge storm closes in with fifty foot waves …

Seeing the Dentist in Italy

As we sat in the waiting room, a rumpled, scruffily unshaven man with fly-away hair passed through frequently. Over his eyes he wore binocular-like magnifying glasses. He turned out to be the dentist. He looked into my mouth and said in a kindly way in excellent English, "Let's see what kind of work they do in America."

"I'm not typical," I pointed out. "I see a biological dentist, and have had all of my mercury removed."

"Ah, do you believe in that?" he asked, skeptically.

"Very much so."

I'm convinced that many people who think they are suffering from illnesses are actually experiencing mercury poisoning. It's a toxic substance that dentists must handle according to special rules and regulations to avoid getting it into the environment. Yet we are to believe, once inside our mouths, it's harmless. I don't buy it.

When Ruth went to Bad Mergentheim, Germany, to Hufeland Klinik for treatment of her breast cancer, we were exposed to a holistic philosophy that holds that cancer is the final defensive response by the body to many lifestyle factors. Just dealing with the cancer tumor without addressing the underlying causes would be inadequate and shortsighted.

One of the prerequisites to be treated there is the removal of all mercury in your mouth. It cost $10,000 for Ruth to have twelve teeth changed. With so many teeth being adjusted, she lost her bite, which was very painful in getting reestablished. Later, I had all my mercury removed too, involving eighteen teeth. Some were filled, others crowned. I guess you could say I put my money where my mouth was.

The Italian dentist said he needed an x-ray for a better look. I thought he was just trying to run up the bill, but I couldn't refuse. A nurse did the procedure very professionally, using digital technology. She pressed a button and the view of the tooth appeared on a flat-screen monitor mounted on the wall. Returning, the dentist looked at the x-ray briefly and nodded his head. He declared that the tooth was fractured and only a root canal would save it. I hesitated to tell him that I also didn't believe root canals were good for one's health, as they often can develop low-grade bacterial infections that can harm one's overall health. One website I visited (holistic dentistry) said nine of ten extracted teeth with root canals show signs of infection.

Accordingly, I once had four teeth pulled solely to remove the root canals. I saw the two front teeth after they were pulled. They came out easily, each with a small black ball on the tip of the root, which indicated an infection. A total of six neighboring teeth around the four pulled teeth were ground down to hold the bridges. So I adulterated ten teeth in my zeal to end root canals. I didn't tell that to the Italian dentist. After such an effort (and expense), I didn't intend to let him do a root canal. I asked if he could do something temporary just to fill the hole and protect the tooth.

"No," he said, "Anything I do might trap germs behind the temporary filling and cause it to become abscessed, which would be problematic while you traveled. How long before you get home?"

"Three weeks," I replied, "the last two on a cruise ship."

"Well, just keep it clean and pray that you don't have a problem in the middle of the ocean."

He charged me only 30 euros, which is about $45, including the x-ray. A month later, in San Antonio, I found a new holistic dentist who built up and crowned the tooth without pulling it or doing a root canal.

Technical Stuff

Day 15, November 9, 2011

The usual: morning power walk (in corridors, due to weather), coffee and pastries at the cafe, fruit at the buffet, and writing for a while. While Linda reads her Kindle, I switch to Day-14's sudoku. Previously, the puzzles were hard to the point of being impossible. Now it's just the opposite—so easy they aren't even fun. Again, they print the puzzle without the dark lines that delineate the larger nine squares. They really need my help.

Today's dance lesson focuses on the cha cha, a simple dance that many people know, including us. However, we want to see if they teach any new variations. Sure enough, she shows one we don't know. And she demonstrates a short routine, doing four basic steps, then the side-by-side figure, followed by four more basic steps, then the chase, and finally four basic steps followed by the step-through. Linda is rather strict in following the given pattern, whereas I tend to be more undisciplined. She prefers to count exactly four repetitions of each step, in proper order. Maybe it helps her predict what I am doing.

Stupidly, I wear my thin water shoes because I have no clean white socks left and the water shoes don't require socks. But they are very flat, with no support and thin rubber soles. They don't slide at all. We are supposed to turn by swiveling on the balls of our feet. Not me. I have to turn my ankles and sort of walk around the turns. By the end of the lesson, my feet are sore. At one point, someone steps on my heel, but I survive.

After a light lunch, we return to our stateroom to nap. As the sun shines brightly and the temperature hovers above 70 degrees, I decide to nap out on our sunny balcony. Usually I sweat when sunbathing, but with the breeze caused by the ship's motion, I feel the warmth without getting overheated. After twenty minutes, I show a little color. Some people on the ship roast themselves daily, achieving an impressive (if unhealthy) tan that will advertise to their friends at home that they have been on vacation.

I initially planned to sit outside for twenty minutes every day to get both my vitamin D and a modest tan. However, this is only my second time, and the cruise is almost finished. Did I receive adequate value in paying extra for a balcony? I think so, because of the night air and ocean sounds. If ocean view rooms had windows that open, perhaps that would suffice. However, they don't.

The captain speaks at 3:30 p.m., an event we expect will be crowded because it isn't being held in the theater. Apparently, rehearsals make that impossible. We go to the Lotus Lounge thirty minutes early and barely get a seat. Paul, the cruise director, introduces the captain by thanking him for the good weather and rather easy crossing.

The captain presents slides showing different parts of the ship, basically a mini version of my ship's tour, but at no cost. He passes out a sheet giving some of the ship's statistics. Very interesting are the photos of the electrical control room, which wasn't on the tour. It's a large, spotless room with rows of meters and readouts. The telemetrics can be read from the bridge, the control room, and the electrical room. Think of the task and the miles of wiring necessary to monitor every stateroom, every smoke detector, every electrical device—in three different places! It boggles the mind how they could keep it all straight.

The call letters for the ship are C6FV9, spoken as Charlie Six Foxtrot Victor Nine. The captain tells us the maximum capacity of the ship, including passengers and staff, is 5,020. On this cruise the total is closer to 4,300. We overhear a man behind us saying he had signed up only a few weeks before sailing and paid under five hundred dollars. I presume he has an inside cabin.

The captain describes the size and capacity of the engines and generators, the azipods and fixipod. The engines produce 103,000 horsepower, far more than would ever be needed. The ship burns heavy fuel oil, which is almost as solid as asphalt and must first be heated to be used. The engines produce electricity, which powers the propulsion, making this a diesel-electric system.

He talks about the five 1,500 horsepower air conditioning compressors. If the air conditioning quit, he points out, within hours the enclosed spaces would not only be warm, but also very humid, and they wouldn't smell very good. I think back to the Golden Era of ocean liners before the invention of air conditioning. Whew. No wonder people stayed outdoors on the deck.

The captain tells of the time the lookout on the bridge saw a distant red flare in the night sky, around 3:00 a.m. He called the captain, who directed him to head in the direction of the flares. Two additional flares, spaced apart, allowed them to get within distance of a very weak radio signal. It was from a one hundred-foot yacht with three people aboard that had been struck by lightning, destroying all of its communication and guidance systems. They had only flare guns and a small, battery-powered radio. That was enough. When the cruise ship was half a mile away, they sent out a small boat and retrieved the three yacht passengers, taking them aboard and depositing them in Civitavecchia. He didn't say what happened to the yacht that they left behind.

A Seabourn ship did the same thing in the Pacific Ocean when the spotter saw a drifting lifeboat. They altered their course and discovered three fishermen who had been adrift for three weeks, surviving on fish and rainwater. Not only did they luck out with being found, and in such a luxurious manner, the four hundred people on the cruise took up a collection and gave them several thousand dollars to buy a new fishing boat. What a reversal of fortune.

As the captain describes docking procedures, he shows a photo of the side of the ship taken from the bridge wing, similar to one I had taken. Docking procedures include referring to a satellite global positioning system that shows the dock and an outline of the ship. The speed and direction of the whole ship, the bow, and the stern are also displayed. So if they were turning the ship to come parallel to the dock, the overall speed might be one knot, but the bow would be going 0.3 knots to the starboard while the stern would be doing 0.5 knots to port. It seems incredible that satellites, orbiting the earth six or more thousands of miles away, can be accurate to within a foot or two.

In his photo, I see something from the bridge wing I hadn't noticed before—an area on an upper deck that cantilevers quite a ways outward. What is that? Little did I know that I would find the answer in just a few hours.

Someone asks how many years it takes to recover the cost of the ship. The ship cost $850 million in 2003, but the captain didn't know the time to recover the cost. I would suspect that it would take decades. If the ship were financed like a house, amortized over twenty years at 5 percent interest, the monthly payment would be $5.6 million. That calls for many paying passengers. If the average were twelve thousand passengers a month, it would take almost $500 per passenger just to pay for the ship.

He next tells us about the water we consume. We can't take enough on board nor store the effluent. Fresh water must be produced and used water must be treated and expelled. The ship produces water in three ways—Two Alfa Laval Desalt Flash and Energy Recovery Evaporators and one Pall Rochem seawater desalination unit (reverse osmosis) "Rosmarin" 80404-50/300-A-SW. Got that? A quiz will follow. With all methods combined, the water production totals 540,000 gallons a day, to meet the per capita usage of fifty-eight gallons. (I find no signs or other requests that we conserve on water usage.)

And don't forget the ice cube production—sixty-five thousand pounds per day. Wait a minute, wait a minute. How can we use sixty-five thousand pounds—32.5 tons—of ice a day! That equals more than fifteen pounds per person. That can't be a correct number, unless they use that much ice in the buffet lines under the food.

I can't even imagine what the sailors of old would think about all of this—ships of this size, moving at this speed, producing their own water and electricity. Such technology reflects the endless possibilities of human ingenuity.

One more universal maritime topic remains: navigation. For centuries, charts were kept and distances mapped. The magnetic lodestone gave way to the compass. In the eighteenth century, John Harrison, a clock maker, invented a chronometer that allowed the calculation of longitude (latitude was already available). Thus, sailors could identify their precise location. That was only a few hundred years ago—a mere blip in time considering the previous millennia. We have fulfilled the prediction of the Roman writer Seneca who wrote in the first century:

> *There will come an age in the far-off years*
> *When Ocean shall unloose the bonds of things,*
> *When the whole broad earth shall be revealed ...*

I heard that quotation on a *NOVA* program on public TV about searching for longitude. Very informative, the program is easy to find online and a great resource for more details on navigation.

Now, of course, we have exceptional technology for navigation. There is no concern about being lost or going astray. Here is a description of the electronics on a cruise ship of the same class as this one:

> *Interswitched BridgeMaster E S-band and X-band radars, docking radar, Voyage Management System (VMS) with DNV type-approved ECDIS, docking system, weather station, doppler speed logs, fiber optic gyrocompass, adaptive autopilot, weather routing software, a complete GMDSS-compliant communications system, Voyage Data Recorder (VDR) and Automatic Identification System (AIS).*

Think of the explorers, traveling for months on unknown oceans in search of new routes and lands, sleeping in hammocks, no fresh food to eat, facing scurvy, pirates, and mutiny. One Norwegian explorer released hungry ravens to see if they found land or returned to the ship. If a sea bird had a fish in its mouth, it was likely heading for its nest on land. Follow it. If there are no sea birds, if the hungry ravens return, and you are running out of food—then what? Eat the ravens, I guess. Many explorers died of starvation.

We, certainly, are not worried about running out of food. For dinner we are going to Portofino, one of the specialty restaurants for which there is a $20 per person cover charge. We make the earliest possible reservations, right at 6:00. Getting there a few minutes early, we are the second party to be seated, following a party of four. They lead us into the second dining room to a table—you guessed it, with our good cruise karma—right next to the window, and not just any window. This part of Deck 11 cantilevers outward—the very windows I noticed in the photograph from the bridge wing during the captain's talk. Now we know what they are.

Again, we occupy the best table in the whole restaurant. Soon the sun sets and the sky darkens, but the moon is almost full, creating a wide zigzag path on the water. The setting couldn't be more romantic.

Eschewing wine, we order a bottle of San Pellegrino sparkling water. Our waiter comes from the Dominican Republic. We ask to make a few changes to the dishes on the menu to better suit our vegetarian and specialized diets. Linda starts with a small bowl of soup, minestrone alla Genovese; then half a portion of two different pastas, *taglierini al pesto* and *pappardelle al funghi.* I start with half a portion of the appetizer for two, *Frittelle di patate e zucchini;* then *Spiedino di mare.*

Linda asked for half-portions of two different main courses simply because she was unable to choose between them. Likewise, I asked for half of an appetizer usually served for two. The waiter didn't object. Linda's soup arrives in a typical bowl, about half full. She finds it tasty and hot. She must eat slowly, as she tends to get full quickly. To my dismay, I receive the full appetizer for two—not half, as I had requested. While excellent, it comes in an obscenely mountainous quantity. Worse, it tastes so good, I can't stop until I've consumed most of it.

We find the service friendly and polished but rather sparse. When removing the dishes, the waiter doesn't ask, "Are you finished?" as most waiters would. Since we both have left food uneaten, such an inquiry might have negative implications. Rather, the waiter more appropriately asks, "Shall I clear the dishes?"

As a tour director in France, I once took a group to the town of Vézelay. Nearby, in Saint-Pere, famous chef Marc Meneau runs a Michelin three-star rated restaurant, L'Espérance. Everyone should experience cuisine of that level at least once. Lunch (five courses) lasts until 3:30 or 4:00 p.m., and costs around $150. I gave the group free time to see Vézelay or go to the restaurant. On this occasion, three women from the group decided to splurge.

Knowing there would be numerous courses, one of the women didn't eat all of the first course, just as Linda and I haven't, even though portions at the restaurant were small. The waiter cleared the table, and then after a modest wait he brought another dish to the woman who had not finished her first course. "This isn't on the menu. What's this?" she asked. The waiter replied: "Madame, Monsieur Meneau regrets that you did not like his first dish, so he has made something else for you." After that, they all ate everything. The portion sizes were small enough to allow full consumption.

Fine restaurants don't inundate their clients with mountains of food. That's a trick cheap restaurants use, to give customers the impression they're receiving extra value (but often at the expense of quality). Huge servings give customers three choices: eat it all, which would leave you over-full and unwell; leave some of it, thus wasting food or insulting the chef; or ask for a doggie bag, a concept that doesn't exist in France, or in fine restaurants, or on a ship. Dining at a high level should present an enjoyable artistic venture into pleasure, not an opportunity to eat enough for the next week, like a camel gorging with water at an oasis.

Either our waiter, not a native English speaker, misunderstood, or the kitchen ignored our requests. Our surprise and dismay continues with Linda's main course. She hoped for a taste of two different items on the menu. Instead, she receives two complete dinners, one entire plate piled high and one large bowl full to overflowing. If we were in San Antonio, we would take most of this home and eat it over several days. For one person, especially one of Linda's size, these portions make no sense. In addition, the courses are not artistically presented. Instead of, "Oh, what a delightful sampling of the pasta," our response is, "Oh, my God, there must be a mistake." Later, I realized I should have sent it all back and insisted on what we had ordered.

One of the pastas is quite good, the other a little strange. Linda hates to leave so much food. I keep urging her not to over eat, as we still have dessert coming. But she keeps chipping away at it. Meanwhile, my dish, a mixed seafood brochette, arrives at the table dramatically hanging from a stainless steel hook on a stand, more than a foot high. The waiter removes the items from the skewer and puts them on the plate. He then separates the lobster from the shell. I count half a small lobster tail, two shrimp, two large scallops, and a generous portion of salmon, accompanied by asparagus and Ligurian-style potatoes with tomato sauce.

My food, dramatic presentation notwithstanding, is ordinary. A cup contains a thin pinkish sauce with little taste. When I dip a scallop in the sauce, it doesn't enhance the taste it in any way, possibly detracting from it. Why bother?

Other tables have ordered the seafood brochette, as several hanging skewers go past us. In a subtle way, the presentation works against the success of the dish. They seem to almost acknowledge, "Since the dish itself is only average, we will try to distract and impress you with the presentation." Of course, at that Michelin-starred restaurant in France, everything was right—artistic presentation, quality, taste, and portion size. Then again, it cost $150, not the $20 each we have paid tonight.

After dinner, the waiter brings a dessert appetizer: a small, two-tiered tray with cookies and pastries on it, perhaps ten items total. He then takes our coffee order, decaf for me, tea for Linda. The coffee, delivered in a tall cup, arrives in advance of the dessert. Once, in Cortona, Italy, when I specifically asked for coffee *with* my dessert, the waiter said, "After." I repeated, "With." The waiter countered with "After." I assured him I meant "With." "OK," he said. Then brought it after. Tonight I find it a bit disorienting to get coffee *before* dessert, but I save it and drink it, a bit cooler now, with the dessert, as I prefer.

I order the *tiramisu alla Portofino* and Linda orders a special Ligurian dessert called *torta di ricotta*, described as being made of ricotta cheese and pine nuts. We had a similar dessert in Levanto during our stay there. It indeed has pine nuts on the top, but it is quite fruity with no trace of ricotta. Linda eats most of it and shares a piece with me as well.

It just doesn't seem to be my night. The ambiance here is exceptional, but the food doesn't measure up. Although the presentation is fantastic—quite the work of art, the *tiramisu* disappoints. It's served in a chocolate bowl and has two waffle-like chocolates on top, one dark and one white, two spiraling pieces of white chocolate in the shape of antelope horns, a dot of whipped cream, and a shot glass filled with a dark liquid.

I discard the white chocolate—too sweet and, in my mind, not really chocolate. Although it starts out being processed like chocolate, the dark cacao bean solids are removed, leaving just the fatty content. Supposedly, the dark part has beneficial antioxidants. The remaining white cocoa butter sometimes has to be deodorized to make it palatable. In other cases, white chocolate is simply manufactured from hydrogenated oils and other horrible things. Legally, the standard for white chocolate specifies that it must be at least 20 percent cocoa butter, 14 percent milk solids, and 3.5 percent milk fat. Should we be comforted that it shouldn't contain more than 55 percent sugar or other sweeteners? To me, the phrase "*white chocolate*" is an oxymoron.

I love the liquor-soaked cake in *tiramisu*. The standard recipe goes something like this. Start by soaking *Savoiardi* biscuits (ladyfingers to us English-speaking folks) in very strong espresso, preferably with alcohol added, such as a dark rum. Personally, I would use Kahlúa, a Mexican coffee liquor. Next the soaked sponge cake fingers are layered with a cream filling made from mixing mascarpone cheese, egg yolks, beaten egg whites, sugar, and sometimes a little wine. A little pure cocoa powder may be sprinkled on top to counter the sweetness of the filling.

Many variations exist, of course, but I am truly puzzled by the liqueur served separately tonight. Am I to soak my own cake? That would be difficult, as this one contains only minute traces of cake (my favorite part) that usually forms the foundation. The chocolate bowl contains a mascarpone mixture and virtually nothing else. It's like being served only the frosting of a cake. I eat only about one-third of the filling and a few chunks of the bowl, and I drink the liquor.

By contrast, at a picturesque restaurant in an old theater back in Cortona, I had the second best *tiramisu* ever. The chef coated a bowl or half-round mold with chocolate and then put in some filling. Next, he filled the bowl with a solid row of soaked ladyfingers. To serve, he inverted the bowl, producing a chocolate-covered half-dome on the plate, decorated with a little cream. It had just the right amount of filling (in the small top part of the dome) and cake (in the larger base). The imaginative presentation differed from the normal rectangular shape.

If that was the second best I have ever had, what was the best? Once, in a small, forgettable town in western New York State (Wellsville), the only respectable sit-down restaurant was L'italia, an Italian one. The meal was ordinary, but the dessert! The owner's grandmother made *tiramisu*. That was the best I have ever had. Linda, who normally doesn't like this dessert because of its sweetness, also loved that one. Grandma just plunked the dessert down on a plate. No pretense or even artistry. Here, Portofino isn't in the same league as grandma, despite the excellent presentation.

The bottle of water turned out to be $7. With gratuity (15% they included, 5% more I added to reach my customary 20%), the meal cost $55. I have no complaint about the price, but the meal could have been much better.

One of *Mariner's* other specialty restaurants, Chops Grille, features steaks. Considering all the Texans on board, they must be packed. Portofino was only half full. If anyone asked our advice, we would say to save the money. The food didn't surpass the quality in the dining room. The waiter was very welcoming and thanked us profusely for coming. However, he was absent for longer stretches than I would have liked, including when it was time to get the bill— so long that I had to get up from the table to look for him.

We loved the moon and the window and the setting and even the service, when it happened. Overall, we had a good time. For better or worse, I guess you could still call it memorable.

Alas, my criticism continues into this evening's entertainment, featuring Merrill Osmond, one of the Osmond brothers. He clearly bases his act in the past. Big screens show photos of the young Osmond brothers, fifty years ago, on the Andy Williams Show where they played for eight years. They have sold over one hundred million records, which is no slouch. Now they are taking over for Andy

Williams in his theater in Branson, Missouri. Which brings me to another story.

I once picked up a friend at the airport in Springfield, Missouri, where a retired couple wearing matching cowboy hats ran the information booth. I told them that we were driving to Arkansas and would pass through Branson at lunchtime. From all of the restaurants, we needed to pick one. Where should we go to eat? Without hesitation they said, "Go to Andy Williams's restaurant, called Moon River, after his greatest hit." So we did.

It was quite large, located across a sprawling parking lot from his theater. On the walls hung dozens of gold and platinum records from Andy's long career. We enjoyed the food. Wandering through the restaurant greeting people was Andy Williams himself. Past eighty, he had just returned from a concert tour in England.

Then living in Saint Louis, I also remember the building boom in Branson. The word was to go to Branson where work was plentiful and profitable. In 2005, for example, they had $121 million in building permits. Besides theaters and restaurants, the town has a large capacity of hotel rooms for conventions and a thriving time-share industry that brings in about 20 percent of the visitors. The former main attraction for Branson, Silver Dollar City, continues to expand to keep from being overshadowed by the neighboring big-name sponsored venues.

I don't know how many theaters they have in Nashville, but Branson, with fifty of them, calls itself the Entertainment Capital of the Midwest. Tickets for these theaters cost from $30 to $50, generally, depending on the entertainer. I think my old college mate, John Davidson, used to sing there. It would be fun to go there for a week and sample some of this great variety of entertainment. Now I notice there are several theaters for sale, no doubt due to the recession.

Osmond is now white-haired and has fifty grandchildren and sixty-seven great-grandchildren. Can that be true? That's what he says. Sadly, Andy died of pancreatic cancer in September of 2012, less than a year after this cruise.

Osmond's performance is almost like karaoke, with a prerecorded background track that includes other singers, his brothers, violins, and so on. In one song, I think he might be mouthing the words and not really singing. The *Mariner* band adds drums and a few trumpet riffs, but it really has little to do. One set that I like is a medley of tunes by other groups of brothers, from Everly to Doobie to Righteous to Gatlin and several more. They are just short segments of songs, often suddenly changing rhythm or key. He clearly has this program down very well—he recently toured with it in Europe. The audience really likes it. Maybe I'm just too full of pasta.

After the show I'm ready to make up for my danceless sluggishness yesterday. We go up to Deck 14 to Ellington's, where a dance band is playing, and our dance teacher is in attendance. It isn't yet crowded, which is good, because the dance floor is minuscule. We dance several songs, trying out our new rhumba moves. The meringue, however, we just can't remember. We have some new moves for the cha cha as well, but I forget the correct sequence, which frustrates Linda.

About 11:00 p.m., well past our bedtime, we leave, thwarted in dancing by a very fast jive number. We feel that they should offer recorded music during the daytime down in the disco or in one of the lounges, where people could practice dancing.

As we wind down, we acknowledge how great the trip has been. We would offer some suggestions, but we have few gripes. This has been a magnificent cruise on a beautiful ship. We have been fortunate to have our special dinner table, our balcony stateroom, time together, and the project of writing this book.

Last Day At Sea

Day 16, November 10, 2011

In *Freighter Odyssey—Around the World in 130 Days,* Dale Stenseth describes traveling for months on a freighter. Every day is the same routine. He describes the size of the swells, the nature of the weather, and his visits to the bridge. The meals are copious but basic and everyone has the same thing. Stops in ports rarely lasted more than a couple of days. After reading half the book, the days become totally predictable. I had no reason to continue. So I didn't.

Similarly, our routine is quite predictable, with dance class and naps and meals. Every day we walk, and I go to the fitness center. In the evenings we sit at our window table, see the entertainment and generally go right to bed. That sameness is OK with us. Routine is comforting, familiar. Through a certain amount of repetition, my purpose has been to establish the rhythm of our days.

In *Cruise Ship S.O.S.: The Life-Saving Adventures of a Doctor at Sea,* Ben MacFarlane portrays his first cruise as a ship's doctor. At the end, he reveals that the book doesn't really describe his first cruise, but an amalgam of experiences that took place over an unspecified number of years, written as if it were a single cruise to make it more readable. I felt tricked. It wasn't real. It didn't happen that way.

This morning, I'm contemplating the nature of this book. It's centered on me and Linda, of course, but it's also more than that. As pampered passengers, how do we get past the fact that cruising is mostly about "us?" Oh sure, there are lectures to enrich, high tech to be learned, cooking to be demonstrated, napkins to be folded, boards to be shuffled, pools to be swum, tea to be sipped, tangos to be danced, pings to be ponged, but the focus and main attraction remains hedonism, as touted in most advertisements. Descriptive adjectives come to mind—sybaritic, extravagant, lavish, indulgent, voluptuous, epicurean, libertine, decadent, seductive, sensual. You get the idea. Can this be justified, morally?

I believe I'm more than a consumer or a vacationer being manipulated by clever marketers. We *all* are. I find our best moments are when Linda and I unite in a deep bond of joining. My particular spirituality is demonstrated in how I am as a person within social contexts, not by hiding in some safe cave contemplating my navel. (Instead, I'm onboard a beautiful ship contemplating my naval. Get it? Navel. Naval.)

Linda cruises for relaxation and attending to her spiritual life, which includes meditation, writing poetry, and painting. I feel content, having arrived at a very good place in my life, yet there remains a tinge of guilt. One writer questioned whether he could long withstand such uninterrupted pampering. I feel that this unrelenting attention to my needs brings time and freedom, so I can do my writing and contemplate and prepare for important and relevant work.

However, the time must come when I actually do that work. If writing is to be my life, my next career, then perhaps cruise ships are a suitable workplace. Otherwise, cruising must necessarily be an exception, not the rule. I have repeatedly taken a stand that says we aren't on vacation, we aren't trying to escape from our lives, we aren't animals who have escaped our cages and are running wild. I would like this to *be* our life, but how can I justify that with a clear social conscience? This is my dilemma.

Once I come aboard, life's requirements and endless errands and chores fall away. No one expects or demands anything of me. I can mold my days as I wish. I feel wealthy, but I have no intention of imitating the stereotyped role of the idle (and bored) rich. Will I ever get tired of this? I hope to get a chance to find out.

I think of a woman featured in a Cunard magazine who signed up for her eighteenth world tour. My first reaction is, "My gosh, how much is enough?" My second is, "My gosh, that would cost over a million dollars." My third reaction is, "Geez, I'm trying to figure out how to afford *one* world cruise." Finally, I say, "Good for you, girl. I envy you. Go for it."

Walking a labyrinth, for example, is not only about getting to the center (which is assured, as there is only one path), but rather, about the quality of the journey itself. In the same way, a cruise can serve as a metaphor for our journey on the sea of life. Confinement offers many benefits. We find not just a microcosm of the outer world, but also a magnifier of the inner one. Shipboard can make us fat and lazy, or it can be an alchemical crucible to burn off the dross and realign our priorities. Here we can make choices. What are our values? What are our moral obligations? No matter how far and wide we travel, as Emerson said, "Your giant goes with you." We can't escape ourselves.

The seemingly infinite depth and presence of the ocean can awaken transforming spiritual sensitivities. In such instance, I can use other adjectives, such as meditative, contemplative, pensive, reflective, introspective, meaningful, transcending.

No cruise company advertises, "Come on a cruise and face your existential angst," yet travel can encourage that. Travel can change you, although maybe not on a brief, sterile, harmless, non-threatening cruise of only a few days. It must be longer, to give you time to settle into yourself. So far, as of 2013, our longest cruise has been twenty days. I don't feel that was long enough.

I am reminded of *bastides*, which were medieval planned towns built to populate and protect the political border of Aquitaine in medieval southwest France. In the midst of a completely isolated and rural setting, they would build a walled city and entice people to live there. Fortified gates guarded the entrances. In the center was a marketplace and a church. One side of the wall was completely rural, the other, totally urban. Not only did the wall keep out the invaders, it kept the energy in. Containment was beneficial and efficient. In a similar way, this ship encloses a body of energy. On one side of the railing is the limitless, mysterious sea. On the other, the hull-bound community, the citizens of *Mariner*. The difference couldn't be more stark.

Compared to ocean liners, cruise ships have slowed the pace, dropped out of the race. Their purpose is no longer utilitarian. With awesome spaciousness, with vastly improved technologies for navigation and communication, without the soot and the stifling lack of air conditioning and crowded conditions, we are privileged to move upon the sea more nonchalantly than anyone in history. Still, when the eye scans that unending curved horizon, land a distant memory, flying fish skimming the parted waves, the only trace of our passing a roiled white wake—time stands still, as it always has.

Not everyone shares my positive experience of cruising. One example is an article written for *Vogue* a number of years ago by David Foster Wallace, entitled "A Supposedly Fun Thing That I Will Never Do Again." He derisively describes cruise ships as being so white and clean that they look boiled. Wallace's writing is quirky and articulate. He spends a considerable amount of space talking about his own idiosyncrasies, which puts the cruise within his personal context—just as I have done.

Somewhat humorously, he suffers from agoraphobia (fear of places where escape is impossible, fear of being in public, fear of leaving a safe place) and spends much of the cruise in his cabin watching old movies on TV. Watching the passengers disembark in Cozumel (he stays on the ship, observing from the 12th deck), he is dismayed by the incongruity of overfed Americans dickering with malnourished children over trinkets. He can't escape painting everyone with the same brush, writing:

> *I am an American tourist, and am thus* ex officio *large, fleshy, red, loud, coarse, condescending, self-absorbed, spoiled, appearance-conscious, ashamed, despairing, and greedy: the world's only known species of bovine carnivore.*

He had never previously traveled outside of the U.S. and it shows in his writing. Life is filled with drudgery and hopelessness, he writes darkly. Any distraction proffered by a luxury cruise is necessarily only temporary, infantile, and artificial. Beneath all the glitter and festivity, he finds only sadness and despair, identifying with those who throw themselves overboard.

Being unfamiliar with Wallace, I look up some details and confirm my suspicions. A highly talented writer, he suffered from persistent depression and ended his own life at age forty-eight. His writing is astute, but in the end, his experience of cruising depended on what he brought to the party. He found it depressing because he was depressed. The same applies to all of us. Travel isn't anonymous and impersonal. Just the opposite. It is affected by our personalities, our self-regard, and our world view.

That's what I have tried to describe in this book—how my past affects my present. The context of our voyage is indeed set by the ship, the itinerary, and the ports. Yet, they constitute only the blank canvas. The final work of art, a life well lived, depends on each of us.

We are all actors and here the stage is a restless blue ocean. We all share the bonds of passengerhood. Whether soot black or boiled white, the basics remain: anticipation and preparation, embarkation, shipboard, distraction and pampering, port visits, sea days, debarkation, memories. These are our raw materials. What we make from them remains up to us.

Being cruisers puts us into a privileged fraternity. John Maxtone-Graham reports, "It seems apparent to me that among the most pleasurably remembered episodes of lives crammed with riches are those involving ocean passage." He has noticed, in talking with others, they are generally interested in travel tales, but when he starts talking about cruises, people's attention especially perks up and the energy builds. We find exactly the same phenomenon. Cruises are fascinating.

The editing of this book continued in December of 2012 during our next transatlantic cruise aboard *Crown Princess* from Venice to Galveston. To my utter surprise, the lecturer for that voyage was John Maxtone-Graham, whose work I admire and frequently quote (as above). A note from me to him resulted in a casual lunch among the four of us: John, his wife, Mary, Linda, and me. At eighty-three, he still spends half his time at sea, lecturing. He finds shipboard perfect for working on his writing, just as I do. His next book will be about the legendary American ship, the *S.S. United States*. He's got fifteen years on me, plus hundreds of cruises, totaling more than ten years at sea. Would that I could be in his position.

Julia Cameron in *The Right to Write* suggests that everyone is a writer, naturally. We should write because "writing claims our world. It makes it directly and specifically our own." That's true for my cruise writing. It turns an anonymous event into something personal, as if injecting me into a photograph.

You would think our final day at sea would be less than casual, rushing around to do all the things yet undone, but such is not the case. We awake in the Gulf of Mexico. White caps and wind escort us home.

We go to dance class, which features the cowboy one-step. In other words, walking. Nothing could be easier. Country-and-western dancing has a direction, counterclockwise, around the perimeter of the room. The various turns and other figures are all done while moving forward at a uniform pace. Back in San Antonio, our Thursday morning line-dance group went to Midnight Cowboy, a place for country dancing. It has a huge dance floor shaped like a race track. The center area contains tables and chairs for sitting and even a bar. Quite the efficient use of space, sitting in the center as the dancers circle around the perimeter of the room is rather like being in the infield during the Indianapolis 500.

Today's dance class takes place in the disco, which is small. Because of the teacher's popularity, the classes have been growing. We end up dancing between the tables and chairs, not on the dance floor. Like every other lesson we take, this one will likely soon fade from our memory.

Linda wants to check in online for our boarding passes from Houston back to San Antonio before we go to lunch. We wait until 12:45 p.m., but she's still too early, as Houston, is still an hour earlier. Apparently you must check in less than twenty-four hours ahead in the time zone of the departure city. So, we go upstairs to the Windjammer Cafe for lunch. They are featuring ethnic foods of several nationalities. For me the choice is between sushi or Tex Mex. The latter wins out.

We wait in line. The serving bowls aren't very big. Behind the serving table they continuously mix and prepare more food. Scrambling to keep up, they have clearly underestimated the demand for

Tex Mex from all of these Texans. The refried beans are a bit thin and the guacamole is wimpy. I put tortilla chips on my plate and cover them with beans and cheese and avocado. Not bad. Then I discover the rice pudding, so I have some of that. It isn't fluid, like kheer in an Indian restaurant. I can hardly pry it out of the serving bowl.

At 2:30 we go watch the finals for the karaoke contest. Each of the finalists came in first or second in the four previous karaoke semifinal sessions. I have never really gotten into karaoke, myself, but it seems quite popular. The theater is three-fourths full.

The first performer sings a classic older song, big band style. The second man sings "Sixteen Candles." The audience generally claps and acts supportive. The fourth contestant, to my surprise, is Mr. Horror. His level of involvement in activities is admirable, compared to which we seem like wall flowers. His chosen song, "Just a Gigolo," lends itself to interaction with the audience. During one musical interlude, he leaves the stage and dances a few measures with someone he picks out at random.

Mr. Horror follows the popular American version of the song, such as was sung by Louis Armstrong, Bing Crosby, and others. The original composition dates back to the social collapse in Austria after World War I, describing the turmoil and the memory by a dancer of once parading in a military uniform. The Tin Pan Alley rewrite changes the scene to a Paris cafe, although it retains the sad story. "Just a Gigolo" appeared in a 1932 Betty Boop cartoon and in a 1979 movie, in which Marlene Dietrich made her final film appearance. It is a classy choice of song and done very well.

The other performers, seven men and one woman, do their numbers. The sole woman sings the theme from *Phantom of the Opera*, which is a hard song and doesn't come off very well. Before her was a Texan who sang "Grand Tour," a country-and-western song. Even before he began, people from all over the theater were calling out his name and clapping. Once he started and the steel guitar riff came in, the Texas audience went wild.

Judging criteria included singing talent, stage presence, and audience response. Considering those criteria, Mr. Horror should clearly win. Sadly, Bill, the guy from Texas, wins, due to the exaggerated audience response. It turns out that he is part of a large group who were primed in advance to stir up a ruckus. The judges fall for it. Mr. Horror is denied his rightful recognition.

Back in the stateroom, I prepare our tips for certain crew members. I slip twenty-dollar bills into four envelopes. Royal Caribbean automatically bills us each approximately $12 per day for gratuities, which are divided between the room stewards and the dining room staff. That totals more than $400. Nothing more is required, unless you want to reward someone for special service. We feel that Michael de la Cruz, our room steward, did a great job. Even better was Jeffry, at the desk in the dining room, who assigned us to our romantic table for two by the window.

On other cruises, we sat in many different places, each time with different people, served by different waiters. But this time, we got to know Valentin and Jude, our waiters, as we saw them every evening. So Michael, Jeffry, Valentin, and Jude each receive a little envelope from us, modest as it is. As frugal as we may be, tipping is a necessity for the underpaid staff and crew.

For our last supper, we each have the cold gazpacho, which is disappointing. Linda makes a great raw gazpacho in our Vita Mix. This one was cooked and then chilled, with too much tomato. It tastes like tomato sauce for spaghetti. Linda has the oven-baked sea bream, which is copious, and I have the ricotta and spinach quiche, which has a very flaky crust. For our last desserts, I have the caramel flan and Linda orders the chocolate sensation. You can't go wrong with chocolate. Seeing Mr. Horror arrive, we tell him that the fix was in, which thwarted him from rightly wining the karaoke contest. He agreed, confessing that he had been very nervous. How often do you get to perform in front of eight hundred people? This was his first time. He reflected, "I should have told them I'm from Austin."

As we sit looking out the dining room window, the full moon rises. An orange tanker passes in the other direction, probably on its way to an oil platform. It has a very small superstructure, so it probably doesn't have extensive crew quarters, like a seagoing vessel. It just transports the oil from platform to refinery.

We go back to the stateroom to pack. The heavy things go into the smaller, brown suitcase. Linda has her scarves and other purchases to pack. The dirty clothes go into my suitcase. We get everything under wraps without much trouble, but I worry that our suitcases may weigh more than fifty pounds, the limit for Southwest Airlines. When the time comes, we go down for the last evening's entertainment. We have attended every program during the cruise. What a change it will be when we get home.

The entertainer tonight is Jeff Bradley, another performer who missed the ship earlier and joined us in Nassau. He tells some very clever cerebral jokes that go over the heads of much of the audience. He performs some dexterous moves with eleven blocks of wood, designed after an act that W. C. Fields did with cigar boxes. He tells a joke, and when there is weak response, he looks at his watch and says, "No hurry, I have plenty of time," meaning people were taking a while to get it.

At the end of the show, the cruise director shows excerpts of an official cruise CD made from a compilation of videos taken during cruise events. I think they cost $35. There are scenes from the sail away party, the belly flop contest, the Halloween parade, dancing under the stars, and a game show called Quest. We aren't shown in the video, because we didn't go to any of those events. It's surprising what a different experience a cruise is, depending on what events one attends (or not). One lady said she spent quite a bit of time in the hot tub and took all the origami classes. To each her own.

Cruise director Paul relates some humorous questions asked by passengers. When told that the walking track required five laps to go a mile, one man asked, "Which direction?" Another asked, "Does the crew live onboard?" One teenager asked if the ship had ever sunk before. Hm-m-m-m.

Then, to finish the evening, crew and officers from all the departments file down the aisles and onto the stage, perhaps forty or fifty of them, all dressed in their work clothes, chef's hats, and so on. The room stewards hold a hanger from which hangs a monkey made from towels. We clap our approval of the hard-working crew and for all they have done to make this a wonderful cruise.

Debarkation

Day 17. November 11, 2011

Approaching Galveston in the early morning hours, we wind our way through hundreds of oil platforms. At one point, in just the sliver of water that I can see from bed, I count ten brightly lit platforms. The ship is running an obstacle course.

When we go to early breakfast, Linda makes some observations about the cruise. She is struck by the fact that all of these thousands of lives, from fifty different countries, converged at the same time in Civitavecchia and got on the same cruise ship. For these seventeen days, we've been a seagoing family. In a few hours, everyone will disperse to all parts of the globe, never again to meet in this exact configuration. For these seventeen days, and only these seventeen days, our lives have been intertwined with each other.

I add that I was impressed by how well the ship keeps track of me. There are diagrams of the deck plan placed throughout the ship. Every time I look at one, there is an arrow pointing to a red dot and a caption, "You are here." Amazingly, they are always right! I *am* there. How do they always know where I am?

Disembarking from the ship can be done the easy way or the hard way. We always choose to do it the hard way. Most people pack their bags and put them in the hallway the evening before, marked with tags indicating certain colors and numbers. During the night, the crew loads the luggage onto pallets according to the tags. The moment the ship arrives, they begin unloading the pallets with fork-lifts, taking them to a large space inside the terminal, where the bags are grouped by color and lined up in numerical order. We have heard humorous stories of people who forgot to leave out clothes for the morning, sending their bags away only to find they have nothing to wear for debarkation but pajamas.

Passengers report to an assigned lounge or other area to wait until they hear their group departure announced. Then they file out, scan their room cards one last time, go into the terminal, go through passport control, find their bags, pass through customs inspection and then leave the terminal to locate their ground transportation. Those with suites or diamond status disembark first or at their leisure.

Choosing the hard way, we handle our own luggage, a process called "express" disembarking. This presumably circumvents the wait for luggage in the terminal while also reducing the work required by the shore personnel. This do-it-yourself method usually means we get off quickly and avoid the lines through passport control and customs. Usually, but not this time.

The ship docks about 5:30 a.m., anticipating the express people to disembark around 6:45. They ask people not to congregate on Deck 4 until after the announcement that the ship has been approved for debarkation by authorities.

We choose to break the rule. At 6:40 a.m. we roll our luggage down the hall and onto an elevator, exiting on Deck 4. Having the same idea, a group of others have arrived ahead of us. We position ourselves close to the debarkation doorway. But nothing happens yet. We see 6:45 come and go, as do 7:00, 7:15, and 7:30. The crowd soon fills the available space near the exit door with a conglomeration of passengers, rolling suitcases of all description, backpacks, carry-on bags, shopping bags, and even art work wrapped and roped for protection. All the passengers could never debark like this. The chaos would be overwhelming.

To their credit, two crew members protecting the rope across the exit door instruct those passengers getting off the nearby elevator that they must to go around to the end of the line. Occasionally, the impatient crowd gets its hopes up as the walkie-talkie crackles and the crew member listens. Still no signal to depart. Around us we notice that the expressers are a younger crowd than the general demographic. That makes sense.

Many are already on their smart phones. Little do they know, their calls may still be going through the ship's equipment. When they see their next bill, they may have a big surprise. It's wise to wait until you are off the ship before making calls.

This is the most hectic day for cruise ships. Within only a few hours, hundreds of tons of luggage must be removed, staterooms cleaned and readied, garbage and recycling discharged, supplies brought onboard and placed in the appropriate storage areas, and then tons of luggage brought on, distributed to the staterooms for a whole new batch of passengers. This process has been fine-tuned through years of experience. How different from the several days it once took ocean liners to do the same thing.

Size creates certain efficiencies. Once the forklifts are charged up you may as well load up a thousand suitcases as a hundred. You need only one set of officers, for example, whether you have two hundred passengers or two thousand. Cooking fifty gallons of soup does not require ten times the effort to cook five gallons. Size matters. Size creates profit. Despite their sleek profiles and rakish stacks, ocean liners were puny in comparison to cruise ships. Their amenities were a fraction of what we have available on this ship. Yet, some of the later liners, built just before and after World War II, had an elegance of interior design not seen before or since.

I have some statistics that help put *Mariner of the Seas* into perspective. The deck area of the ship totals around thirty-five acres—more than a million-and-one-half square feet. Of this, one-third is carpeted and one-tenth comprises the outside decks. The 4,100 works of art onboard are valued at over $12 million.

On Day 11's tour, I pondered the amount of wiring it took to connect the three control centers to everything on the ship. I find the answer: almost two thousand *miles* of electric cable. The water pipes make up an additional eighty-six miles. For those of you who appreciate such things, the air conditioning moves some twenty million cubic feet of air per hour. *Mariner* has more than an acre of windows. Of the 15,500 seats for passengers, one-third are in the cabins and some two thousand are on the outer decks (accommodating two-thirds of the passengers at one time—far more than is ever likely to be needed). The remaining 8,300 seats are distributed among the theater, dining rooms, and lounges. For three thousand passengers, this number of seats explains why the ship never seems crowded. The swimming pools and Jacuzzis hold some 320 tons of water.

All of these thoughts pass through my mind as we wait amidst a crowd of impatient people. I'm a numbers person. These kind of statistics help me understand what an amazing artifact this ship represents. For those of you who don't get numbers, take my word for it—it's really, really big.

Subsequent to this cruise, in April 2012, *Mariner* underwent complete refurbishment. New eating venues include Boardwalk Dog House and the upscale Giovanni's Table. Activities for youth were expanded, featuring specially designed Fisher Price activities. Facilities for babies and tots were also enhanced. They made Vintages wine bar more intimate, and a venue for buying art, Kinkade Gallery, was added. The Lido Deck now has an outdoor movie screen, plus all cabins have been upgraded. The wonderful digital interactive maps that we experienced on *Rhapsody of the Seas* after its refurbishment have been installed on *Mariner*, along with shipwide Wi-Fi. We love this ship, and now it's even better.

No one forced us to come early and stand uncomfortably for this long. We could have ensconced ourselves on a comfortable couch in one of the bars, reading or playing cards, until they made the announcement. For our trouble standing in line, we are among the first to leave. We exit out onto promenade Deck 4 at 7:50 a.m. After they scan our room keys to verify that we are leaving the ship, we walk across the sky ramp into the terminal building. The long, hard-floored corridors slope slightly downhill. In charge of both suitcases, I find that they roll easily in their upright position, each resting on all four wheels. At one point Linda goes down the escalator, whereas I wait for the elevator, which takes an interminable time to arrive, fill, and descend.

The ground feels solid and steady under our feet. We land creatures feel more secure on *terra firma*. Passport control goes quickly. "Welcome home," the agent says. We don't even see a customs agent, except to hand in our cards showing that we have spent around $100 each on souvenirs. I suspect that the nonresidents are scrutinized more closely. Shortly, we exit into the sixty-eight–degree morning.

Linda signed us up with a nonofficial shuttle company, so we walk past the row of big buses and, with a little trouble, find an obscure Ford van that says Galveston Limousine on the side. It takes another thirty minutes of waiting for all of us with reservations to show up. I snap a few last photos of the ship, and then off we go.

Everyone in the van seems excited to be back in Texas. During the hour-long ride to Hobby International Airport in Houston, we talk among ourselves. Many others say that they, too, prefer the sea days. They, too, just walk around unaccompanied in the ports, such that after a while the memories become indistinguishable. They, too, think any entertainment that requires loud volume needs to be reconsidered. I wrote the same sentiments on my evaluation form.

Two years ago, Linda and I were on a similar shuttle to the same airport, having completed our first cruise together, on *Voyager of the Seas*. During those magical two weeks we grew from good friends into a romantic couple. Marriage followed and more cruises. The thrill has never subsided, for cruising and for each other. To our continuing wonder, we have become dedicated cruisers and transatlantic crossers. That's exactly how we plan to keep it.

Postscript

We took a year off from cruising because in January 2013 we moved into our new home in San Antonio. Getting ensconced there, traveling to make a few labyrinths, visiting grandchildren in Anacortes, and other activities kept us occupied. However, 2014 looks good for cruising, with one already scheduled and others being considered.

The website originally intended only to hold the photos and comments relating to this voyage on *Mariner of the Seas,* www.retiredgonecruising.com, now covers all of our cruises. *Retired Gone Cruising* was the original working title for this tome. The photos of this specific voyage are located at www.cruiseoftheheart.com. My company, Labyrinth Enterprises, LLC, the company I started almost two decades ago for building labyrinths, has now become the publisher of my books (see www.labyrinth-enterprises.com).

In the writing of this book I learned much. First, because I worked on the book in my spare time, it took far longer to finish than I ever imagined. To write all of the books in my head, I will either need to live to 120 or dedicate more time to writing. Second, all of my peripheral and extraneous curiosities expanded the memoir considerably. I originally thought it was going to be a short book.

Third, through the editing and rewriting, I became a better writer. I sent out several early copies of the manuscript for comment. My favorite maritime author, John Maxtone-Graham, read only as far as the second chapter, writing that he found the book too scattered and confusing to follow. As I was tightening things up, our friend Barbara Diamond suggested moving the lengthier asides to the end of the chapters, which helped the narrative to flow better.

Then Jay Herring, author of *The Truth About Cruise Ships*, called and offered suggestions. He had similarly sent his manuscript to Brian David Bruns (*Cruise Ship Confidential*) who told him it was far too long and needed to be cut in half. He looked at my 125,000 words and made the same suggestion. As a result, I decided to expand my material to two volumes, thereby reducing this memoir to a svelte 86,000 words. The second book will come closer to 60,000 words.

The greatest influence on this book was the amazing proofreading done by Kathy Clayton of Greenbelt Editing Services in Austin, Texas. I was tempted to depend on my own efforts, being impatient to get the book out, but wisely decided to engage a professional. Wow! It was worth every penny (and the subsequent two-month delay). Rare was the paragraph that didn't have some correction or suggestion. It took me several weeks going back through the manuscript page by page making the changes. I was irritated at first by that necessity, but when I was finished, I was glad the book was so improved and presentable.

Linda encouraged and supported me through the entire creation of this book, even when I "abandoned" her during our cruise to take so many notes and photographs. She introduced me to cruising, as you have read, which has been a great joy of discovery. This memoir is at heart a love story, hence its title. Without Linda, neither this book nor my wonderful life (nor the gift of grandchildren) would have happened. Thanks, Sweetie, I love you.

During this process, I taught myself how to self-publish. Finding advice wasn't hard. Just the opposite. There are so many resources that I was inundated with information. To keep it straight, I took notes from beginning to end. Believing that others would find those notes of interest, I plan for it to be a concise book named something like *How Grandpa Self-Published His Book: And How You Can Too*.

Many companies and individuals stood ready to assist me to get published. The cost of their services varies according to the extent of their involvement.

> *I chose to design the interior of the book myself. In doing so I eliminated the conventional header that repeats the title of the book and name of the author on top of alternating pages. It seemed too redundant and egotistical.*

For the text, I chose 12-point Garamond Premier Pro as my typeface, which dates back to Claude Garamont (with a "t") in the sixteenth century (died 1561). Comparing this type to several others, I found it slightly darker and more distinct, hence, easier to read.

For the script used in the chapter titles and subtitles, nothing on my computer seemed right. On the Internet I found a lovely typeface called Good Vibes, free for the using, designed by Rob Leuschke (see www.typesetit.com). I am not alone. Some 1,112,099 people previously downloaded this typeface. Thanks, Rob.

For the record, I have no connection to Royal Caribbean other than being a frequent customer. I have been straightforward in both my compliments and criticisms. Linda and I find cruises such as this repositioning cruise on *Mariner* to be the best combination of price and value, especially since we love sea days. Would we prefer one of the more luxurious cruise lines? Maybe so, if we could afford it. Would we be willing to cut the cost and travel on a party ship? Not likely. So here we are, right in the middle. I should mention that we have also enjoyed cruises on Holland America, Norwegian, Princess, and Cunard.

Vacations to Go (www.vacationstogo.com) has served us very well in booking cruises. I also prefer their website, which allows searching by cruise, ship, company, port, or embarkation/debarkation city. Our agent, Judy Hastings, is the best, so I want to share her contact information:

Judy Hastings
Email: jhastings@vacationstogo.com

US and Canada: 1-800-338-4962 ext. 7152

Finally, thanks to you, my readers. I hope you have enjoyed this book. It would help me immeasurably if you would express yourself by submitting a review or making comments to my blog. Instructions are available on my website, www.robertferre.com.

Robert D. Ferré
November, 2013

Bibliography

Books I Have Read

A Man and His Ship: America's Greatest Naval Architect and the Quest to Build the S.S. United States, Steven Ujifuss

A Trip to the Orient: The Story of a Mediterranean Cruise, Robert Urie Jacob

A World Cruise Log, Joseph H. Appel

Abandoned Ship: An Intimate Account of the Costa Concordia Shipwreck, Benji Smith

Building the Biggest: From Ironships to Cruise Liners, Geoff Lunn

Burning Cold: The Cruise Ship Prinsendam and the Greatest Sea Rescue of All Time, H. Paul Jeffers

Captain of the Queens, The Autobiography of Captain Harry Grattidge, Former Commodore of the Cunard Line, as told to Richard Collier

Crossing and Cruising: From the Golden Era of Ocean Liners to the Luxury Cruise Ships of Today, John Maxtone-Graham

Cruise Confidential: A Hit Below the Waterline: Where the Crew Eats, Sleeps, Wars, and Parties—One Crazy Year Working on Cruise Ships, Brian David Bruns (I guess he couldn't decide on a title. This is the first of a three-book series.)

Cruise: Identity, Design and Culture, Peter Quartermaine and Bruce Peter

Cruise Savvy: An Invaluable Primer for First Time Passengers, John Maxtone-Graham

Cruise Ship Blues: The Underside of the Cruise Ship Industry, Ross A. Klein

Cruise Ship SOS: The Life-Saving Adventures of a Doctor at Sea, Ben Macfarlane

Devils on the Deep Blue Sea: The Dreams, Schemes, and Showdowns That Built America's Cruise-Ship Empires, Kristoffer A. Garin (A fascinating and detailed account of the rise of the cruise lines.)

Doomed Ships: Great Ocean Liner Disasters, William H. Miller (Miller has dozens of books on ships which are well worth investigating.)

Exposed: The Cruise Industry, David Feeney Duncan

Fire at Sea: The Mysterious Tragedy of the Morro Castle, Thomas Gallagher

Freighter Odyssey—Around the World in 130 Days, Dale Stenseth

Liners to the Sun, John Maxtone-Graham

Normandie: France's Legendary Art Deco Ocean Liner, John Maxtone-Graham

Notes Made During A Cruise Around the World in 1913: On Board the Hamburg-American Line Steamship, Cleveland (1914), R. H. Casey

Nothing Can Go Wrong, Captain, John H. Kilpack with John A. MaxDonald

Pictorial Encyclopedia of Ocean Liners, 1860–1994, William H. Miller, Jr. (417 historic photos)

Poems of the Sea, J. D. McClatchy, editor

Queen Mary 2: The Greatest Ocean Liner of Our Time, John Maxtone-Graham, photos by Harvey Lloyd (Besides the spectacular photos and amazing tale of construction, the book includes history and other material of interest.)

Seamanship: A Voyage Along the Wild Coasts of the British Isles, Adam Nicolson

Selling the Sea: An Inside Look at the Cruise Industry, Bob Dickinson and Andy Vladimir

Ship for Brains, Brian David Bruns (The second in a three-book series.)

Stern's Guide to the Cruise Vacation: Descriptions of Every Major Cruise Ship and Port of Call Worldwide, Steven B. Stern

Super Ship, Noel Mostert

The Big Ship: The Story of the S.S. United States, Frank Braynard

The Captain's Log: Around the World with Cruise Captain Hans Mateboer, Hans Mateboer

The Essential Little Cruise Book: Expert Advice for Planning and Enjoying a Perfect Vacation at Sea, 4th Edition, Jim West, Ann Carol Burgess, editors (This is the advice book I liked the best; in addition to practical advice, they suggest that you stretch your horizons and try new things on a cruise. Eat food you don't usually eat. Do things you don't usually do. To make your vacation an adventure, be adventurous.)

The Innocents Abroad, Mark Twain (Twain's description of a voyage almost 150 years ago makes observations about passengers and shipboard that still pertain today.)

The Liner: Retrospective & Renaissance, Philip Dawson

The Only Way to Cross: The Golden Era of the Great Atlantic Express Liners, John Maxtone-Graham (Maxtone-Graham is my favorite maritime historian. You will see a number of his books here. Chronologically, this is the first of a trilogy. Check out his interviews on YouTube.)

The Outlaw Sea: A World of Freedom, Chaos, and Crime, William Langewiesche

The Queen Mary: Her Inception and History, Neil Potter and Jack Frost (I liked the original title better, *The Mary: The Inevitable Ship.*)

The Truth About Cruise Ships: A Cruise Ship Officer Survives the Work, Adventure, Alcohol, and Sex of Ship Life, Jay Herring

The Truth About the Titanic, Archibald Gracie

Titanic Survivor: The Newly Discovered Memoirs of Violet Jessop, Who Survived both the Titanic and Britannic Disasters, Violet Jessop, edited and annotated by John Maxtone-Graham

Triumph Over Calamity, C. Peaden

Unsafe on the High Seas—Your Guide to a Safer Cruise, Charles R. Lipcon

What Time is the Midnight Buffet? Tales from the Cruise Adventure of a Lifetime, chesterh

E-Books and Articles

"A Supposedly Fun Thing I'll Never Do Again," David Foster Wallace
Cruise Ship Stories, Guy Beah
Cruise Ship Tricks: How To Break the Rules, Equip Your Cabin, and Not Spend Money, Kate Harper
Cruise Travel Secrets: Discover What the Cruise Ship Brochures Don't Tell You, Mora Frederick
The Ship Dwellers: A Story of a Happy Cruise, Albert Bigelow Paine

More Books of Interest

At Sea with God, Margaret Silf
Berlitz Complete Guide to Cruising & Cruise Ships 2012, Douglas Ward
Bonsor, N.R.P. North Atlantic Seaway: An Illustrated History of the Passenger Services Linking the Old World with the New, Brookside Publications, 1975-1980, 5 vols., revised edition
British Passenger Liners of the Five Oceans: A Record of the British Passenger Lines and Their Liners from 1838 to the Present Day, C.R. Vernon Gibbs
Cruise Vacations for Mature Travelers, Kerrie Smith (I had great hopes, given the topic, but found this book dated and only marginally interesting.)
France/Norway: France's Last Liner/Norway's First Mega Cruise Ship, John Maxtone-Graham
Great Passenger Ships of the World, Patrick Stephens Ltd., 1975-1977, 1986, 6 vols, Arnold Kludas
Hurtigruten—Detailed 11 Day Voyage Guide: Nature, Culture, History, Legends, Berit Liland (See my description of this book on Day 11, pages 162-163.)
Modern Cruise Ships from 1931-2008, Fatih Takmakl
Permanent Passenger: My Life on a Cruise Ship, Micha Berman
Ships of State: The Great Atlantic Liners, E. Mowbray Tate
The France and the Queen Elizabeth 2, John Maxtone-Graham
The Unsinkable Mr. Brown, Brian David Bruns (This is the third book in the author's memoirs. I enjoyed the other two, just haven't gotten to this one yet, feeling it may be a bit redundant.)
Titanic Tragedy: A New Look at the Lost Liner, John Maxtone-Graham

Websites of Interest

www.+

retiredgonecruising.com My website with photos and descriptions of this and subsequent cruises.

cruisecritic.com One of the largest cruise websites, with reviews, articles, and more.

cruiseclues.com A privately maintained site with more links to cruise and ship information that I have ever seen. You can contribute more.

vacationstogo.com My preferred site for ships and cruises and for booking cruises. The website allows users to look up cruises by any criterion, from dates to specific ships or companies to ports of call, departure cities, and more.

cruises.com Another major vendor of cruises.

cruisenow.com Another vendor of cruises, whose goal is happy customers. Whose isn't?

voyager-class.com A detailed site about the design and features of Voyager-class ships, which includes *Mariner.*

travltips.com (Note: there is no "E" in "travl"). Book freighters, barges, and other unique cruises. Also has a printed magazine.

ssmaritime.com The website of Reuben Goossens, maritime historian, author and lecturer who worked for fifty-one years in the passenger shipping industry. He has written about 420 classic liners. Very opinionated.

savetheclassicliners.com Related to the above site, to encourage the saving of classic, aging liners.

cruisebruise.com Reports on what can go wrong on cruises, including missing passengers, murder, death, overboard, rape, injury, etc.

internationalcruisevictims.org Covers crime issues, offers support to victims and their families.

cruisejunkie.com The website of Ross A. Klein, the cruise industry's biggest critic.

livecruiseshiptracker.com This websites tracks all major cruise ships in real time and shows on a map where they are located. If you are on a cruise, your friends can keep track of exactly where you are.

sailwx.info/shiptrack/cruiseships.phtml Another site with ship tracking, as well as information about tides, air and water temperatures, visibility, wind speed, and waves.

shipboardcruiser.com A non-commercial site with numerous links to newsletters and websites.

thecruiselines.com One of an almost infinite number of websites selling cruises. Lists the ten best reasons for taking a cruise: value, romance, cuisine, variety, activities, simplicity, new horizons, family, pampering, satisfaction, and you. Of course, that's eleven reasons, but who's counting.

seatrade-insider.com This industry website is frequently quoted by other so-called cruise news websites. So why not go directly to the source.

cruisingdoneright.com One of several Canadian cruise-related websites. They have better than normal articles and blogs. They have a close connection with portsandbows.com.

portsandbows.com The website of Canadian Phil Reimer, who writes a cruise blog and weekly articles for Postmedia and canada.com.

cruisemates.com They call themselves the online cruise community.

cruiselinefans.com Has an amazing list of cruise cams (live, onboard video)

cruisedeckplans.com This website contains what its name implies: deck plans. There are a number of other sites in which this information is available, such as Vacations To Go. Nevertheless, here is another source.

thegreatoceanliners.com Great site to look up historic ocean liners.

theparbucklingproject.com A site dedicated to covering the salvage operation of the Costa *Concordia*.

maritimematters.com Called "Martin Cox's Maritime Matters," the site seems to feature the blogging of Peter Knego. Has a wonderful list of live bridge cams for many cruise ships. See where they are at this moment, in real time.

avidcruiser.com Aaron Saunders started this blog, "From the Deck Chair," two years ago. He initially paid for his own cruises, but now has enough visibility that he is starting to get invitations from cruise ships to come and write about them. (Hello, I'm available, too.)

ocean-liners.com Another website about ocean liners, this time by Louis Mancini.

theblueriband.com A site dedicated to the history of the Blue Riband, the prize for the fastest crossing of the Atlantic by an ocean liner (or, apparently, any other ship).

cruisecompete.com This site offers a way for cruise companies to bid for your business. I'm suspicious. The typical deals listed seemed pretty ordinary to me.

prowsedge.com Called *Prow's Edge Cruise Magazine*, this site has articles written by travel writers on subjects beyond just cruising.

cruiseshipstories.com As the name implies, stories told by cruise-ship crew members and passengers.

cruising.org The site of the Cruise Lines International Association (CLIA), the official group representing the cruise industry.

cruiseporthotels.com A travel agency specializing in hotels near cruise ports.

www.ingramcontent.com/pod-product-compliance
Lightning Source LLC
Chambersburg PA
CBHW071524040426

42452CB00008B/870